# Secret SAS Missions in Africa

*To Rex,*
*After everything, finally brought down by cancer on 30 April 2017.*
*Good man, great soldier and a fine friend.*

# Secret SAS Missions in Africa

## C Squadron's Counter-Terrorist Operations 1968–1980

Michael Graham

Pen & Sword
**MILITARY**

First published in Great Britain in 2017
and reprinted in this format in 2018 by
**Pen & Sword MILITARY**
An imprint of Pen & Sword Books Ltd
Yorkshire – Philadelphia

Copyright © Michael Graham, 2017, 2018
ISBN: 978 1 52674 844 7

Printed and bound in England by CPI Group (UK) Ltd, Croydon, CR0 4YY

Pen & Sword Books Limited incorporates the imprints of Atlas, Archaeology,
Aviation, Discovery, Family History, Fiction, History, Maritime, Military, Military
Classics, Politics, Select, Transport, True Crime, Air World, Frontline Publishing, Leo
Cooper, Remember When, Seaforth Publishing, The Praetorian Press, Wharncliffe
Local History, Wharncliffe Transport, Wharncliffe True Crime and White Owl.

For a complete list of Pen & Sword titles please contact
PEN & SWORD BOOKS LIMITED
47 Church Street, Barnsley, South Yorkshire, S70 2AS, England
E-mail: enquiries@pen-and-sword.co.uk • Website: www.pen-and-sword.co.uk
Or
PEN AND SWORD BOOKS
1950 Lawrence Rd, Havertown, PA 19083, USA
E-mail: Uspen-and-sword@casematepublishers.com
Website: www.penandswordbooks.com

# Contents

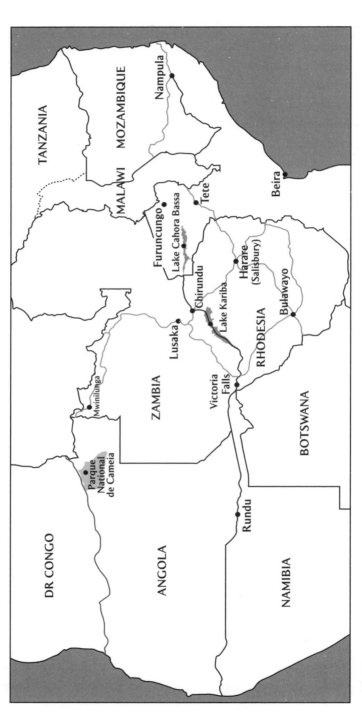

C Squadron SAS operational area.

# Author's Notes and Acknowledgements

I walked into the Air New Zealand Koru Club lounge ahead of a flight to Wellington and sitting on his own in a corner was Wilbur Smith. I went over to him to say hello and after introducing myself said I had a question.

'Is it true that my mother used to do your medical prescriptions at Highlands Pharmacy in Salisbury back in the 1950s?' I asked.

'Absolutely true,' he replied without any hesitation. 'And how is Mrs Graham?'

We ended up sitting together on the hour-long flight from Auckland and chatted about Africa. He was especially interested in my time in the SAS.

Before going our separate ways he said, 'Mike you should write a book. It was an extraordinary time in Africa and the world should know what part the SAS played in shaping history. It will be a great story.'

It took me a few years but after regular prompting by good friend André Louw in Sydney I eventually got started. Wilbur Smith had said it would be a great story and that's what I wanted to write. I had no wish to write a precise accurate history.

I needed help to achieve this so joined the New Zealand Society of Authors. Government department Creative New Zealand give the society some funds every year to assist and encourage new writers and they use this to pay for manuscript appraisals.

I applied twice without success, but after the second time the secretary called to say my problem was genre. I'd said my work was fiction but that was firmly rejected by the committee who said it was non-fiction.

I argued that I thought non-fiction was the truth, the whole truth and nothing but the truth, and while most of what I'd written was based on actual events I'd mixed things up and added detail to suit the narrative in each story.

I was told about 'creative non-fiction' or 'faction' as one of the committee put it. I changed my genre and got the grant.

That put me in touch with Caroline Martin. After retiring from the *Otago Daily Times* Caroline now helps new writers like me with professional editing. Caroline has been wonderful to work with and her contribution has been immense, not just with the writing but also with the critical presentations to get the attention of potential agents and publishers.

Matt Perkins helped with the latter by producing some great graphics showing where the action took place in Africa. Feedback confirmed the positive impact this had with the many submissions we made to agents and publishers in the UK.

My sincere thanks to you all.

Mike Graham

# C Squadron SAS

Serving in the Long Range Desert Group and with the original SAS during the Second World War, Rhodesians had proved they were good Special Forces material, and it was this background and the offer of 100 trained men that in 1950 persuaded the British government to add C (Rhodesia) Squadron to the newly formed Malayan Scouts – later to become 22 SAS.

A and B squadrons in the new SAS were English-based units with D Squadron formed in Scotland.

At the same time, both New Zealand and Australia formed SAS regiments and while there was close liaison with 22 SAS they retained control by keeping them as part of their own armed forces.

Three years later, at the end of a campaign to contain the spread of communism into south-east Asia, the members of C Squadron were returned to Africa.

Here trouble was brewing, with a Mau Mau uprising in Kenya, with rebels in the Katanga province of the Belgian Congo, and with what was seen as communist-inspired dissent in other regions. The squadron was initially based in Ndola, Northern Rhodesia – now Zambia.

There were ups and downs in the years that followed before C Squadron eventually moved to what was then Southern Rhodesia and that became their permanent base. The Rhodesians had an air force with helicopters and DC3 Dakotas for parachute operations – both critical to SAS operations.

At the height of the Cold War the Russians, the Chinese and to a lesser extent the North Koreans were actively courting dissident political and tribal factions throughout Africa, training and arming them, and backing so-called 'liberation' struggles. Not that liberation interested them in the slightest – their eyes were firmly fixed on the vast mineral riches of the region, and nowhere more so than in central Africa: oil in Angola; copper in Zambia; gold, chrome, asbestos, nickel and coal deposits in Zimbabwe and Mozambique; platinum and diamonds in Botswana.

Ultimately they wanted South Africa but first they had to establish themselves in central Africa, and our job in C Squadron SAS was to make that as difficult as possible for all parties involved.

We operated with the Portuguese forces in Angola and made sorties into Botswana and the Caprivi Strip in Namibia, but predominantly our offensive was in Mozambique and Zambia where the terrorist camps were established for training and infiltration into the southern targets – starting with Zimbabwe.

We had three sets of gear.

Most often used was our NATO-style gear, which in terms of hardware was the Belgian-made 7.62 millimetre Fabrique Nationale (FN), a 'GT' version of the SLR used by the British Army and others. The FN was a beautifully made firearm. It was simple enough and robust enough for servicemen and was exceptionally reliable. Most of all, though, it was high velocity and the round was heavy, so it packed a serious punch. If you hit someone with an FN round they stayed hit and down – which was more than you could say for the AK-47 and its predecessors with the shorter, less powerful round. However, the AKs have undoubtedly killed many more people than the FN ever will.

We contributed significantly to that statistic because we also used Chinese gear, including the basic AK-47, and we also had their 'bamboo bazooka' – the RPG – which, like the AK, has been an absolute icon for any terrorist group – they've all had them.

Thirdly, we also had Russian-made gear: the AKM was a more modern version of the AK-47 but used the same ammunition; and similarly their RPG7 was way more sophisticated than the bazooka made in China but used the same rockets. We added more Russian gear to our armoury as the campaign progressed and as we captured it, including light anti-aircraft weapons such as the 12.7 millimetre cannon that we mounted on a couple of our Mercedes Unimog combat vehicles.

Having three lots of gear was a premeditated plan we hoped would disguise our identity and perhaps deflect the interest of intelligence agencies.

We used the different weaponry and equipment to take advantage of the ideological and often tribal differences between factions caught up in this Cold War struggle. So when we attacked a Russian-sponsored training camp, for example, we would deliberately dress and arm ourselves with Chinese gear and made sure we left some clear sign suggesting the involvement of a rival faction.

We'd then wait and watch the newspapers for reports of retaliatory raids instigated by our victims, and they seldom let us down. Raids and counter-raids sometimes went on for weeks and in one case the Zambian government had to intervene to stop the mayhem. Once it settled down we would start planning the next raid, and next time round we would target a Chinese-sponsored camp and use our Russian gear. And so it went on. Several years later, Zimbabwe leader Mugabe was told about it and said that throughout the long campaign they'd had no idea an SAS regiment was operating against them.

C Squadron was disbanded in 1980, but has remained on the organisational spider of 22 SAS. It may again be resurrected but the Rhodesian connection is now history.

It was originally formed on the back of 100 troops offered to the British by the Rhodesian government of the day, but was never truly Rhodesian thereafter. In my time the first two COs were British followed by a South African. The 2 I/C (author) was born in Burnley, England, and the troops were a real international mix. The New Zealand SAS had no operational commitment at this time and several of their team came over to join us and, along with a couple of Australians, made a big impression. We had a few British from our parent regiment 22 SAS who were then busy countering urban terrorism – especially in Northern Ireland – but the best of the Brits came from the Parachute Regiment, which I still rate today as the best bunch of fighting men on the planet. We had a couple of Germans – one with an extraordinary record with the French Foreign Legion – a couple of Poles and a good number of great South Africans who slotted seamlessly into the bush warfare role. We had a few Americans – veterans from Vietnam and 101st Airborne – and they too made a great contribution.

So this international mix of SAS soldiers, using an international mix of equipment, ambushed terrorist infiltration and supply lines and attacked and destroyed training and battle camps. We blew up bridges, roads and railways, boats and ships, fuel dumps and stores to disrupt the logistical effort – often deep inside unfriendly country.

Night parachute drops were a frequently used means of reaching these targets, we sometimes were deployed by French Alouette helicopters, and occasionally we were able to use our very versatile Klepper kayaks which could be carried or air-dropped in kitbags and assembled before taking to the water. The terrain of central Africa did not lend itself to vehicle operations although we did a couple with our Mercedes Unimogs, but generally we moved around in our purpose-built Sabre Land Rovers.

These long-wheel-base 4 x 4 vehicles were open-top; they had a windscreen for the driver while the front passenger seat was a GPMG position with the 7.62 millimetre machine gun mounted over the bonnet. At the back, between roll bars and the rails, to which we could strap our Bergen packs, was a second GPMG mounting with a 360-degree traverse. These modified Land Rovers were highly capable vehicles with an intimidating display of firepower if ever we needed it.

Most of all, though, we walked – a lot of the time at night, concealing ourselves during the day in observation posts or ambush positions. And we did a great deal of this in serious big game country.

Lion, leopard, hyena, wild hunting dogs, elephant, rhino, buffalo, hippo, crocodiles and deadly snakes were regular companions and sometimes dangerous adversaries. Birds, baboons and monkeys could compromise our hiding places.

There were tangled vines with razor-sharp, backward-pointing barbs that would rip your clothing and flesh, bean plants with toxic fine hairs that caused an agonising burning itch.

There were malaria-carrying mosquitoes; tsetse flies, which caused sleeping sickness; aggressive wild bees; and the dreadful, minute, salt and pepper ticks that crawled into and embedded themselves in the inner ear.

As crazy as it may sound this environment was the big attraction. We mastered it and loved every minute of it. And in doing that we were, without question, the bush warfare elite force.

There were many adventures with the wild creatures of this environment, but if you knew and understood them the risks were minimal.

Keeping out of trouble in this sort of country required a combination of knowledge and concentration – you had to be incredibly alert. A bird call, for example, could signal the imminent arrival of a herd of buffalo and would give you time to get out of the way. You would hear lion not too far in front and instinctively check the wind direction to see if they would get your scent and hopefully retreat. If they didn't and you stumbled across them at close quarters anything could happen. If you had to use a shot to get out of trouble that could give away your position and compromise the entire mission.

Quite simply, I reckoned the very nature of operating in big game country gave us a huge advantage over any human enemy. If we could avoid conflict with lions, buffalo and elephants there was no way we would be caught out by a bunch of people trained in Russia or China. We were the bush warfare specialists – we were playing on our home ground, there was no referee and we never lost a game!

We were the African Cold War killers.

# SAS Africa – the Team

## The Major – Mike (Mick) Graham

Mike was born in Burnley, on the Lancashire side of the northern moors in England, but raised in Rhodesia where his father was an instructor at an agricultural college with 350 African students. A life-long interest in birdlife started when he was 10 years old and from this early age happiness was wandering across the 6,500 acres of college farm and woodland with his pointer dog companion.

After school Mike went to university in Natal, South Africa, where he studied zoology and botany with a dream of becoming a game ranger.

Called up for national service in Rhodesia, he enjoyed the army environment from the outset. He was commissioned as an officer and served in a commando unit before applying for SAS selection. He was duly awarded his wings and admitted to this elite unit.

After a number of years as a troop commander he was promoted to captain and posted to the position of intelligence officer at an operational brigade headquarters.

It was a turning point in his career. The job required close cooperation with senior officers in all the military branches as well as the air force, police and civil authorities and sometimes politicians. Mike made a mark and was decorated for his contribution.

Military staff college followed and a year later he graduated in the top three of his class.

He returned to the SAS as major and second in command of the regiment.

Vital statistics: height 1.8 metres (5 feet 11 inches); weight 82 kilograms (180 pounds).

## Rex – Warrant Officer Rex Pretorius

Born in Pietersburg in the Northern Transvaal, South Africa, but raised on a massive 250,000-acre game ranch in the southern Matabeleland province of Rhodesia, Rex had a traditional Afrikaans family upbringing with a focus on hunting and living off the land. As a result he developed an environmental awareness akin to the animals they farmed and hunted.

He became a proficient mechanic and spent hours working on the open-top, short-wheel-base Land Rover that was the love of his life.

A big, powerful man, Rex worked as a professional hunter on another huge game ranch in the lowveld of the Limpopo province before being called up to do national service in the army. His professional hunting work was seasonal and like the Major he too was attracted to the SAS and predictably had no problem with the selection course.

Rex led two lives, the first with the SAS and the second as a professional hunter. R and R for him was being reunited with his beloved Land Rover and going hunting. He was a true bushman.

Vital statistics: height 1.95 metres (6 feet 5 inches); weight 105 kilograms (230 pounds).

## Horse – Sergeant Maurice Greenfield

Born in Launceston, Cornwall, England, he was the second of three sons in a farming family that had tilled the land close to Bodmin Moor for centuries.

Mum and Dad and the three boys from the marriage were, without exception, big people: big hearts that gave them stamina, determination and compassion; and big smiles because the Greenfields loved being the clowns. They seemed to have a never-ending repertoire of jokes they recounted with an infectious laughter that got everybody going.

As there were too many of them for the farm in Cornwall, 'Horse' as he became known through his school days, decided to join the British Army.

Looking for adventure, Horse ended up in the famous British Parachute Regiment and served in Ireland where the fight was with IRA terrorists. The Paras did well but their no-nonsense approach offended the left-wing politicians of the day. Stagnation and boards of enquiry followed.

Horse had better things to do with his life while this was going on and one night in London's Earl's Court, he met a group of Rhodesians having a good time and enjoying their 'OE' (overseas experience). They spoke of Africa and the wonderful land and wild animals of the bushveld.

'You should come and join us,' one voice piped up. 'We can always use men from the Brit Paras!'

It was Karate, on leave, full of beer, and he brought us one of Britain's best.

Vital statistics: height 1.95 metres (6 feet 5 inches); weight 106 kilograms (233 pounds).

## Karate – Sergeant Tony Caruthers Smith

Born in Bulawayo, Rhodesia, Karate, as he later became known, lost his father in a road accident when very young and was brought up by his mother who worked with the education department. He had a good academic record at school and was interested in electronics but had no specific career ambition.

Called up for national service with the army, which he enjoyed, Karate became a skilled radio operator. After joining the SAS, he took this to new levels with his mastery of Morse code and an uncanny knack of knowing just how to set up an aerial to ensure communications.

Karate and the Major were on the same advanced demolitions course and the two subsequently worked together on many operations involving the use of explosives. They were especially known for their skill in the tricky business of melting down Pentolite and moulding it into deadly 'bunker bombs' – family sized plastic Coke bottles filled with the high explosive that were used to great effect on many occasions.

Karate had a cool head: relaxed when laying charges, calm under fire, and calculated and proactive during crises.

His slight stature and crooked, toothy grin disguised a hard, sinewy frame and tireless stamina. This physical strength combined with his mental resilience and technical skills made Karate one of Sierra One Seven's vital assets.

Vital statistics: height 1.725 metres (5 feet 8 inches); weight 75 kilograms (165 pounds).

## Simmo – Corporal Peter Simmonds

Born in Perth, Western Australia, where his father worked for gold mining giant Newmont. A small gold mining operation at a place called Penhalonga in the eastern highlands of Rhodesia was looking for a mine manager and his father got the job. After years of working in the heat of the Australian outback and in the steamy conditions of Papua New Guinea the family were looking forward to living in a cooler climate and enjoying the picturesque

environment of the eastern highlands. Simmo's mother was a horticultur-
alist and conditions at Penhalonga were perfect for growing flowers. They
bought a small holding and started growing gladioli.

Simmo had just turned twenty and in Perth had worked as a builder's
apprentice. He was able to help with the construction of the sheds and
greenhouses and the initial planting of the gladioli corms. The business
flourished and soon the flowers were being exported across the world. In
Penhalonga, the Simmonds family had found another source of gold. But
for Simmo it was all too tame and he decided to join the regular army.
After training he was posted to a commando regiment. The Major – then
a lieutenant – was his troop commander.

When the Major announced he was off to try his luck with the SAS,
Simmo put up his hand and said he was going too. He'd proved his worth
on operations and as a very efficient organiser. Together they conquered the
rigorous SAS selection course and inevitably he became one of the team.

Vital statistics: height 1.75 metres (5 feet 9 inches); weight 86 kilograms
(190 pounds).

## Jonny – Corporal Jonasi Koruvakaturanga.

Jonny was born in Lambasa, Fiji, the son of a *ratu* (tribal prince) who was
general manager of the local sugar mill. He did his initial military training in Fiji and then joined the New Zealand Army, serving in an infantry
unit. Jonny heard about C Squadron through Pig Dog and joined him in the
adventure to Africa.

Tall and with massive strength and stamina, Jonny was known as the best
MAG gunner in the regiment and handled the heavy weapon as if it were an
air rifle. Working in small numbers as we usually did, we relied massively on
Horse and Jonny who carried the firepower in our group.

Vital statistics: height 1.95 metres (6 feet 5 inches); weight 106 kilograms
(233 pounds), but nimble and quick with it.

## Pig Dog – Corporal Verne Conchie

He was born in Riverton in Southland, New Zealand, of part Maori parents. The family owned a deer farm on the narrow wind-blown plain at the
southern extremity of the South Island, between the tumultuous seas of the
Foveaux Strait and the impassable inland peaks of Fiordland.

By the age of 10 Verne was hunting red deer and wild pigs alongside his father. They fished the streams together, put pots out for crayfish and collected shellfish. They would drive feral goats on to their property from neighbouring forests and either milked them to make cheese or slaughtered them for the Halal market.

Vern walked out of school at the age of 14 and initially worked full-time with his father before moving on as a deer hunter and seasonal hand at the local meat works. He was good at his job and managed to send a useful monthly contribution back home to his parents.

At the meat works he met Des and Amy Coles – an older man and wife team who had met while serving in the army together, and both saw the potential in Verne as a soldier. Des, who had been a regimental sergeant major, still had plenty of connections in the army and it wasn't long before he had talked Verne into giving it a try. The New Zealand SAS was on a recruiting drive at the time; Verne took up the challenge and thrived in the environment.

Vietnam was over and a chance to serve with an operational SAS regiment was there for the taking: the Kiwi found himself in Africa.

The name 'Pig Dog' has its origin in New Zealand where wild pigs are hunted with insanely tough breeds of dog that can have a gentle side to them. Bull terrier and bull mastiff crosses are popular. Verne looked a bit like a pig dog, he was built like a pig dog, and he had the strength and determination of a pig dog.

Verne Conchie was also incredibly loyal and devoted. We all knew he would put his body on the line for his comrades without any hesitation or consideration for his own safety. And with bush skills that rivalled Rex the two were an invincible lead-scout pairing with an instinct for danger that could not be taught.

Pig Dog was a legend!

Vital statistics: height 1.75 metres (5 feet 9 inches); weight 86 kilograms (190 pounds).

## Fish – Corporal Paul Fisher

Paul was born in Ndola, Zambia, where his father was manager of a large copper mine. A combination of falling copper prices and political corruption disrupted the economy and the family moved into Rhodesia.

Paul had a good education and did well at school. Not a great sportsman, and branded an academic for no reason other than he wore glasses, Paul was determined to prove that physically he could hack it with the best of them.

No better place to do that than with the SAS and Paul was exceptional.

He announced one day that what he particularly liked about the SAS was that in spite of all the heavy physical stuff demanded we were 'Soldiers who used our brains!'

Amen to that.

'Fish', as we called him, used his brains to enrol for every course going, but discovered a special skill as a paramedic and the SAS subsequently channelled his focus on that.

When not on operations, he'd work as a male nurse at the local hospital accident and emergency ward.

Vital statistics: height 1.77 metres (5 feet 10 inches); weight 80 kilograms (175 pounds).

## Mack – Corporal Angus McCrimmon

Born in Leith, Scotland, Mack came from a fishing family in this town on the Firth of Forth to the east of Edinburgh.

With the introduction of the smelt (kapenta) into Lake Kariba, some commercial fishing skills were needed in the land-locked country of Rhodesia. Mr McCrimmon senior responded to the international call and the family moved to Africa. Mack was 16 at the time and already a competent sailor with a good knowledge of boats and fishing learned from working with his father.

Joining the SAS seemed like a good way to continue his interest in boating, and the Zodiac inflatables and the collapsible Klepper kayaks used by the unit duly became his speciality. He was sent on courses in South Africa to become an outboard motor mechanic – the logic being we couldn't call the AA or the coast guard in the places we operated if our usually reliable 40-horse Evinrudes packed up for some reason.

Mack brought mechanical engineering skills to our group that were invaluable and on several occasions saved us from serious trouble, but more than that Mack was supremely confident on the water.

Mack would lead the unit through nights paddling on mirror-smooth inland lakes where there was no horizon, where the lake surface blended seamlessly with the sky, and where flares of methane gas danced across the water ahead of them. He would lead them in missions launching their Kleppers from submarines at sea and paddling through the waves into unfriendly territory 1,000 kilometres away from home.

Mack was yet another star in the call sign Sierra One Seven.

Vital statistics: height 1.77 metres (5 feet 10 inches); weight 80 kilograms (175 pounds).

## Nelson – Nelson Ogadu

Born and educated in Kampala, Uganda, with a degree in economics, Nelson became a victim of the irrational tribal-based violence that enveloped his country. He fled as family and those he'd grown up with were being slaughtered by rebel gangs that manned roadblocks and invaded villages.

After months on the road he reached Rhodesia where he got a job as a labourer loading containers with sacks of maize to be shipped to countries to the north that were engulfed in civil conflict and could no longer feed themselves. The Major visited the site (that was run by a friend of his) and saw Nelson at work. He saw something different in the man. He pulled up alongside the container being loaded and greeted him. Nelson told his story but at the end he added: 'Perhaps God has guided me here to meet you? I speak many languages. Will that help you?'

'What time do you finish your work, Nelson?' asked the Major.

'4pm, Sir.'

'I will be here at that time to pick you up.'

He breezed through the selection course and the parachute training, revelling in the environment of physical and mental challenges. He became a vital part of our Sierra One Seven team and gave us a point of difference: he was African and an amazing linguist.

Vital statistics: height 1.95 metres (6 feet 5 inches); weight 100 kilograms (220 pounds).

# SAS Call Sign Sierra One Seven

I knocked hesitantly on the open door of the brigadier's office where he sat at his desk engrossed in some paperwork.

The red emblems of rank on his collars and the rows of medal ribbons added colour to the pale khaki shirt he wore. His dark, curly hair was longer than most would have in the army, and his characteristic bushy, black eyebrows twitched as he concentrated on the sheets of paper spread across his desk.

Peter Tremain had moved from his training role with 22 SAS, in Hereford, to take over command of C Squadron in the early days of our bush warfare campaign in Africa. He had seen action in Korea and in Malaysia, and then later on he was one of a small number of covert operators whose job, in the event of war, was to infiltrate behind East German and Russian lines and locate the assembly areas of armoured divisions preparing to advance. Once they had found a target, they would radio back the details and location and then it was 'Goodnight nurse' as he put it, because within minutes a missile with a tactical nuclear warhead would be launched and on its way.

There would be no escape option for the SAS men who delivered the critical information, and they were not expected to make it home – which goes to prove suicide bombers have been around for a while and are not exclusively Muslim.

'Come in, Mick,' he said without looking up. 'Take a seat while I finish the last details of the proposed budgets for next year.'

I sat down while he worked out what it was going to cost to run an SAS regiment for another twelve months.

'Plastic explosive?' he said to me suddenly.

I'd got used to his abrupt questioning style and knew he was asking how much we'd need in the coming year.

'In your budget I'd allow for the same as last year, but this year we should buy from the South Africans. Their PEA is as good as our traditional ICI brand, but it's half the price and a hell of a lot cheaper to ship to us up here in Rhodesia.'

'Good. Agreed, but we'll add on ten per cent to give us some negotiating room if those bloody bean counters want to give us a hard time again.'

He fiddled around with the papers, adding a few written notes, then bundled them all together and put them inside a manilla folder.

The brigadier picked up the phone. 'Jock,' he said, 'we need two cups of tea down here. The major and I have some discussions that might take a bit of time.'

'Yes, Sir,' replied the cookhouse. A few minutes later, two mugs of steaming tea and a plate of sandwiches arrived.

The brigadier left his desk and sat opposite me in one of the more comfortable loungers beside the low coffee table where Jock had put the tea and sandwiches. We enjoyed the refreshments and swapped some friendly notes on family.

We had served together for ten years, starting when he was a major and I was a young lieutenant troop commander in his commando regiment. He had seen me in action for the first time and, liking what he saw, guided me into the SAS.

'Mick,' he said, 'you know as well as I do that in the SAS we get all sorts of odd jobs and strange missions. We never know what's coming next and invariably we are under the spotlight in these situations, so it's important for the regiment that we handle ourselves really well. With your experience and ability, I can't think of anyone better suited to lead these forays. As a major, you have the rank and credibility to deal with whoever and whatever we meet up with, while at the same time, you are not too senior to be leading from the front in the field.'

I nodded in appreciation, but wondered where this was leading.

'In 22 SAS we set up special task forces consisting of teams with expertise in unusual situations. We had one, for example, that dealt with aircraft hijacking, and another for hostage situations. Here in Africa we are already recognised for our bush warfare skills, and to showcase this I want you to lead a team that is the best of the best.'

The brigadier paused to let this new twist in my SAS career sink in for a moment. My mind was racing. Who would make up the rest of this new team? Would I have a say in its composition or would the brigadier simply give me the other names?

'This morning, I received a message forwarded from the Portuguese Embassy, requesting help in an area well north of the Zambezi River towards the border with Malawi. A well-organised Frelimo cadre is giving their national service conscripts a hard time and they don't have better trained regular army troops to do anything about it.

'No better time to kick things off with our own special task force. You and I have worked with Colonel Costa da Silva before, so we know we can count on him to support us as best he can in the circumstances.'

A shiver of excitement ran down my spine at the prospect of going into action against this terrorist group in what would be a new part of Africa for all of us, and a hundred questions flooded my mind.

But before I could say anything, the brigadier held up his arm in a silent gesture that signalled wait and listen a bit longer.

I smiled, nodded and remained silent as he continued: 'Mick, I will leave the selection of your team to you, but there is one exception. I have intervened to appoint your second in command. I know you'll be happy with what I've done. I have ordered the transfer of Rex Pretorius from training troop to join you. You and Rex go back a long way and have been a great combination together. You're both older and wiser now and in this new role it's my belief you'll take your achievements to a new level.'

'Brilliant. Thank you, Sir. Rex would have been my first choice,' I replied.

'Rex doesn't know about this at the moment,' said the brigadier. 'But I'll call him in now and then it's up to you two to pick your team. You will be leaving on your Mozambique mission at first light day after tomorrow. A Rhodesian Air Force DC3 Dakota has already been organised. I will be getting further information about the operation through the day, so I want to see you and your new team for an updated briefing in the Ops room at 17.00 hours.

'One last thing, Mick,' he added. 'Your exclusive radio call sign will be Sierra One Seven. I have let Jimmy Munro, our signals officer, know that and he will be organising your code books. Jimmy will help you with any equipment needed to ensure you have comms with us no matter where we send you.'

I saluted and left the office.

I walked towards the bird bath I had installed beneath the colourful bougainvillea vines on the lawn of the office area and sat on a bench in the shade. A pair of red and black firefinches watched me, and then, deciding I was no threat, ducked into the water.

It was a good place to think.

At 1.95 metres tall and weighing in at 105 kilograms, Warrant Officer Rex Pretorius was somebody every human instinct said you didn't mess with. He was a sergeant in our training troop when I did my selection course and pushed everyone hard, especially potential new officers like me. The big South African with black, curly hair like the brigadier wasn't vindictive, but his job was to test would-be SAS men to the limit of their physical and mental strength.

I'd climbed the mountain with my big pack and then done the forty-two-kilometre marathon endurance part of the trial that followed with the sergeant alongside me every step of the way. At the end I'd sat down to rest and made a brew. I'd done it in record time.

Just as the water started to boil, the sergeant came over and told me there was an emergency and I had to take a heavy radio battery and some explosives to a patrol at a grid reference about ten kilometres away. He picked up the billy and was about to pour the water on to the ground when I stood up and grabbed his arm.

It took him by surprise. I was 15 centimetres shorter and 20 kilograms lighter, but it was time to exert my own strength and personality. I looked him in the eye: 'Sergeant, your delivery is no problem, but it won't be happening until I've had a brew.'

I was a lieutenant at the time so, with some firmness of voice, I said to him, 'Get your billy, Sergeant. We'll share the brew and a muesli bar and that should be enough for us to make this extra mission.'

There was a twinkle in his eye and a barely discernible smile on his face as we drank the hot tea. He added the extra weight to my pack, then we made the delivery in another record time.

Rex appeared at the edge of the lawn and, seeing the finches enjoying the water, did a detour so he wouldn't disturb them as he joined me at the bench.

'Last week, when you were away, I saw a grey, stray cat that had concealed itself in a pile of leaves the gardener had raked up around your bird bath,' he said.

'It was very confident as I approached, but it didn't reckon on me having the Tokarev pistol you keep in your desk drawer. I've now got a new Davy Crockett hat drying in the sun behind the vehicle workshops and you've still got your firefinches.' He laughed, shook my hand firmly and sat down next to me. 'It's good to be back, Mick.'

'Ha!' I cried. 'Good job, Rex. Yes, it's great to be back together again. It looks like the brigadier already has some fun and games lined up for us, starting with an operation in northern Mozambique. I've had about ten minutes more than you to think about this new team. So far all I've come up with is we have to have guys with us who understand the way you and I operate. Bushcraft is what we hang our hats on.

'So, who do we need?' I asked.

'Mick, you're good up front leading us through big game country and into action, but you can't be there all the time, so my first choice would be the Kiwi, Pig Dog. We need someone else who sees everything and whose instincts can predict danger in front of us. Pig Dog is the best we have had from New Zealand, and he will put his body on the line without hesitation.'

'Agreed,' I replied. 'And with that last bit in mind, Karate would be my next choice. He's as cool as a cucumber and one of the best with the radios. Also, he and I were on the same advanced demolition course and we are bound to be using explosives at some stage.'

'My choice too,' said Rex. 'But now we need to look at firepower. We need big boys for the machine guns, and the more they know about communist weaponry the better. There are two specialists that I'd pick: first would be Horse. He's as strong as his name suggests and with his British Parachute Regiment experience, he's a great team player. And he has a sense of humour – he'll always be good for morale no matter what's happening.

'My second choice would be the big Fijian, Jonny. He doesn't say much but he takes a pride in his weapon skills that I've seldom seen. Jonny's weapon will never have a stoppage and on the shooting range he is invincible. He's big and strong, so physically will handle anything we throw at him.'

'Excellent,' I said. 'We also need a medic. Fish would be my choice. And he will give us more firepower with the bazooka he has made his speciality weapon.'

'That's seven,' said Rex, 'and thinking ahead, I'd make Mack number eight. When it comes to operations on water there's nobody better. Mack's smart and a great all-round soldier.'

'Agreed. Great choice. That leaves us with just two more to select, and my last pick would be Simmo. He's good in the bush but he mainly gets my vote because he's an organiser. While you and I are with the brigadier planning an operation, Simmo and Mack can take over and get all the gear organised.'

Rex laughed. 'A combat store man. I like it. OK, the final call is Nelson. He's another big man – like Jonny and Horse – but he has one unique talent that is bound to serve us well. He's African and he's a linguist. He's one of those lucky people with an ear for languages. He doesn't speak much Portuguese but he speaks all the regional African languages with remarkable fluency. With Nelson we can communicate with the locals anywhere the brigadier is likely to send us.'

'No brainer,' I replied. 'That's the team. Let's get them together and ready for Mozambique.'

# Madness in Mozambique

It was late November, the rainy season had begun and the parched African bush was already transformed. I was in the co-pilot's seat of a Rhodesian Air Force DC3 looking down on the thick, green canopy of the low woodland as we headed north towards the untidy town of Tete on the Zambezi River.

'Twenty minutes out, Mick. Time to get George back here to help me with the landing.'

Co-pilot George Walker was at the back, chatting with Rex and the brigadier. He returned to the front and I strapped in as the aircraft descended towards the runway.

We crossed the wide expanse of the Zambezi River that sparkled in the bright sunlight. A dozen hippos, enjoying the morning in the shallow water close to the road bridge, made threatening gestures as we disturbed their peace on short finals to the runway.

The elderly DC3 bounced once then slowed down as we passed a row of parked Portuguese military aircraft: Fiat jets, old Harvard trainers and some newer looking Dornier light aircraft. We stopped outside a hangar and disembarked as a small tanker came over to refuel the aircraft.

After refuelling, our next stop would be the Portuguese military headquarters located in Nampula, another two hours flying time east towards the Tanzanian border. Here we would meet Colonel Costa da Silva for an updated briefing on the military situation and find out exactly what he wanted us to do.

We had worked with the colonel before in Angola. Our actions there splintered the Russian-backed MPLA terrorist groups and for some time afterwards they were ineffectual, so it was no great surprise when a request for similar help came in from Mozambique.

All we knew so far was that a Frelimo terrorist gang was harassing a Portuguese garrison at a small trading post known as Furuncungo, located to the north-west near the border with Malawi. We guessed that would be our ultimate destination.

While the DC3 was being refuelled, Fish and I walked over to the nearby military garrison where three big, French Berliet trucks were being loaded with troops and equipment. The men were new conscripts that had literally just been flown in from Lisbon. Several of them were carrying their personal gear in brown, cardboard suitcases with travel stickers on them, and I could tell from the way they handled their G3 rifles that training had been minimal.

I approached the lead vehicle, waved to the guys on the back and in my best schoolboy French called out, '*Bonjour, mes amis. Comment ca va?*'

There were smiles all round and comments in Portuguese I couldn't understand, then a solidly built young man replied in good English, 'Good morning, Sir. We are well, thank you. We are about to leave for the Furuncungo base – wherever that may be?'

I told him we would probably be joining them there, and asked his name and where he had learned such good English.

Guido Batista was a medical intern in his second year when the call-up papers arrived; much to his disappointment, the Portuguese military would not defer his service until after he had completed his training to be a doctor. I introduced him to Fish – our own medic – and could see an immediate rapport.

Guido turned and held the arm of a very similar looking man sitting next to him on the back of the truck: 'This is my elder brother, Eduardo.' The man's big, friendly face lit up with a smile and he too greeted me in passable English.

'Are you a doctor as well, Eduardo?' I asked.

'No way,' he laughed. 'I'm just a peasant farmer, and it will be hard work for our mother and father with me being away.'

He suddenly turned serious. 'Excuse me, Sir,' he said. 'Can you please tell me where we are? We were on a plane through the night from Lisbon – and now we are here.'

'Eduardo, you are in deepest, dark Africa,' I replied. 'I'll find you at the base and show you a map. It's good you speak English. We are probably going to be with you on operations for the next week or so and it will be good to have you close if we need to communicate to your comrades. I'll explain this to your officer, but are you OK with that?'

'It will be a pleasure, Sir. I am thinking we are lucky to have you with us.'

'*Obrigado*, Eduardo. I hope that turns out to be true.'

As I walked away, I could hear Guido and Eduardo explaining our conversation to the other bewildered Portuguese conscripts and was glad I'd gone over to say hello. Fish stayed with Guido for some time explaining to him the possibility of this convoy taking a landmine hit on the way forward and what he'd be faced with if that happened.

Poor buggers, I thought. Peasant farmers with cardboard suitcases, who had no idea where they were or what they were here for.

I mentally wished all of them on that convoy well; but events would soon show that nobody with any influence was monitoring my thoughts.

The DC3 rumbled east over a stunning landscape of massive, bare granite features, thrust up from a flat plateau at a time when the Great Rift Valley was getting itself sorted out. With that came deep layers of mineral-rich, red soils nourishing hardwood trees that formed a dense, green canopy. I liked it. We would have no trouble being invisible in that environment.

We touched down in Nampula and were taken to the military headquarters, located in a grand building with a marble staircase that lead to the equally palatial office of Colonel Costa da Silva.

In contrast to the boys on the French Berliet truck I'd met in Tete, the colonel knew exactly where he was and what was happening.

'The general situation is not unlike what you encountered in Angola,' he began. 'But this time you are up against the Front for the Liberation of Mozambique, known as Frelimo, and they have Chinese – not Russian – backing.

'The Chinese established a major training base for Frelimo at a camp called Mgagao, near Iringa in southern Tanzania; from there guerrilla groups infiltrated the northern Cabo Delgado and Nyasa provinces of Mozambique. They met little resistance as we had no real military presence. Since then we believe they have established bases on or near the Malawi border and have been launching operations south into the Tete province.

'Lisbon responded to my request for assistance by sending troops called up for national service.

'Brigadier, we need your help to protect these ill-prepared and barely trained conscripts from a well-organised Frelimo cadre operating in the Furuncungo area. They are gaining confidence as we fail to counter their strikes with mines in the roads and mortar attacks on our camps. I fear for my troops. And while we here are limited to using what we are sent by Lisbon, the casualties that result are never seen to be a Lisbon problem.'

The brigadier nodded.

'Colonel, we fully understand your position. This morning the major spoke to some of the new conscripts now on their way to Furuncungo. He said they looked like good men, but they didn't even know where they were!

'After this briefing we will fly back to Tete, where we will be joined by two Rhodesian Air Force Alouette helicopters. Tomorrow morning we will fly up to Furuncungo and commence our search for the gang.'

The discussions continued until it was time for lunch. The colonel was a generous host and our visit was probably a good excuse to indulge a little more than usual. While we were busy with grilled langoustines washed down with an unending supply of chilled Mateus Rosé, and while Guido and Eduardo trundled towards their new home on the back of the big, French trucks, there were sinister things happening near Furuncungo.

Frelimo leader Regone Mwanza was now feeling confident, as Costa da Silva had suggested he would be. He had blown up two Berliet trucks with landmines that inflicted casualties, but he knew the two mortar attacks on the camp were mostly off-target. He was determined to do better this time.

He had picked an open area in the woodland, ideal for his 82-millimetre mortars and the frightening 122-millimetre rockets he had recently been supplied with via a new logistical route through Malawi. Regone thought it was less than two kilometres to the base, but he wanted pinpoint accuracy for this attack, so he and one of his group walked carefully towards the Furuncungo garrison.

In broad daylight and without any fear of detection, the two terrorists reached the edge of a clearing made by the Portuguese around their camp. As a defensive measure, they had cut down all the trees and cover in a 100-metre circle around the base.

Regone and his comrade crouched down in cover to observe.

They could see the trenched perimeter with sandbagged pillboxes where the machine guns were located and they watched with interest as troops moved here and there around the base.

The Portuguese had guards posted but nobody saw them.

Regone looked at the camp buildings. 'I think it is 150 metres from here to the centre of the garrison?' he whispered to his comrade. The older man, who carried an SKS rifle, studied the ground for a moment and nodded in agreement.

Regone took a compass bearing, then the pair started to walk back towards the baseplate position. His companion was there to pace out the distance, so Regone said nothing as they retraced their steps.

Two thousand one hundred and thirty-two steps later the pacer and Regone reached the clearing with his weapons; 2,132 paces on the ground, he estimated, should convert to a firing range of around 2,050 metres. He added on the 150 metres to the centre of the garrison. In the late afternoon they carefully set up the rockets and mortars, using the compass bearing and an elevation to give them 2,200 metres range.

There was nothing left to do except have some food and then sleep in the shade and await the planned attack time of 02.00 hours, which was when their Chinese trainers had told them the enemy would be at his lowest state of alert.

Regone took the hand of his small-breasted, Chinese political commissar, Yui Zin, and led her away from the other twenty terrorists brought here for the mission. They found a deep, shaded gully where the ground was softened with the fallen fronds of a huge fig tree, and there he gave the Chinese woman an intense pleasure she'd never had back in Shanghai.

The convoy from Tete, with Guido and Eduardo, arrived at the Furuncungo base without incident around 15.45 hours. They didn't see anything through the thick cover but passed within 100 metres of where Regone had lined up the rockets and mortars.

The garrison was about 100 metres square. On the outside the Portuguese had used bulldozers to create a perimeter embankment, into which they had constructed pillboxes with roof cover from hardwood trees they had cut down around the camp. On top of the timber they had placed corrugated iron sheeting and on top of that two or three layers of sandbags. Behind the pillboxes they had dug trenches so guards could move in cover between these defensive positions. It was well done and it would be a difficult assault task for any attacking force trying to wipe out the base.

Within the perimeter, sitting on concrete slabs, was an assortment of timber-frame buildings with grey, corrugated iron cladding. The biggest of these buildings was the barrack room for the troops. The bunks were tiered four-high off the ground and there was a row of lockers against the wall on one side for clothing and personal possessions.

In the centre of the base were the cookhouse and the troops' canteen and a second structure served as a combined officers' and NCOs' mess. Beyond that was the vehicle park with the twisted frames of the two trucks that had found the TMH46 anti-tank mines on the roads around the garrison.

Guido and Eduardo settled into their allocated bunk spaces and listened to the briefing from the garrison commander. Guido was shown the medical room where he would work, but it was pointed out that he would also be expected to do his share of the more routine duties around the garrison.

The two brothers thus found themselves together on guard duty that night, and joked at their luck of getting the 'dog watch' – between 02.00 and 04.00 hours. They were soon to find out just how lucky they were.

At 01.45 they were woken by the duty sergeant. They had ten minutes to get themselves together before reporting at a pillbox on the perimeter to relieve the earlier watch.

Frelimo's Regone Mwanza made a mistake he would never know by sticking to the theory that the ultimate time for an attack was 02.00 hours. Chairman Mao's advisors did not remember, or did not know, that 02.00 was a conventional guard changeover time for most Western forces. If Regone had initiated his plans just ten minutes earlier, or later, his strike would have been even more devastating.

As it was there were two guard rosters in the safety of the pillboxes when Regone gave the order to open fire.

It was all new to these Portuguese conscripts, so they took some time on the handover-takeover routine and it was while that was in progress, under the patient eye of the sergeant, they heard the sounds of multiple explosions in the distance.

'Mortar attack!' screamed the sergeant. 'Get under cover.'

First to hit was a 122-millimetre rocket. It shrieked over the centre of the camp and exploded into the unprotected rear of a pillbox on the far perimeter. The soldiers there would have been looking anxiously outwards in the opposite direction. Six cardboard-suitcase conscripts were killed instantly.

Within seconds of the rocket impact, the 82-millimetre mortars arrived in force with sickening pin-point accuracy.

Mortars were a deadly weapon and Regone had done well with his distance and bearings. The first four bombs smashed through the tin roofing of the barrack room. Exploding on impact, they created what was described as an 'airburst' effect on the bunks filled with sleeping soldiers who didn't even know where they were.

It could have been much worse if Regone had had the training and experience to know that after firing the first rounds the baseplates of the mortars would 'bed-in' with the recoil, and a couple of downward clicks on the elevation sights were needed to bring the next salvo back on target.

The next three 122-millimetre rockets roared over the top of the pillboxes and exploded into the two already wrecked trucks in the vehicle park and some fuel drums that burst into a brilliant red fireball.

The next salvo of mortar bombs fell short, peppering the pillboxes on the perimeter with deadly shrapnel. It was a terrifying ordeal and there was no respite for the Portuguese conscripts who thought the next explosion could be the end of them. They hugged the ground in fear and prayed they would be spared.

It was time for Regone Mwanza to disappear into the bush and get as far away as possible before first light. But before leaving, he ordered a TMH46 anti-tank mine to be buried in the road close to where he had launched the attack.

By 03.00 that fateful morning, they had completed their mission and were heading confidently back to the base they had established in the dense cover by the river that flowed south from the foothills of Malawi. The Portuguese would respond with impotent outrage at the attack and would achieve nothing. Regone would rest, resupply and plan his next raid on the colonial enemy with the reinforcements he was expecting. It would be especially pleasurable, meanwhile, to have Yui Zin with the group. She would keep them focused. At the same time, he would enjoy her personal attention.

Back at the garrison, some of the guards in the perimeter pillboxes started firing at shadows they thought were attacking terrorists. Fuelled by fear and imagination, the panic spread from one pillbox to another and soon hundreds of rounds of ammunition were being fired uselessly into the dark bush.

A lull in the firing gave one of the older, regular army sergeants attached to the base the chance to shout: 'Stop firing! Stop! Cease fire!' And in the brief quiet that followed they could hear, for the first time, the anguished cries of the bunkhouse casualties.

'Oh my God!' said Guido. He took off his web belt and gave it and his rifle to Eduardo, then ran as fast as he could towards the barracks, but halfway there he realised he did not have his medic bag, so he changed direction and ran to the medical room. He grabbed the bag and rushed into the barrack room. Carnage confronted him. He paused in the doorway, shocked at what he saw. What the hell do I do here, he thought?

'In the blessed Mary's name, please help me!' cried a voice beneath an upturned bed next to him. Guido lifted up the mattress and found a soldier lying in a pool of blood. His belly had been sliced open by shrapnel from the mortar bombs and his intestines now lay in the blood on the concrete floor.

As an intern, Guido had worked in the accident and emergency department of the main hospital in Lisbon. Having to deal with car accidents, he had seen gore like this before. He gave the soldier a shot of morphine then picked up and examined the intestinal tract. Remarkably, it didn't appear to be punctured, so he gathered it up in his hands and threaded it back inside the abdominal wound. He poured sterile solution over it then stitched it up. It was rough, but there was no time here for refinement. He applied two thick dressings, taped it all up, wedged a wet pillow under the man's head and left him in a pain- and morphine-induced haze.

Stepping over the man, Guido spotted an arm sticking out from another upturned bunk. He lifted it up, but this time there was nothing he could do. The back of the soldier's head had been blown off with the bomb blast. Mercifully, he would have been killed instantly.

Another dead man lay face down in another pool of blood, and yet another hung grotesquely from the ladder used to reach the top bunks.

Guido heard a cry of anguish and digging through the mess of bedding, clothes and vomit, found an injured young soldier lying on his back in the mire. A large, jagged hole in his chest pulsated and pumped out blood through the smashed rib cage. He lifted the man's head off the floor and propped it up on the edge of a mattress. He gave him a morphine shot and cleaned up the wound as best he could before putting on a dressing and bandage.

Guido was in a shock-induced trance and didn't realise there were uninjured survivors, until he felt a tap on his shoulder and a shaky, young voice asked in Portuguese what he could do to help.

'Get the officer. There may be men in here we can save. Be quick.'

Meanwhile, news of the attack had reached the base in Tete, where we were relaxed and enjoying a strong coffee ahead of the pre-dawn helicopter flight to Furuncungo.

A messenger arrived breathless. We were summoned to the operations room.

The haggard looking base commander, wearing a brown dressing gown and smoking a strong-smelling cigarette, greeted us.

'We've been badly hit at Furuncungo,' he said. 'Sixteen dead and several others with serious injuries. Their only chance is to get to a hospital as soon as possible.

'Brigadier, once the helicopters have dropped you off at the base, is it possible for them to ferry the badly injured back to Tete?' he asked.

The brigadier agreed without hesitation because tactically it was also the right thing to do. Sitting on the ground at the base the helicopters would be a tempting target if the terrorist group was still in the area. Having them flying with casualties made plenty of sense until such time as we had a handle on the ground situation.

We flew fast and low over the woodland canopy, heading north-west towards the massive escarpments that formed the border with Malawi. The country was devoid of human habitation. We caught a glimpse of a leopard as it ducked into cover on one of the bare granite outcrops, and later three large kudu antelopes with massive, spiralling horns galloped away in panic as the aircraft roared over them.

The small trading centre of Furuncungo was located next to the Revubie River, which brought perennial, fresh water down from the Malawi highlands. Large palms reaching above the dense, riverine woodland marked the course of the river. As we approached the settlement and military base, the pilots took the aircraft higher to get a good look at the ground below.

We flew over the garrison and could see the damage done to the pillbox by the rocket, and the torn roofing hit by the mortars. Speaking through my headset, I asked the pilots where the terrorists could have based their weapons, because we were looking down on a thick, woodland canopy and you can't fire rockets and mortars through trees.

The lead pilot obliged by banking the helicopter over the pillbox, which we could now see had been hit from behind, and flew the aircraft in what he guessed would be the direction back to the launch position. And sure enough, we found it: there was a slightly elevated area of sheet rock with low bushes that would have been perfect for the attack.

'Great work, Harves,' I said. 'Can we put Rex and his stick down on the ground, so he can have a look round while we find out what's happening at the base?'

The second Alouette duly descended and Rex and his team dropped their packs then jumped out.

We, meanwhile, landed on a football field next to the camp, and were met by a Portuguese Army captain who drove out in a Jeep. He saluted. Then, emotion suddenly overwhelming him, he broke down: 'Sorry. Sorry,' he said as tears rolled down his face. 'It is terrible. We have sixteen men dead and more than twenty with injuries – some very serious and I think they too will die.'

'Captain, this is our own doctor,' I said and pointed to Fish. 'First, we must take him to your own medical staff, so he can see which of the injury cases we need to fly back to Tete. At the same time, we need to quickly refuel the helicopters so there is no delay.'

He nodded his head. '*Obrigado*.' And with that he regained his composure.

We drove into the camp and followed the captain to the first barracks. We walked past sixteen black plastic bags lying in a row on the ground. Sixteen boys who didn't know where they were, now heading home to Lisbon.

Inside the barracks, I struggled to cope with the horror of it all: the madness of the tiered bunks inside an elevated tin shed, the blood-stained walls and upturned mattresses. The stink of vomit, urine, sweat and fear was overwhelming.

I recognised Guido, working on a soldier lying on the floor in a puddle of puked-up tinned octopus. I put my hand on his shoulder to get his attention and pointed to Fish, and that was all I could do. I had to get out. I couldn't stand being in there any longer. Fish knew what to do. I had to get out and join Rex. I needed fresh air and to be well away from the stench and the carnage.

The Portuguese captain was obviously as glad as I was to get out of the barrack room and he led us across a small parade ground towards the mess building. A tattered Portuguese flag was draped over the flag pole, limp in the lifeless morning air. Cockerels scratched amongst some chilli bushes growing against a wall. A goat was tethered to a tree on the corner of the mess building: it looked downcast and seemed to know there would be more killing before the day was done.

While I set up our VHF radio to speak to Rex, they brought a big plate of hot bread rolls – fresh out of the oven – and coffee with a bottle of *aguardiente*. It made us all feel much better.

Communication with Rex, just two kilometres away, was no problem and his news was all good. The clearing was, indeed, the place from which the attack had been launched. They had found the firing positions and there were tracks of at least twenty terrorists who had carried in the mortars and rockets used in the attack. Rex said there was one very small set of prints, suggesting there was a woman or adolescent involved in the attack.

The tracks, he said, led to a game path that headed north-west up towards the Malawi border. Finally, he had followed another set of tracks that led them to the bush road between Furuncungo and Tete, and there found where the terrorists had planted a TMH46 anti-tank mine. Rex carried a small packet of PEA plastic explosive, a detonator and a short coil of safety fuse. He placed it over the mine and waited for communication with us before blowing it. 'Good thinking, Rex,' I said. 'Another unannounced explosion would create chaos here. We'll spread the word so there is no more panic and I'll join you shortly at the clearing.'

I then asked the captain if he could find Eduardo, Guido's brother, whom we had met in Tete, and after some delay a sergeant showed in a nervous looking Eduardo.

'Relax, Eduardo,' I said. 'This is a terrible time for everybody, but we are already on the tracks of those who did this attack and we will find them. While we are doing this, I need your help.

'Eduardo, I need you to act as an interpreter for the brigadier, so he can communicate with the captain. Please explain my request to the captain and ask if that is possible.'

The captain agreed at once and rattled off instructions in Portuguese.

I decided to leave Mack and Simmo with the brigadier. I gathered up the remaining bread rolls; Rex and the team would enjoy them. The bottle of *aguardiente* we'd save for a more appropriate time, because there was no telling where this operation would take us.

Harves put us down in the clearing, wished us well, then pulled out. We braced against the wash of whirring rotors, engulfed in the noise and the heady smell of avgas. I was already feeling a zillion times better.

Rex and the boys came over and I gave them the still warm bread rolls.

We turned our attention to the job in hand. The TMH46 mine was a Russian or Chinese-made product, consisting of six kilograms of TNT moulded into a metal casing that looked like a casserole dish. In the centre – where the handle would be on the casserole dish lid – was a threaded cylindrical cavity. Into this cavity was screwed a 200-gram TNT booster charge attached to a pressure-sensitive detonating device.

To detonate the device, more than 200 kilograms of pressure had to be applied, so if locals were to walk over it nothing would happen, but if a car, bus or truck were to go over the mine it would explode with devastating effect.

Regone Mwanza had a nasty streak in him. As bad as the mine on its own could be, it would do even more damage if boosted by other explosive devices. Knowing he was due for a resupply, Regone had dug the hole deeper this time and placed his six remaining mortar bombs and twelve grenades beneath the mine.

In another operation, in another country, we had lost two good men while trying to lift and remove a mine that had been booby-trapped, so these days we didn't take any chances. Rex lit the safety fuse and we all backed off into cover waiting for the explosion.

There was a great crash of thunder as the mine exploded, followed by the sound of deadly metal fragments scything the sky above us. I let the brigadier know the road was now clear and we turned our attention to the more serious business of tracking down the Frelimo terrorists.

It was 09.00, so they were six or seven hours ahead of us and by now would probably have reached one of their bases; maybe a staging base where they would cache munitions to be used on operations like the Furuncungo attack.

As we followed Rex on their tracks, I was thinking about the map and the briefing Colonel Costa da Silva had given us in Nampula.

In addition to the trouble around Furuncungo, he had reported terrorist activity around the settlement of Tembue, not that far to the west, and at Mulomba, an equal distance to the east of Furuncungo. The direction of the track we were following headed towards a bulge on the geographical border with Malawi, where part of the Great Rift Valley mountain chain thrust southwards. It would be an ideal location for a main base camp. There would be permanent water and dense cover in foothills where the locals were supportive. It was a remote location that would not attract unwelcome political attention to the host country Malawi, but the town of Lilongwe was not that far away so the logistics of resupply would be easy to arrange.

Somewhere in that mountain chain was a big camp from which all operations into the Tete province were launched. The Furuncungo gang we were following could lead us all the way there. Best of all and luckily for us – given we were only eight in number – they didn't even know we were coming.

The track was easy going and led us through a belt of low canopy woodland. The grass was still low as it was early in the rainy season. Flame lilies decorated the understory; we saw some game spoor. Leading the way, Rex disturbed a large, black snake that was in the process of killing and eating a rat. We detoured around the snake and kept moving.

Rex put up his hand and we immediately dashed forward into cover. A big black and white sable antelope bull with massive swept-back horns trotted towards us, knowing we were there but unsure if we were friends or foes. He cantered away as the human scent reached his nostrils.

I called a halt at midday. It was now very hot and humid, but we had found a pool in a small stream where we could see the terrorist gang had refreshed themselves, and we did the same. We backed off onto a small rise where we could observe the track and rest in the shade for an hour or two. In the next three or four hours it was highly likely we would be closing in on a terrorist base. We would need to be as alert as possible.

Rex, Pig Dog and I took turns in leading as we continued following the track through the afternoon and into the early evening. It was tough mentally, but it was nothing new; we had many times before followed tracks used by the bad-tempered and dangerous African buffalo. There were no buffalo here so in a way it was probably a bit easier, but then again buffalo don't carry AK-47s!

As daylight faded, we moved off the track and on to a low rise where we had a view of the surrounding country. I spread the map out on the ground and we lined it up with the compass to work out where we were. Looking ahead and to the north we could see a long, low ridge.

'Eighteen kilometres,' said Rex. 'I can still make out the shape of the trees on the ridge and that means eighteen kilometres away.' He pointed to the close contours on the map: 'That's it. And that's where they will be,' he said, pointing to what the map showed as a gap in the ridge where two rivers met and had cut through the feature.

It was a good guess and we'd work on that.

With the ridge for reference we could work out roughly where we were, so I called base to give the brigadier our location and a brief situation report, including our guesswork. I told him we were going to rest where we were until the moon came up at 20.30 hours. We would walk through the night, aiming for a recce base on top of the ridge about two kilometres east of the gap where the rivers met. From the top of the ridge we would have a good look around during daylight tomorrow and would report back before going further.

The brigadier acknowledged, and told us the helicopters had done two trips taking the badly wounded back to the hospital in Tete, while Guido had cleaned up the less seriously injured. The captain had organised a detail to hose down and repair the barrack room while Simmo and Mack, with Eduardo and a patrol of thirty men, went to the mine explosion and attack site. They had then done a wide, circular clearance patrol around the base and settlement.

There would be nightmares in the camp that night, but nothing more serious than that.

The boys had heard the radio conversation, so knew the score, but once we had closed down I said to them, 'Guys, the truth is we don't really know what we will find up ahead, but the good thing is these Frelimo bastards are not expecting us because they know the Portuguese troops do nothing other than defend their base. We know there are at least twenty of them and there may be many more. There may only be eight of us, but they don't know that.

'Once we start the action, they will not know if there are 8 or 800 attacking them and they won't know who we are. My guess is that most of them won't hang around to find out. That is a huge advantage to us, but to have that advantage we have to be invisible until it's time to squeeze the trigger. Are we all happy with that?' It was quite unnecessary for me to ask; I just wanted to be sure we were, as usual, all on the same page, and to offer a chance for anyone with a better idea to let us hear it.

'Rex? Karate? Jonny? Horse?'

Rex looked around then spoke for the others: 'Sounds like a winner to me.'

Meanwhile, eighteen kilometres ahead of us, Frelimo leader Regone Mwanza was also making plans; and his too involved physical exertion as he and Yui Zin lay naked in the cool water of the river next to their camp.

After the mortar and rocket attack, the terrorists had disassembled their weapons and shared the load amongst themselves. Led by Regone, they then made haste along the well-worn track to the north. They walked at a brisk pace, without stopping, until about an hour after sunrise when they reached a small stream and Regone called a break.

They drank from the stream and shared some caked maize meal they had wrapped in newspaper. When it was finished, Regone took one of the news-paper wrappings and used it to roll a joint filled with dried marihuana leaves. *Dagga*, as they called it, grew naturally in Malawi and was widely used by the indigenous people, so Regone was easily able to secure a supply. He enjoyed it. It calmed his nerves; it seemed to enhance his already hot sexual desire. And in the absence of anything like morphine, it would at least give some comfort to anyone unfortunate enough to be wounded.

Regone took a deep drag on the smouldering joint then passed it to Yui Zin. She inhaled tentatively then passed it on to the man sitting next to her. It was passed from one person to the next until all had drawn on the joint and the remaining stump was given back to Regone. Holding it delicately between finger and thumb he sucked out one last drag then dropped it to the ground and extinguished it with his foot.

He stood up, the signal for all to do the same and start moving again.

It was a beautifully calm African morning. A golden oriole called from a nearby tree – liquid clear notes, a deep, melodious call. Yui Zin stopped and put up her hand for everyone to halt.

She pointed in the direction of the calling bird and said to Regone, 'In my village in China we have these birds. They are lucky for us. They will be lucky for us here.'

She looked back at the men, who were all watching with interest, and she started to sing. Yui Zin had a sweet voice and her village song about the ori-oles had a simple but pleasing rhythm. Still singing she started moving for-ward again and they all followed. In the front Regone had picked up the tune and joined in with his deep, base baritone. Not knowing the words, he impro-vised with his own, in his own language, and soon the rest of the group had joined in. Others took the lead, sometimes with new words, and a repetitive chorus developed based on Yui Zin's original theme; the natural harmony of the African voices merged with impromptu descants that would subtly lift or suppress the tempo before skilfully reverting to the original. Tears came to Yui Zin's eyes as the harmonies enveloped her and she remembered home. Eyes streaming, she put her head down and sobbed. The oriole flew off as the singing group marched towards the eighteen-kilometre camp.

About an hour after we resumed our pursuit, Rex found the *stompie* that Regone had discarded; in the bright moonlight it was hard to miss. He picked it up, took a sniff and passed it to me: 'They are on *dagga*,' he said.

We walked through the night, accompanied only by the calls of small owls and nightjars. Where there were clearings, we could see the outline of the ridge we were heading for and as we got closer, we could see that in addition to the trees it was strewn with large boulders. It would be a good place for us to hide.

We reached the ridge just as the first light was dawning. We were all very tired and in need of sleep, but we didn't know if we would be secure. It would not be the first time we had gone into a hide at night only to find a local settlement close to us as it got light. We took up defensive positions and waited.

Yui Zin's orioles were calling above us, along with the metallic rasping of a drongo. A flock of francolin partridges suddenly burst out of cover below us in an explosion of noise. I saw Rex, on my right, swivel his aim in that direction then, grinning at me, he pointed up to an early black eagle that had caused the panic.

I took first watch while the others settled themselves into hides between the boulders.

We had found a good place.

We spent the day trying to get some sleep, but in spite of being in the shade of the trees and boulders, by 11.00 it was very hot and humid so we sweated it out. We had filled our water bottles at a small stream at the base of the ridge, but there wouldn't be much left by the end of the day. Karate got out the HF radio and tapped a Morse message back to the brigadier, letting him know where we were. The black eagle returned and spiralled upwards on the hot air lifting over the ridge. I wondered what it could see from up there.

By 16.00 the sting had gone out of the hot day. Staying close together we moved cautiously along the top of the wooded ridge towards the gap.

An hour later we had reached the edge and could see the river line and some well-used tracks less than 500 metres below us. Two figures, dressed in what looked like blue overalls, appeared carrying black, plastic barrels in each hand. Both had an AK-47 slung over their shoulders. It was a water detail.

Back-tracking in the direction they had come from, I was sure I had seen a wisp of smoke wafting through a dense thicket of figs and mahogany trees.

I handed my binoculars to Rex. Through the glasses he followed the water party back towards the thicket. 'There's smoke there,' he whispered. 'They have a cooking fire.' And he pointed to the same thicket of trees I had been watching. We motioned for the others to close in and have a look, while Rex and I tried to work out how best to get down off the ridge for a better look once it got dark.

Looking south we could see parts of the track we had been following, the main track into the camp. As it approached the ridge, it wound up through some boulders into a narrow saddle and from there dropped down into a wooded basin, where we had seen the water party and the smoke. If the camp was attacked from the north, any fleeing terrorists would be chan-nelled by the ground into this narrow saddle: with that realisation our best offensive option was suddenly obvious.

All day I had been thinking we would do a close-in recce that night, pull back to our camp amongst the boulders and then attack the base with the helicopters the following morning. But now the camp location was suffi-ciently clear to us that a close-in recce need not be risked.

We wouldn't wait. We'd move down and position ourselves in two groups in ambush on either side of the saddle that night. At first light in the morn-ing, I'd get the helicopters to come in from the north and attack the camp with their machine guns. That would get the terrorists running our way and we'd take them out at close range in the saddle.

'OK guys,' I said, 'this is what we are going to do ...' And while Karate and I called the brigadier to give him the plan, they all took turns with the binoculars to get themselves familiar with ground they would be crossing in the dark in an hour or two.

Rex was busy with Jonny and Horse, who carried the 7.62 millimetre MAG machine guns, discussing where best they should position themselves.

We were all carrying our NATO weapons – FN rifles and the MAGs – so we could use Portuguese ammunition if we ran out, which suddenly looked a distinct possibility.

Regone, meanwhile, was comfortable in his camp. There was plenty of water, the camp was well concealed beneath tall, densely foliaged trees, and he was well provisioned with food being brought from the main supply base in Malawi.

He currently had twenty trained guerrillas, plus another fifty semi-trained men who carried the ammunition and weapons. They were also used to ferry provisions and to bring in new recruits from Malawi. He had sent thirty of them away that morning to replenish the mortars, rockets and mines used in the Furuncungo attack.

And he had his political commissar, Yui Zin.

When the moon came up, we started our descent from the top of the ridge to our selected fire positions in the saddle. We picked our way quietly around the strewn boulders, stopping every so often to look and listen, and some-times we used the passive light intensifier scope to check the way ahead. We used it for half an hour when we reached the saddle and the track and once certain there were no guards or night patrols, we split – I stayed on the ridge side of the track while Rex took his group across it and into cover on the opposite side.

With the moon and our night vision equipment, we had the freedom to try various fire positions before eventually settling in between some granite boulders that were elevated above the track and gave us the widest view while at the same time offering concealment and cover.

Karate turned on the VHF radio and put on his headset. He gave me the thumbs up indicating that Rex was in position.

It was not long after midnight and all we had to do now was to wait.

Jonny and I took the first two-hour shift while Karate and Pig Dog slept. Jonny and I were both tired, but we had been in ambushes together before and knew the routines. A rustle in the grass – he'd touch my arm and point. We would both go into the aim and focus on the noise. A small owl would call in the distance. He'd point and smile, aware that as a keen bird watcher I'd know exactly which owl it was. Probably, the scientific name of it as well. Small distractions like that kept you awake, alert and alive.

Our next guard was at 04.00 and by then it was quite cool. I longed for a cup of coffee.

By 05.30 some of the birds had started to call. I saw Pig Dog move silently into his firing position. Karate moved in next to me, put his headset on and tapped out a call to Rex. He gave me the thumbs up. All good. Not long to wait now.

The sun was still rising when the familiar voice of the lead helicopter pilot, Ian Harvey, came over the air, advising they were ten minutes out and would be looking for our flares and smoke in about five minutes. He said they were flying low on the north side of the ridge to limit the noise and would initially attack out of the sun.

Rex and I acknowledged. We both had orange smoke grenades that we would let off next to our positions. At the same time, we would both fire a red mini-flare in the direction of the camp to indicate the target.

We heard the hum of the engine noise just as Harves called for smoke. I pulled the pin and threw the smoke grenade a few metres behind us. An orange cloud erupted on the opposite side of the saddle as Rex did the same.

The noise suddenly increased and from behind the ridge the two Alouette helicopters appeared, the rotor noise changing as they climbed and went into orbit. We fired the red flares in the direction of the camp and, breaking silence, I told Harves to look for the patch of big trees.

'Got it,' he said in an instant. The helicopters angled to one side and the gunners in the back seats opened fire.

At first the gunners fired into the thatched, A-frame shelters that had been built under the trees, but as the camp woke up to the horror that had suddenly engulfed them the terrorists started running. The helicopter gunners cut them down as they ran in every direction, but by keeping to the north of the camp the aircraft drove many of them, unwittingly, towards our position in the saddle.

The first one bounded into view. He was wearing no more than a tattered pair of shorts and carried an AK in his right hand. Rex let him get to within fifteen metres of us then dropped him with a single shot.

Moments later a loose group of six terrorists rushed up the track towards us. They were close enough for us to see the wide-eyed fear in their faces when we opened up and cut them down in a deadly crossfire.

Two more appeared over the rise and stopped when they heard the firing: they half raised their AKs and were looking ahead, wondering what was happening. I got one of them with a quick shot, a fraction of a second before Jonny blew both of them away with a brilliantly controlled burst from his MAG.

There was a lull in the firing. The helicopters continued circling. A short burst of fire from the lead aircraft and another terrorist died. We lay still for some time, waiting for those who had hidden to sneak out and try to escape.

Harves' voice came over the radio, advising they needed to refuel and were returning to base. He said they would come back once we had cleared the camp and told us there was a clearing where both aircraft could land on the north side of the camp. 'And Mick,' he added, 'there is a highway leading north. It looks like this camp may just be a staging base. My guess is there are still bigger fish to fry.'

I acknowledged and returned my focus to the ambush position. We had done this often enough to know that the biggest risk was to show ourselves too early. A desperate RPD gunner could be hidden and waiting for us.

Fifteen minutes passed. Mentally, I had just decided to give it a couple of minutes more, when Pig Dog touched my arm and pointed. He had seen a slight movement in rocks off to one side of the saddle, at about the same level as Rex's fire position. Karate tapped out a warning to Rex.

We sat hardly daring to breathe. The terrorist was careful and patient. He would have known we were there somewhere. We waited another ten minutes and again saw movement. This time it was quite a bit closer. We tapped another warning to Rex, who would not have our view.

Another ten minutes passed. Then, no more than twenty metres away from Rex's position, a big man in blue overalls stood up slowly. In his hand he carried a Chinese stick grenade. He pulled the pin. As he lifted his arm to throw the grenade, all four of us opened fire at the same time.

Jonny was still firing his MAG when the grenade exploded next to the fallen body. Shrapnel and bits of bone and flesh flew through the air towards us.

Regone Mwanza would never again trouble the Portuguese.

I went on the radio immediately to Rex. I suggested he send Horse higher up and further forward to give cover, while he went forward himself to check out the bodies strewn across our ambush position. We'd keep watch from the opposite side of the track while this happened and then we'd move as a team through the saddle and down into the camp. I'd put Jonny with the MAG up higher and keep him forward and abreast of Horse with the big gun on the other side.

We all knew the routine. The MAG gunners would stay above and ahead of us as we advanced through the saddle towards the camp: left top MAG would move forward 5 maybe 10 metres and duck into cover; right top MAG and both lower fire positions would watch, ready to fire instantly if there was any opposition to the left top movement; right top MAG would then move with cover from the rest; then it would be the turn of the lower pairs to 'pepper pot' forward in the same way.

It was laborious, but in high-risk situations like this we only ever exposed 25 per cent of our resource to a watching or waiting terrorist group, while the other 75 per cent of us were poised to react with withering fire at the slightest threat.

No words were spoken as all this happened. There was, perhaps, the rustling of leaves underfoot and a muted thump as the big boys with the MAGs went to ground, but no more.

Rex reached the fallen and dismembered body of the man with the stick grenade.

In a bloodied shirt pocket, he found a copy of Mao's *Little Red Book* with the name, Regone Mwanza, written in the front pages. Inside was a small black and white photograph of a young-looking Chinese woman and written on the back was, 'To Comrade Regone with love from Commissar Yui Zin Que'.

Commissar Yui Zin Que had not only lost her lover. We found her body later inside one of the thatched, A-frame shelters hit by helicopter fire. She had an AK-47 with the usual webbing belt that held spare magazines and in a pouch she also carried a bundle of RGD-5 blast grenades. She too had Mao's *Little Red Book*, with her name written in it, and I kept that with Regone's book to send on later to Colonel Costa da Silva.

We moved carefully through the saddle, checking the bodies and collecting all the weapons. Most had Chinese-made AK-47s, but we also picked up a couple of older SKS rifles and a single bamboo bazooka. Nearly all of our victims had fled from the helicopter attack without their web belts, so there was not much ammunition and only one or two grenades.

The ground dropped down and levelled out as we moved into the camp itself. It was located in a bend of the river and under the dense canopy of riverine woodland. The deep shade did not encourage much undergrowth so the area was clear, and with flowing water just metres away, it was the perfect campsite.

Under each tree as far as I could see were A-frame bivvies: thirty, forty, maybe more? Freshly cut green foliage had been tied on top of the long grass used to thatch the sloping sides to help conceal them from the air. The Portuguese had a squadron of old Harvard aircraft based in Tete and two Fiat jet ground-attack fighters which they had used against these Frelimo, so such precautions were good practice.

I called a halt and again put Horse and Jonny forward on the flanks with the MAGs. The first thatched bivvy was closest to Rex, so I signalled that Karate and I would cover him while he and Fish checked it out. A few minutes later Rex emerged with an RPD machine gun and a pack full of ammunition. He signalled there was one more dead terrorist to add to the list, then he and Fish got down to cover Karate and me as we moved on to check the next bivvy.

It took us a good hour to work our way through the camp in this way and we weren't challenged. All up, there were eleven dead bodies in the camp area: that meant we'd accounted for twenty-one of the gang thus far. The tally was rising.

While I reported back to the brigadier, Rex took the others on a wide-sweeping patrol around the camp. The helicopters would have engaged any fleeing terrorists on their side of the saddle, so we were sure there would be more casualties.

He returned an hour later having found another four dead, an underground arms cache and the 'highway' that Harves had seen from the air. He said they'd seen tracks – no more than a day or two old – of twenty to thirty terrorists heading north on the path. They had also found several tracks made that morning by individuals who had managed to elude the deadly fire from the helicopters.

It didn't bother me that several had escaped. We had accounted for twenty-five terrorists in the attack and had captured a pile of weapons. Furthermore, in the game we were playing it was only half-time. The highway north suggested there were bigger things ahead of us. We'd follow it and find out.

I thought of burning the camp then changed my mind. We'd leave it intact with the bodies where they lay, as a grim warning to any terrorists that might venture back.

The brigadier came in with the helicopters that brought fresh food, new batteries for the radio and the ammunition I had requested. He handed me a small canvas bag, saying, 'The Portuguese had nothing like what you wanted, but then I thought about the helicopters and the rescue gear they carry. They look quite good …' There was a question mark in his voice.

I opened the bag and found six fireworks. They were magnesium distress flares that burned with an intense white light.

'Perfect. Brilliant. Thank you, Sir. Sorry I couldn't explain over the air, but this is what I have in mind …'

I had asked the brigadier if he could find me at least six light grenades. I had been thinking about the logistics of our tiny band – a mere eight of us – attacking a big camp and how much damage we could really inflict, however much we took them by surprise. At the same time, I was still struggling to get the horrific images of the barrack room hit by mortars out of my mind. Putting the two together, I had come up with the idea of giving them a taste of their own medicine: we'd attack them at night while they were sleeping, but instead of using rockets and mortars, which we didn't have, we would employ the services of Number 5 Canberra Squadron of the Rhodesian Air Force. We'd bomb the camp from the air.

We would find the camp, pass back the location and details, then on the night of the attack we would move in close to the camp and indicate the target for the bombers with the flares. Once we had lit the flares, we would get the hell out of there as fast as we could and into whatever cover we could find.

'It's a good plan,' said the brigadier, 'but it's risky for you on the ground. Aerial bombardment is not a precise science at the best of times, and you want to do it at night. To mark the target properly you will need to get in bloody close. You'll be well within the danger zone.'

'But that's what we do, Sir,' I protested. 'And with due respect, it's not nearly as crazy as what you were trained to do against the Russians. At least we aren't guiding in a nuke!'

The brigadier laughed, knowing he had no answer to that: 'It's your show, Mick. Let's give it a go.'

Simmo and Mack had come in on the second chopper and were busy collecting the weapons and making them safe. Rex showed Simmo the arms cache. There were stacks of TMH46 anti-tank mines, boxes of grenades and ammunition and, surprisingly, four cases of gelignite, a commercial explosive we knew well from working with the mines and public works department from time to time on demolition jobs.

While we got ourselves reorganised, Simmo set about laying charges.

We had been on the go solidly for three nights, and with the adrenalin flow of the attack now gone fatigue set in quickly. I just wanted a wash in the river then to lie down and have a deep, uninterrupted sleep.

To get us out of the area and give us a start on the next leg, the choppers dropped us off in a clearing fifteen kilometres north of the camp. We followed a heavily wooded gully away from the main river line where the track ran and, happy we were far enough away, I called a halt. We found resting places in cover where we could defend ourselves, then I called everyone over. From my pack I pulled out the bottle of *aguardiente* I had been carrying, took a swig of the fiery, clear liquid and passed it to Rex: 'Cheers, guys! Good job today.'

Karate folded up eight small pieces of paper and tossed them around in his cap. He held it out to Jonny. 'Number one!' he exclaimed. 'First guard. I reckon I can just hang on for another hour.' With that he set up his MAG next to a tree on the anthill above us.

The moon didn't rise until after 20.00 hours and we were well rested and keen to move again as its light started to filter through the trees. Looking at the map, I thought we had 50 to 60 kilometres to cover before reaching the foothills of the escarpment. Logic said that any camp would not be too much further on from that. It was cool at night and there was no shortage of water. The track was wide and well used – a blind person could have followed it – and there was no big game around to trouble us. We'd get there comfortably in two nights. Then we would have to find the camp and plan the attack.

The terrorists who'd escaped from the camp attack would have been in a big hurry to leave. They would not have seen us, so would have no idea who we were or how many there were of us. All things considered, we still had the advantage; so long as we remained invisible we would again give Frelimo a nasty surprise.

Rex pushed the pace that night and we made good ground. We moved off the highway an hour before first light and followed one of the many densely wooded side gullies off the main river for another forty-five minutes then based up. The ground could not have been better for us: densely wooded to give us both concealment and shade through the day as we rested, we were slightly elevated above our tracks leading in, and there was cool, fresh water just a few metres away.

I'd drawn a midday 'stag' from Karate's cap and was enjoying watching a pair of brightly coloured barbets feeding on figs in the tree above the guard position, when the VHF radio crackled into life.

It was the brigadier. He was in one of the helicopters that had dropped off Mack and Simmo along with the Portuguese captain and a few of his men, including Eduardo, to see the camp we had attacked and to do a wider search of the surrounding area. The helicopter gunners were sure they had scored a couple more hits than we had accounted for, and also thought they should check the saddle where we had done our damage.

Having dropped off the ground force they had climbed, hoping to get VHF reception through to us, because there was urgent news that couldn't wait until our next twice daily HF sched.

I picked up the mike and acknowledged the call.

'There have been major developments,' replied the brigadier. 'A group of Russian-trained ZAPU terrorists, armed with SAM7 missiles, shot down an Air Rhodesia Viscount on the tourist route between Lake Kariba and Victoria Falls. Eighteen of the seventy-four passengers somehow survived the crash-landing. Four of them moved away from the aircraft, fearing an explosion, then watched in horror as the ZAPU group involved came to the wreckage and bayoneted the survivors, including a mother with her baby girl in her arms ... It doesn't bear thinking about.'

I heard the emotion in his voice.

He paused for a moment then continued: 'As you can imagine the country is shocked, hurt and angered by this action and the Rhodesian Government wants retribution and wants it fast! They – the politicians – and equally the Combined Operations chiefs – need to bolster morale in the country quickly. Their credibility is also on the line.

'Troops are on the trail of the ZAPU gang responsible, but they may not catch up with them before they cross back into Zambia. Meanwhile, the authorities and the country need a big result and they need it as quickly as possible, and when our request for the Canberra reached ComOps HQ to attack what we believe is a significant and substantial terrorist camp, they jumped at it.'

The brigadier paused: 'Roger so far?'

'Roger so far. Go ahead, Sunray,' I replied, my mind already racing with imagined pictures of the horror of the air crash, before the fickleness of the brain brought back the real pictures of guts hanging out of the Portuguese soldier and the puked-up tinned octopus on the bloody floor of the barrack room hit by the Frelimo mortars. I reached for my water bottle.

'Your request has been approved,' said the brigadier, 'but there are a few slight changes to the plan. Firstly, 5 Squadron, with your friend Bernie Vaughan, are running a high-altitude photo recce over the general area where you think the camp is located. That may already have happened earlier today before the cloud build-up. If they find anything, we'll let you know and guide you in on the target.

'Secondly, they want us to follow up the bombing with the helicopters and with you on the ground at first light. It's a good plan,' he said. 'Any survivors should be in a state of shock, but that aside what they really want is a count of casualties. Today they are going to let the media know that we have killed at least twenty-five terrorists and they will also say we are far from finished. With this sort of advance publicity they are desperate for us to deliver news of a big kill.

'You still with me, Mick? Roger so far?' he asked again, making sure I fully understood the implications that had now been added to our mission.

I acknowledged.

'It's political now, Mick. You are centre stage and everyone is watching. They wanted to send a Ministry of Information TV team to interview you guys after the attack. I told them that wouldn't happen, but that I'd be happy to front it myself later so they would get their story. I know this has nothing to do with the aircraft attack, but that's politics, Mick.'

'No problem, Sunray,' I replied. 'It doesn't change much for us. Judging from the tracks on this highway we have been following I'm sure we'll find the camp, and it looks like there will be a good number of terrorists there. But who knows? They come and go, so giving them the casualty numbers they are obviously looking for is another matter altogether, but rest assured we'll give it our best shot.'

'The situation is such that we could have got anything we asked for,' the brigadier went on, 'but I told them we had everything we needed. I want to be in the air somewhere close, so I called Colonel Costa da Silva. I told him that being overhead in a light aircraft during the follow-up attack would be very useful, so he has organised a Dornier and is coming down in person to join me in that role. He is really excited about it.'

I acknowledged again in a neutral voice. It was great we were getting the support we needed, but we still knew nothing about our target. Everything we had seen so far suggested that it was substantial, but we didn't know for sure and we didn't know where it was. If we were wrong, or if the terrorists had moved out of the camp, it normally wouldn't have mattered much, but now it was different. I shuddered, feeling the pressure for the first time. I knew sleep would not be easy, as the next number from Karate's cap took over the guard.

We had to find a big camp and we had to kill more than 100 terrorists. With that whirring around in my brain, I eventually drifted into sleep as the red and black barbets ate more of the figs above me.

Before setting off again that evening we made Morse contact with the HF radio. There was a lengthy reply and we recognised the rhythmical style of Simmo at the other end, tapping out the coded message. The Canberra photo-run had located the camp. The terrorists had taken over a disused mining complex. Estimated numbers: 300-plus. They wanted to attack the following night and suggested a time of 03.00 hours.

Karate tapped back, 'wait', while we dug out the maps and worked out if that was a practical proposition. We would have to cover twenty-five kilometres that night, which was possible, but we'd have to push it along to give ourselves enough time to reach the camp area before daylight.

I looked at Rex, who nodded: 'Even if it gets light before we reach the hills overlooking the camp, there is plenty of cover for us and we'll still be some distance away.'

'Agree. Let them know, Karate.'

With not having to carry extra water our packs were a lot lighter than they often were, which was just as well, because we could see the ground was getting steeper and we all knew Rex would push the pace.

We didn't wait for the moon so the first three hours were, from necessity, fairly slow, but Rex picked up the tempo through the middle of the night and we made good progress. At 05.20 hours the sky was starting to lighten and we were at the base of a steeply ascending ridge that would take us up to where we had planned to spend the day. The cover was a lot thinner on the ridge top and we were no longer on the well-worn path. Rex kept us below the skyline to avoid silhouetting as we picked our way up and around scattered boulders. Our senses were on high alert – we couldn't afford to mess things up now. We had to stay invisible.

It took us just under two hours to do that last climb and by then it was broad daylight. We found a good hiding place amongst rocks in a narrow gully and called it quits. While Karate sent back our position, Rex and Jonny did a 360-degree sweep to see if there were tracks and to assess the likelihood of us having visitors. There was nothing so we settled down to sleep.

We heard gunfire a few times in the direction of the camp and presumed they had a firing range and were training, but otherwise the day was uneventful.

At 16.00 hours we had packed up and started to move carefully further up the hill towards the terrorist camp. The tree cover was fairly sparse, but there were plenty of boulders and we made good use of those. We reached the top and crept forward.

On level ground below us was the camp. We could see a number of old, iron-clad buildings and numerous thatched structures. People were moving around and all of them were armed. Two trucks were parked off to one side. There was no sign of any defensive positions and no big guns like the 14.5-millimetre KPVs we had encountered at other bases. There was a Chinese-made 82-millimetre recoilless rifle parked under a tree, and under another tree I spotted the familiar tripod of the 122-millimetre rocket launcher. This was definitely a training camp, and judging by the number of terrorists we could see, it was clear that a major offensive in the Tete province was about to happen.

Below the camp we could see a ridge running parallel with the one we were on. Through the trees we could see the highway track winding up it towards the camp.

In a straight line we were no more than 400 metres away from the camp, but between us and the ridge with the highway track that led into it, the ground descended steeply into a thickly wooded gully.

Having had a good look at the ground around the camp, we pulled back into cover to consider our options.

The steep-sided gully between us and the track was not a good obstacle to tackle in the dark. This was no place to roll an ankle or worse. The highway track we had used so far seemed the better option and I was keen to use it again. I decided we'd go back down the ridge retracing our steps of the morning, pick up the highway track and follow that up towards the camp. It was a lot longer but we had plenty of time. Moonrise was at 21.30 and we'd make good use of that in our final approach to the camp.

By using the highway track, we wouldn't have to worry about locating the camp in the dark. It would lead us all the way there. It would give us an escape route to safety when the bombs were on their way down. Finally, we could organise a reception party on the track for any fleeing terrorists, just as we had done in the saddle at the first camp.

To mark the target for the Canberras, we would organise the flares as an inverted 'V' pointing towards the camp, but I'd need to tell the aircraft how far it was between the point flare and the edge of the camp.

Rex and I went back to our observation position, to work out exactly where we wanted to be with the flares and where we would position our ambush on the track.

I had no idea what ordnance the Canberras would use, but suspected it would be the 'Alpha bomb'. The aircraft would attack over our heads and the bomb's angled descent would be away from us and in the direction of the camp. However, the Alpha bomb was sphere-shaped, and when released they spread apart both laterally and vertically as the air pressure that built up between them pushed them away from each other. That natural dispersion pattern was good news for a bomber, but it could be bloody bad news if you were underneath and trying to direct a night attack while only 100 metres away from the target.

The outer case of the bomb was packed with hard rubber balls and when it hit the ground they bounced the bomb forward for up to 20 metres before exploding between 3 and 4 metres above the ground. It was a deadly weapon and each aircraft would be carrying 300 of them.

I had already made the decision that I would illuminate the point flares. The question was just how close could I sensibly get to the camp without unduly compromising my own safety?

Looking back at the camp again with my binoculars, the ground provided the answer. The highway track climbed quite steeply up to a crest before levelling out on the flatter ground where the camp was located. If I positioned myself on the edge of the crest, within three steps of retreating back down the slope, my head would be below the level of the camp. This wouldn't protect me from a bomb falling short, but so long as they hit the target I should be safe.

Forty metres below this crest the ground was open and it would be a good place for the two back flares. From my position at the point of this 'arrowhead' Rex and I agreed it was no more than 150 metres to the edge of the camp. It was very close.

Another 150 metres back from where we'd light the flares, we could see the track ran over a rocky outcrop. With good firing positions and cover it was ideal for our ambush position.

We backed off the ridge top and I sent a last radio message to the brigadier outlining our plan and giving him the grid reference of where we would be at attack time. I told him to let the air force know there was nothing we could see in the way of air defence that they should be afraid of.

As the light faded we started moving back down the hill.

We reached our ambush position at the top of the highway track just before midnight. We shook off our packs and got our fire positions organised amongst the rocks.

This time we were all together, so I decided to try something different and put Jonny and Horse with the two MAGs right in the middle on either side of the track.

If a big group came down the track, Horse would wait until they were just about upon us and open fire. Jonny, meanwhile, would have his gun aimed higher at those further behind and descending the track towards us. The rest of us would spread out on either side and cover the flanks and pick off whatever we could once the big guns had opened fire.

With the ambush position organised, I got out the flares and gave two each to Rex and Fish, who would do the back positions, and kept two for myself. Karate would come with me to the 'point' position up front in the danger zone.

The flares looked like those Roman candles we'd fire off on Guy Fawkes Night. There was a fold-out plastic base and a small metal ring that when pulled detonated a cap which in turn ignited the magnesium. The label I had read during the day warned about looking at the light – bloody good thinking, I thought, given we would need our night vision big time to scoot down the hill away from the bombing.

The flares would burn for forty-five seconds. We'd each light one on command from the Canberras to guide them in, and wait until it had fizzled out before lighting the second, at which point we would hightail it back to our ambush position as fast as we could. If a first flare failed to ignite, we had the second flare as backup.

By 02.00 hours we were all in position. We all had radios and were listening anxiously for the voice from the Canberras. They would be airborne by now and heading towards us at a little over 400 miles per hour. We waited tensely.

I whispered to Karate: 'Sorry, I never give you a choice in where you go, but you're my right-hand man and we've been through a lot together over the years. I hope this works out OK for us.'

Karate – otherwise known as Tony Caruthers-Smith – was anything but a martial arts expert and would be a liability in a barroom brawl, but when the air was humming with RPD fire and RPG rockets, he was as cool as a cucumber.

He looked up and gave me his crooked-tooth smile. 'Don't you start going soft on me, Mick. We're in control here and the blues are good buggers. They won't hit us. We'll be just fine.' And as he said that, a voice came over the radio: 'Sierra One Seven, this is Cyclone Five Green Leader. Do you read me, over?'

I recognised the voice of Squadron Leader Bernie Vaughan. His widowed mother came from Morecambe, in north-west Lancashire, where my own parents had lived at the end of the Second World War. His father and mine had both flown Lancaster bombers in a Pathfinder squadron over Germany. Both were shot down. My father survived but Bernie's dad didn't make it home, so our families united in what was then a young, peaceful and prosperous Rhodesia.

I had always liked Bernie, but we had different interests and were very different personalities. I knew he always appreciated me taking him out hunting with our pointer dog to bag a guinea fowl for dinner, but he had nothing of the passion I had for wildlife and birds. During the day Bernie was a quiet, almost subdued individual, but at night he shed this image and a different personality emerged.

Bernie was a stars man. He loved astronomy. We would sit outside away from the lights and he would walk me through the night sky: the inverted Plough rotated on its own axis during the night, but the front stars always pointed due north. Orion's belt was generally north-west and he showed me how to get a true due-south bearing off the Southern Cross. He pointed out the different planets and explained how their orbits and proximity to earth influenced our compasses.

We ended up in different schools and universities and lost touch for a number of years before reuniting again in a far from peaceful environment that our hopeful parents could never have anticipated.

'Reading you fives, Bernie. Good to hear your voice,' I replied into the whisper mike. 'No problems here. We are in position and are ready to ignite the markers. We will be presenting an arrowhead indicator and your target starts 150 metres forward of the front flare. All three positions have two flares and they burn for forty-five seconds. We will await your orders for firing the flares, but would recommend an early indication to help you while you are still some distance out. I don't believe that would compromise anything. We will then wait for your request to ignite the second flares when you are on short finals.'

'Couldn't be better,' he replied. 'We have six aircraft for this mission. We will now split up into three two-aircraft formations for the attack. The first two aircraft will drop 600 Alpha bombs over the target area, twenty seconds later the second wave will drop sixteen 250-kilogram bombs to destroy any heavy stuff and twenty seconds after that another 600 Alpha bombs will follow in a wider spread than the first salvo. You with me?' he asked.

'Sounds good to me,' I replied. 'And don't worry about us; we will be well out of the way.'

'Never gave it a moment's thought,' was the response and I could hear him chuckling into the microphone. 'Stand by for first flares in nine minutes.'

'OK, Rex? OK, Fish?' I queried. Two clicks on the mike confirmed they were all set to go.

'Sierra One Seven, this is Green Leader. Stand by for first flares. Over.'

'Rex? Fish?' I said into the whisper mike. Two double clicks back.

'Ready when you are, Green Leader.'

There was a pause of about two minutes while the incoming bombers adjusted their flight paths.

Looking back from my position I still couldn't hear the aircraft, but I could make out the navigation lights as the close formation pairs homed in on the target.

Bernie's voice came over the air again: 'Sierra One Seven, stand by for first flares. Counting down: ten, nine, eight, seven, six, five, four ... Mick, fire them now!'

We pulled the pins and the flares burst into life. An energetic, pulsating, white light engulfed us and we instinctively turned away and ducked down. The light flares hissed and spluttered.

'Got you visual, Sierra One Seven. Perfect. Stand by for the second flares,' commanded Bernie, who would be belly-down in the nose of the

Canberra, lining up the bombsights at an invisible target just 150 metres forward of our flares.

'Second flare now!' he shouted with urgency. 'Mick, get the hell out of there.'

We pulled the pins and moved as quickly as we could over the crest and down towards the ambush position.

The bright light had affected our night vision so we took our time, knowing there was nothing we could do about a short-falling bomb but, by being a bit slow and careful, we could at least give ourselves a chance of getting back to the ambush position in one piece.

We were halfway down the slope that Jonny was covering with his gun when all hell broke loose above us.

The two lead Canberras flew alongside each other; passing over us we could see they were no more than twenty metres apart. The Avon jet noise increased as they released 600 Alpha bombs over the camp and then opened the throttles to climb up and away from the target and the surrounding high hills.

Our second flares were still burning brightly when the next pair of Canberras released their individual payloads of eight 250-kilogram high-explosive bombs. As the flares flickered and died, the third pair of Canberras flew over dropping another 600 Alpha bombs on either side of the first run.

It was all over in less than two minutes and they didn't hang around. Bernie's voice came over the radio: 'Green Leader to Sierra One Seven. You guys OK down there?'

'We're fine, Bernie,' I replied. 'Glad you are on our side.'

Bernie acknowledged, and with that the familiar soft whistle of the Avon jets disappeared into what remained of the night.

We sat in our ambush position waiting for a target. Our ears were still ringing from the noise of the 250-kilogram bombs, and if I blinked my eyes there was still the lingering image of the first flare I had inadvisably looked at when it started to splutter.

Nothing happened. We lay there in anticipation until first light and with it the sound of two helicopters heading our way.

'Sierra One Seven, this is Charlie Seven. You guys OK?' The familiar voice of Ian Harvey was a welcome relief to the tension of the night.

'Good to hear your voice, Harves. Yes, we're all fine but still on red alert. No action so far though,' I added.

'We'll be over in a few minutes. Give us a smoke so we know where you are.'

I gave an orange smoke grenade to Pig Dog, who quietly lobbed it off to one side of our position. Harves acknowledged the smoke and I told him we would follow the path up into the camp once he had given me the OK.

I told the boys we would stay where we were until we knew exactly what had happened at the camp. We were safe in our ambush position and with all the overhead aircraft activity I was in no hurry to move. We were again invisible. We were very tired, but still highly alert because at times like this anything could happen.

But nothing did. There were a few bursts of fire from the helicopter gunners in the time that followed, but nothing came our way. Horse was a bit pissed off because he reckoned I had given him the best fire position ever but he didn't get the chance to use it.

The drone of a light, fixed-wing aircraft in the distance, and the brigadier's voice, got us back into action. I told him we were all OK and that before we did anything we were going to have a brew and some food because it had already been a long day.

'Negative, Mick,' he replied with urgency in his voice. 'I want you to pack up now and be ready to be uplifted in the next five minutes.

'Initial reports back from the choppers say the Canberras were bang on target and there are bodies and devastation everywhere. It looks like we've got the result the country was looking for. You have done a fantastic job, but enough is enough and there is no need to risk anything more.

'Not only that, but according to my map you are now about 1.5 kilometres inside the Malawi border. Given how close Lilongwe is they will undoubtedly find out about this and there is bound to be an international stink. It will be much better for us all if we vacate the area as quickly as possible. Costa agrees and says that is exactly what Lisbon would be telling us.'

As we lifted off, Ian Harvey said he'd do a quick orbit of the camp so we could see the place ourselves. I was curious to see how close we were with the flares and wasn't thinking further than that.

'Oh my God!' I whispered into the headset as the aircraft turned and the camp came into view.

The ground looked like the TV images you saw of places in America that had had a big twister go over them – everything was completely flattened. Everything and everybody had been smashed into small pieces, and those bits of everything and everybody were all mixed together in an awful layer of death and destruction that spread across what once had been a terrorist campsite.

The bombing had been done with pinpoint accuracy and nothing survived. The biggest piece of wreckage I saw was half a truck axle with a wheel still attached that had been blown into a tree that no longer had branches.

We looked down in horror and amazement. Harves pulled back on the stick. It was time to go home.

The Rhodesians got their story and our success did, indeed, provide a good boost to morale and resolve at a time when, in truth, they were running out of hope.

*Take That!* shouted the headline, and went on to describe how a small contingent of 'elite' SAS troops had combined with the air force to inflict 'a crushing blow' on terrorists trained by Communist China, in which at least one of their own kind had been killed. The article quoted the air marshal as saying, 'The SAS were amazing. They came up with a novel idea of marking the target at night, then put themselves at considerable risk by getting close enough to ensure our pilots had every chance of hitting it – which they did – and with pinpoint accuracy. It gave us the result we were all looking for and everyone returned home safely. It was a remarkable operation.'

The euphoria didn't last long. Three weeks later, another Air Rhodesia Viscount was hit by Soviet SAM7 missiles close to Victoria Falls. All seventy-four passengers and crew perished in the crash.

Just over a year later we would eventually get even with the terrorist groups responsible for the atrocities, but these were dark days for the Rhodesians.

For us the story ended about three months later when we were all summoned to the Portuguese Consulate in Salisbury.

We dressed up in our greens and went in our open-top Sabre Land Rovers. Horse and Jonny insisted we put their MAGs on the mountings and they loaded each of them with a belt of 250 rounds. We were not expecting trouble, but I rather enjoyed the security a couple of MAGs brought to a drive around town.

The Portuguese security guards welcomed us at the gate, smiled and pointed with thumbs up to the machine guns. We were escorted into the building and there waiting for us was the Portuguese Consul and the brigadier, resplendent with a chest full of medals. I saw Ian Harvey all dressed up in his blues with the other helicopter crew and standing somewhat shyly to one side was Squadron Leader Bernie Vaughan.

I saluted them all and went forward to shake the hand of the consul. I then stood to one side and introduced each of the boys to him and the other dignitaries and they filed by shaking hands as they went.

With the introductions over, the Portuguese Consul called for our attention then told us how appreciative Portugal was of our military efforts in the Tete province. President Marcello Caetano had agreed with the recommendations from the provincial commander that the main participants should each be recognised with the award of the Order of the Colonial Empire.

A gilt cross hanging from a bright red ribbon with black central and edge stripes was pinned on our chests. It was a great honour and of all my medals I still cherish this one the most. We were each given an envelope in which was the citation for the medal written on a gold-edged card with the Portuguese coat of arms. It said nothing more than 'For service to Mozambique'.

For Frelimo, the two attacks ended their offensive in the Tete province.

The Frelimo leader, Samora Machel, was suspicious of Malawi President Dr Hastings Banda, and was said to have thought the Portuguese were tipped off and subsequently launched the air raid. Nobody was in any great hurry to refute that supposition.

Frelimo didn't have the recruits to replace the loss. Instead they changed their focus to moving south beyond the Zambezi into the Manica province and towards the Port of Beira.

In the end it didn't matter much, because back in Lisbon, President Marcello Caetano was ousted in a coup led by General Antonio Spinola. The latter immediately ordered all Portuguese troops home. They abandoned Mozambique and handed the country on a plate to Frelimo.

Samora Machel couldn't believe his luck!

At Furuncungo meanwhile, brothers Guido and Eduardo hauled themselves up into the back of the Berliet truck for the long drive to Beira, where a TAP Boeing would fly them home to Portugal.

With national service abolished in the coup, Guido could now return to the hospital in Lisbon and complete his internship. The initial bitterness he'd felt at having his service deferment denied had long since disappeared in the happiness of going home. He also realised that the horrific Furuncungo attack had given him invaluable medical experience.

He had gained something from being in Mozambique, but he was glad to be moving on.

For Eduardo, it meant he could head back to the family farm in the Algarve to help his parents with the olives; even more importantly, he could pick up the relationship with the daughter of the neighbouring farmer. He had been promoted to sergeant and had tales to tell of tragedy and heroics with which he had been closely involved in a far-off land. He was in with a good chance.

The two brothers climbed the steps to the aircraft door. At the top Guido paused and looked back over the airport buildings. He waved his arm and shouted, 'Goodbye Africa!'

Behind him, Eduardo pushed his brother gently forward.

'Yes. Goodbye,' he said. 'And this time when we get off the plane we'll know exactly where we are.'

# The Chewore Ambush

The SAS operations centre was built like a university lecture theatre with tiered seats for 200 to accommodate the entire squadron, as it often did for training exercises or in preparing for a major strike somewhere.

The entire front wall was covered by a massive large-scale map of the central African countries that included Rhodesia, Botswana, Zambia and Namibia – the latter through the Caprivi Strip, a curiously shaped, narrow corridor of land that connected these four countries near Victoria Falls. Mozambique and Malawi completed the coverage to the north and east.

The brigadier welcomed us as we saluted and filed into the meeting he had called.

The ten of us that made up the SAS call sign Sierra One Seven, which he had created, sat down in the centre seats.

'Good to see you all,' said the brigadier. 'After your exploits in Mozambique, word has spread and you are now in some demand. The intelligence team and I filter any requests that come in from one organisation or another, so you can be assured we do our best to ensure you are only deployed into situations we are confident you can deal with.

'The request we have now suggests we may have a serious terrorist incursion on our hands. It's an unusual and somewhat unfortunate situation, so I have agreed to send you into the area as soon as possible to find out what's going on.'

The brigadier moved to the impressive map display. With a long pointer, he picked out an area almost in the dead centre of the Zambezi Valley where, on the Rhodesian side of the border with Zambia, the Chewore River flowed into the great Zambezi.

'To explain what I mean, have a look at this,' he said.

'To the east of the Chewore River the police coverage of the valley floor only extends as far as the Sapi River.' He circled the area with his pointer.

'To the west, the Rhodesian Army forces operating out of Chirundu only go as far as the eastern boundary of the Mana Pools Game Reserve.' He again indicated on the map.

'They have made these boundaries deliberately to avoid any confrontation between friendly forces that may not recognise each other. But in creating this safety buffer zone they have, unwittingly, created an open corridor for terrorist groups operating out of Zambia. It looks like some of them have recognised this situation and have used it to infiltrate the country.

'I have been given a report from a game scout who found tracks at the Chewore River mouth twenty-four hours ago. There has been a lot of rain in the area so he was unsure about precise numbers. He guessed twenty or more. He said the tracks were recent and heading inland towards the escarpment.

'Mick, you and Rex know this area well, so I want you to go into the upper reaches of the Chewore River then work your way steadily north towards the Zambezi, to intercept any terrorist groups that may have come into the country.

'To get you in there quickly, we have organised a Rhodesian Air Force DC3 Dakota, and you'll drop into the area by static line parachute. We have found what looks like a good drop zone on a flood plain, and they'll drop you from 400 feet just before first light tomorrow morning.

'At 15.00 this afternoon, there is a meeting with the air force at the parachute school, where they want everything assembled and ready for a 03.00 departure tomorrow. There's no time to waste so I'll leave you to get into it. If there are any special requests between now and then, I will be here to help if I can.'

We filed out and headed for the stores. 'The Chewore,' said Rex with excitement in his voice. 'It's the wildest part of the valley. Masses of game and there'll be no shortage of water.'

It sparked a sudden thought. I turned round immediately and headed back to the brigadier. 'Sir, I do have a request before we go. While we're getting organised, could your staff please get me a long-range weather forecast for the area? It's the time of year when extended wet periods can be expected down there; if that happens it will change how we operate on the ground.'

'No problem,' he said. 'I'll bring it over as soon as I have it.'

January was the height of the rainy season, when the intertropical convergence zone moved south to bring rain to central and southern Africa.

Most days in the Zambezi Valley at this time would be well over thirty degrees with high humidity. From 14.00 hours onwards, there would be a steady build-up of huge clouds as the in-coming warm, moist air lifted over the escarpment. The clouds would build and gain height through the afternoon until between 16.00 and 17.00 when the heavens would suddenly open. Usually the storm would be gone an hour or so later, but sometimes it would not let up for three or four days and, just like the wild animals around us, we would huddle together in whatever shelter we had and sit and shiver in the wet.

In these prolonged wet periods, the smallest dry stream beds became impassable torrents, so there was no point trying to move anywhere. We would sit and wait for the weather to pass, waging a silent battle with the biting insects that thrived in these conditions and were hungry for our blood.

We were loading the truck that would take us to the air force base, when the brigadier came over with my weather report.

'Mick, the good news is the forecast for tomorrow morning's drop is very good. No wind to speak of and clear skies, which will please the pilots given how low they'll be flying. The rest of the day is OK. However, a heavy rain band is spreading south and forecast to be over you early next day and persist for at least two days after that.'

'I'm sorry, but you're going to get wet,' he said.

'That's OK, Sir, and thanks for getting the report. We'll patrol as far north as we can tomorrow, after the drop. There is a huge elephant highway that follows the Chewore River up into the escarpment, where there is permanent water, and it's the most likely route in for any terrorist group. Once the heavy rain arrives there will be little point carrying on, so we'll set up an ambush on the track and sit it out until the weather clears.

'It could work out well. Any terrorist group will not expect security forces to be operating in such conditions, and they'll be happy their tracks are being washed out. We'll let them do the hard work. They can come to us.'

The brigadier nodded in agreement: 'Sounds good to me. Best of luck.'

At 05.00, the aircraft reached the escarpment of the Zambezi Valley and banked right towards the east and our drop zone. The pre-dawn light silhouetted the hills as the pilots slowly descended.

'Twenty minutes to red light,' announced the parachute school dispatcher.

It was the signal for us to pick up our packs and attach them to the steel 'quick release' hooks on the webbing harness beneath our reserve parachutes. The dispatcher worked his way around us all, checking the pack connections and the release device which, when operated, dropped the packs on a 3-metre rope so they were free of our bodies when landing.

'Stand up. Hook up,' he ordered.

We struggled to our feet with the heavy load of the packs and parachutes, made a few adjustments, then attached the large hook at the end of the parachute static line to the strong, steel cable running the length of the plane above us. Again the dispatcher moved among us, checking everything and getting us closer together in a line.

He moved back to the open door of the aircraft, attached his own safety harness to the cable, then stood watching the red and green lights above the exit.

This was the tense time.

It was tense for the pilots as they reduced speed and descended. They watched for their instruments to indicate an altitude of 400 feet, at the same time peering through the early morning gloom to locate our drop zone.

It was tense for us with the nervous anticipation that accompanies every operational parachute jump.

The red light flashed on.

'Stand in the door!' yelled the dispatcher.

We all moved forward in a stuttering sort of shuffle. I stopped with my foot on the edge of the open door and my right hand holding the side. I looked up and could make out the outline of the hills that seemed to be very close to us. The ground below was still in darkness.

'Green light. Go! Go! Go!'

I leapt into space and folded my arms in front of me, on top of the reserve parachute. A second later, I felt the tug on my shoulders as the big, brown canopy of the American T10 parachute opened. I immediately felt for the quick-release device to drop my pack, which fell away and dangled on the rope below me.

Time for a quick look round.

I could now see the ground which was flat and grassy. I was drifting slowly forward, so pulled down on my back rigging lines to further slow the descent. Feet and knees locked together, legs slightly bent at the knee and I angled my ankles for what would be a forward right landing.

My pack hit the ground first. I landed in front of it and rolled forward. The ground was soft with the recent rain. Nice.

I collapsed the parachute canopy while still lying on the ground and struggled out of the webbing harness. I unstrapped my rifle, grabbed a twenty-round magazine from a front pouch and loaded. If there was trouble here I could now shoot back.

The others landed and did the same. We lay on the ground, ready for action, as the drone of the aircraft engines faded and died in the distance.

The sun crept up over the hills and we saw we were in the middle of an extensive grassy plain. A small herd of impala antelope watched us from a distance.

For the moment I could see we were safe, so we got to work bundling up the parachutes into plastic bags that we piled together. They would be recovered by helicopter at the end of the operation. With that chore out of the way, we moved quickly into the cover of the nearest treeline.

Concealed by the woodland, we dropped our packs and set about organising ourselves for the day. While Horse and Jonny loaded their machine guns, and Fish prepared the rockets for his bazooka, Rex, Pig Dog and I looked at the maps.

We were on a side stream of the main river, and by following it down we would soon find the elephant trail leading to the permanent waterholes further inland. If there were terrorist tracks on the trail, we'd follow and catch them from behind. If not – which is what we hoped – we would silently work our way down the track.

We would be invisible. If we met a terrorist group, we'd stay in cover and let them approach. We'd wait until they were upon us before springing the trap, then we'd cut them down without mercy in a hail of close-quarter gunfire.

I put Rex and Pig Dog up front together. While Rex scrutinised the ground for tracks or signs, Pig Dog would watch the area ahead. Looking for the slightest movement. Listening for the faintest sound. Sniffing the air for smells that shouldn't be there.

I would follow at a discreet distance, which would vary with the cover. Right on my tail would be Jonny with his machine gun and Fish with the loaded bazooka.

Keeping in visual distance behind us, the others followed in file. In the event of any action up front, they would run out to one side and bring covering crossfire in from the flank.

We reached the Chewore River. With the recent rains, narrow channels of shallow water twisted across the sandy bed between deeper pools that had formed at bends in the river. Scattered piles of elephant dung were being inspected by some large, black hornbills, while a troop of grey vervet monkeys drank at a pool.

The elephant trail ran under a canopy of tall, flat-crowned acacia trees that lined the river. It was well used: elephant, buffalo and zebra had been there recently, but there were no human footprints.

Rex and Pig Dog moved carefully forward down the track. Every so often they would stop, eyes and ears straining to locate the movement they had seen, or the sound they had heard. Whenever they did this, those of us behind would silently move forward, on the offensive, ready to attack.

Flocks of guinea fowl, baboons and a porcupine thus rehearsed us through the day for the action that could come at any time. But nothing did and at 14.30 I called a halt.

By then it had already been a long day for us. More importantly, to the north over the Zambezi River, we could see a broad band of cloud. The rain wasn't too far away.

I'd stopped us at what would be a great ambush site. The track passed between two anthill mounds in an elevated position, overlooking the trail below as it short-cut between the banks of a wide bend in the river. We could see over 200 metres ahead of us through sparse cover.

'Ambush positions don't come much better than this,' I said, 'and we have time to make a good job of it before the rain arrives. Rex, you take Pig Dog, Horse, Mack and Nelson and make your position behind the left anthill. The rest of you are with me on the right side of the track.'

Once Rex and I had positioned everyone on the two anthills, we all set about making ourselves comfortable and making our fire positions as dry as possible. We carried light-weight, green, nylon flysheets that with twine and sticks we could fashion into low, one-man shelters.

We furnished the shelters with essential equipment from our packs and web belts: the plastic poncho made a good groundsheet for our parachute-nylon sleeping bags. Water bottles, ammunition, insect repellent, our jackets and some snack food were carefully placed where we could reach them with minimal movement and sound.

With the structures built, we set about concealing them with clumps of dry grass, dead logs and leafy branches.

While Jonny kept watch with his machine gun at the ambush position, Rex moved back in the direction we had come and with the others built a bigger shelter where we'd stash our packs and where we could safely have a meal break. Karate and I, meanwhile, went forward of the ambush and moved parallel with the track running through our killing ground.

Karate carried a reel of thin, black wire. He'd given the end to Jonny to hold in the ambush position and was now running it out to the end of the 100-metre spool. Alongside him, I carried two claymore mines that we'd conceal close to the track and using the cable would detonate electrically if we sprung the ambush.

Our bullets would get those in front. The mines would get any others behind them.

The claymore mine was a concave, rectangular plate 200 millimetres wide by 150 millimetres high and 39 millimetres thick. It weighed 1.5 kilograms and sat up off the ground on wire legs at each end. The main body of the plate was a matrix of 700 x 12-millimetre ball bearings, bedded in epoxy resin with a layer of C4 plastic explosive moulded to the back. When detonated, the nature of the explosive force changed the shape of the plate from concave to convex and the steel balls exploded out in a wide-angled pattern. Travelling at 1,200 metres a second they were lethal to anyone within 100 metres.

We manned the ambush in four-hour shifts with half the party resting as the others watched and waited.

The rain started just before last light.

The anthills and the trees above us offered some protection as the first squall engulfed our position and pounded the flimsy shelters. After a few minutes the deluge eased back to a less frantic, steady downpour that continued through the night. It was eerily quiet. There was none of the usual thunder and lightning and thankfully very little wind.

We made up little routines to break the boredom and to remain alert. Every twenty minutes, we would silently stretch out and adjust our body positions, we listened to the frogs and crickets and if they stopped croaking or rasping everyone became doubly attentive.

We listened to calls of the owls and the nightjars, and communicated with sign language to identify small animals that ventured close to our ambush. While it rained, rained and rained.

At first light, we sent two from each team back to the big shelter Rex had built for a brew and some food, while the rest of us watched the trail. It was still raining steadily but visibility was fair.

Another day and another night dragged by and the rain didn't stop.

On the third morning, the sky was brighter and the rain had eased back to a light drizzle. Early morning mist swirled across the track and through the trees on the far side of the ambush position.

I lay stretched out under my shelter between Karate and Fish, both within touching distance. Jonny and Simmo were higher up the mound with the machine gun, but Fish could reach them.

Karate, Fish and I had been on guard since 04.00. As 08.00 and the end of our shift approached, we were all thinking about going back to the big shelter for a coffee and some breakfast.

Suddenly, there was a low crackling from the radio lying next to me, followed by tap, tap, tap. It was Rex's warning call.

We shook the others awake and carefully looked over the edge of the fire positions. Through the mist a column of dark figures had emerged. They all carried weapons and heavy backpacks.

'You got the battery ready?' I whispered to Karate. He nodded and held up the claymore cable for me to see.

I turned to Fish who had the bazooka in the shoulder, ready to fire. Our eyes met and he nodded. We'd spoken about where he should fire the bazooka and decided he should aim about 50 metres away from us. Bullets, bazooka, claymore mines in that order. We had the ground covered for a good 100 metres away from us, but as more and more terrorists appeared on the track I realised it wouldn't be enough.

I risked one last look as the leading group was about 100 metres away, opposite our claymore mines. I saw they were looking down at the ground, working hard carrying bulging backpacks. I realised we were going to take them completely by surprise. But how many were there? Ten, twenty, thirty, forty, fifty, sixty, seventy, eighty I estimated and more kept coming.

I ducked down and pulled the FN rifle into my shoulder. I'd initiate the ambush by killing the leader. The others would then open fire and Karate would detonate the claymore mines.

My heart was racing. 'Stay cool, Michael,' I whispered to myself as they came closer and closer.

A head appeared in my rifle sights. As he stepped towards me the head became a neck. Another step and as the neck became the sternum in my sights, I squeezed the trigger.

*Whoosh*! Next to me, Fish fired his bazooka. I heard the long, sustained firing of the machine guns then *boom*! as Karate blew the claymores.

I jumped out of my shelter and stood on top of the anthill. 'Fire high, Jonny!' I shouted. 'Go for those at the back of the column. Horse, go high!' And I watched with satisfaction as the red tracer bullets from the two machine guns flashed towards the confused figures 200 metres away. Several dropped.

The back-blast of the first rocket blew down Fish's shelter, which was helpful because he could then reload faster. He followed the machine guns and fired his next two rockets into the melee at the back of the column.

Rex and the others had also abandoned cover and were firing down on the running figures trying to escape. Some escaped, but not many.

Kneeling and watching, I realised the rain had stopped.

'Rex, Pig Dog, Horse, Nelson!' I shouted. 'Get after them.'

They bounded down the slope below the anthills and led by Rex, started the pursuit.

Twenty minutes later there was a volley of gunfire. I recognised the heavy report of the FN rifle and knew it was Rex back in action. Sporadic firing followed for some time then silence.

We'd again taken them by surprise. More of them were killed. Already confused and demoralised by the ambush, the survivors would be terrified by this second strike. They would drop their packs and flee towards the Zambezi River, where they had crossed from Zambia. The terrorists had been well and truly terrorised.

From the anthill I looked down on the carnage.

Bodies lay on the ground immediately in front of us, gunned down at close quarters in a deadly hail of fire from our rifles and machine guns.

Beyond were several bodies scattered over a wide area, killed while trying to escape the ambush.

Further away was the devastation of the two claymore mines. I counted seventeen bodies with backpacks still attached lying across the track.

Looking beyond the claymores, I could see more scattered bodies, including a group that had been hit by Fish's bazooka, and further out yet, another group caught by the machine guns as they stood dazed and leaderless, watching the horror in front of them.

Backpacks and weapons were scattered across the entire area. Getting it all together would be a big job and it wasn't a task I particularly wanted, especially when Rex returned with the news of another terrorist group that had missed the ambush.

The four of them had run along the track after the fleeing terrorists and it wasn't long before they spotted a group of twenty or more, hurrying away from the ambush site. Remarkably, they were still carrying their heavy backpacks.

Darting forward through cover, Rex and the team soon closed the gap. Undetected, they moved to within thirty metres of the last man in the file.

Rex had an idea and whispered instructions to Nelson, who moved in front.

Nelson jogged forward on to the track with the others on his heels. As they closed in on the retreating group, Nelson shouted in the African language, 'Comrades! Comrades! Wait for me. Wait. Wait.'

Those at the back of the column stopped and turned round just as Rex and the others fanned out alongside Nelson. In unison, the four SAS men dropped to their knees and opened fire.

Seven more died in that first burst of fire and another four were killed as they struggled to drop their backpacks and run. The lucky survivors dropped everything and scattered in all directions.

Rex opened a backpack out of curiosity. At the top of the pack, wrapped in a thin blanket, was some tinned food, AK-47 ammunition and six fragmentation grenades. Rex lifted out the blanket. Taking up most of the pack space below were three TMH46 landmines.

These shocking weapons were used indiscriminately by the terrorists to instil fear into a local community. The mines would be laid in a country road to kill and maim innocent people going about their business. So much the better if a school bus full of kids ran over it.

Pig Dog led the way along the trail back towards our ambush position. He stopped suddenly and turned to Rex: 'Look at this,' he said pointing to the ground.

Where he stood, the elephant trail branched. The left branch they could see led back to the ambush position, while the right headed off to the west in the general direction of *Chiramba Kadoma* – the Ayers Rock of the Zambezi Valley, a massive, flat-topped feature that rose over 700 metres from the valley floor with sides so steep it was completely unclimbable. Not even baboons could get to the top. And on this track were the boot prints of six terrorists.

Rex and Pig Dog studied the ground closely. The rain had partly obliterated the prints but had not washed them away. 'Day before yesterday, I reckon,' said Rex. 'What do you think?'

The stocky New Zealander agreed at once: 'So, they won't be too far away and I'd bet they heard the noise we made this morning.'

On their return with this news, it didn't take me long to work out what we were going to do about it.

'Rex, you and your ambush team pack up now and start following those tracks. Six terrorists on the loose is six too many, so we need to find them. I'll wait here until the support team I have requested arrives. They will be coming in by helicopter and we'll use the aircraft to catch up with you.

'If there is time and if they have the fuel, we'll play leapfrog. As they drop us off, you jump in with your team. We'll brief the pilot to follow the trail from the air and look for somewhere he can put you down about 10 to 15 kilometres further on. If you find the tracks there, we'll get him to bring us up to you, and if there is still time and enough fuel we'll do a repeat. I reckon they are probably 40 kilometres ahead of us and this is a good way of closing that gap.'

'Like it, Mick,' Rex replied. 'Let's get moving.'

Two hours later, I heard the distinctive sound of Alouette helicopters in the distance. I grabbed the radio.

'Cyclone Seven, this is Sierra One Seven, do you read me, over?'

'Sierra One Seven, this is Charlie Seven, reading you strength five. Greetings, Mick. I have your Sunray on board,' replied the familiar voice of Ian Harvey, the pilot who'd been with us in Mozambique.

'Good to hear your voice, Harves,' I replied. 'We'll mark our position with a red smoke as you get closer; there is plenty of room to land about 100 metres south of us, but before you do, I'd strongly recommend a few clearance orbits with your own guns ready. We have not had time to do a proper clearance of the area and there may be armed survivors lying in cover. We need to be careful.'

'Thanks, Mick. Will do,' the pilot replied. And as the noise got louder, I lobbed a smoke grenade on to the trail behind us.

Two dark green helicopters roared over us and banked to one side as they orbited our position, the barrels of their GPMG guns pointing at the ground, the gunners looking for targets.

'My God, you've done some damage here,' Harves said as he took in the scene.

'There's more,' I said. 'After the ambush, Rex chased after the survivors, caught up with them and had another crack. Follow the trail north for a few minutes and you should find the place. There'll be a lot of backpacks on the ground.'

The aircraft angled off and soon located Rex's contact spot.

'We're coming in now, Mick,' said Harves. 'It all looks OK from up here.'

The helicopters landed and closed down. I went to the lead aircraft and opened the door for the brigadier, who hopped out and shook my hand. 'Great work, Mick,' he said.

'How many do you think there were altogether?' he asked, wasting no time to get to the crux of the matter.

'Well, Sir. I tried a quick count as they came into the ambush area and my guess then was eighty, but after the initial action, Rex ran into another twenty or thirty. We haven't had a chance to do it yet, but a count of the backpacks will give us a better idea. To answer your question, I'd say there were over 100 and I reckon we may have got half of them. It means there are fifty or sixty terrorists on the run back towards the Zambezi. Most are now unarmed and don't have equipment or food, and most will be on their own or in small groups at best. Picking them off on the river line will be the best option.'

He nodded.

'Sorry, Sir, but there's still more for you,' I continued and told him about the second group and that Rex was now on their tracks. I explained my plan.

'Go for it, Mick,' he said, and turning to the pilots asked what they thought. Positive as ever, Ian Harvey said he reckoned they would have enough fuel to do the two leapfrogs I hoped for.

I thanked them all then turned to Phil Hammond, the lieutenant troop commander brought in to clean up our mess with seven of his men. 'Sorry to lumber you with our dirty work, Phil, so thanks in advance. Take it easy out there. We haven't physically checked the wider area and you may find terrorists still alive and armed.'

Rex had stopped at the edge of an area of open grassland. He'd sent Horse and Mack ahead to scout around and ensure we had no unwelcome company. We landed and my team jumped out of the helicopter. We managed a quick briefing under the noise and swirl of the chopper blades. Rex gave me a big grin then joined the others who were already in the helicopter.

I loved the smell of avgas and there was plenty to enjoy as the Alouette powered up and away towards the distant hills.

Fifteen minutes later, Harves called to say Rex had found the tracks and he was on his way back to pick us up. We managed to leapfrog twice more before the aircraft had to leave.

We'd covered over thirty kilometres in a little less than two hours and were now much closer to the towering cliffs of *Chiramba Kadoma*. The tracks we were following were now much more distinct: a day old or less, Rex estimated.

Looking ahead, the ground was far from inviting. Tactically, the terrorists would have the high ground in what was very difficult, broken country. There would be permanent water for them and shelter in caves and rocky overhangs.

We realised they had probably seen and heard the helicopter. They would be nervous about it and alert, but it had gone away and not returned. They would be happy with that, but would take precautions. They would suspect it had dropped troops on the ground, but they would not have seen anything as we were still too far away, so they would have no knowledge of how many we were and who they were up against.

However, we had undoubtedly lost the element of surprise and they were, in all probability, waiting for us. Compared to this morning, the boot was now on the other foot. We would be walking into their ambush.

For the next two hours the going was easy and we made good progress. The trees in the open woodland were in full summer leaf and gave us both shade and concealment as we got ever closer to the hill slopes where we expected our reception committee to be waiting.

As we closed in on the massive, flat-topped feature, we could see a change in the vegetation. The ground was steep and stony. It would retain less water so only dense, stunted thorn trees would survive there. Even on the game trail it was hard work and uncomfortable to get through.

I went to the front as we moved silently and slowly through the tangle of thorns. My eyes were straining, looking ahead for any slight movement, all senses alert for a sign – anything that would give me warning.

I heard what sounded like a metallic click. I dropped to my knees, rifle in my shoulder, and peered through the thorns and leaves trying to locate the sound. There was another click then suddenly an eruption of sound as with whirring wings and raucous alarm cries, a flock of crested guinea fowl took flight above us.

Glancing over my shoulder, I saw Rex grinning and pretending he had a shotgun. He knew these guinea fowl were rare and protected.

It was a good opportunity to have a short mental break and a quick swig of water. As good as it was to see the guinea fowl, I couldn't help thinking that anyone with half our bush sense would now be looking in our direction and wondering what spooked the birds.

Another hour passed and by now we were well into the foothills. The thorn scrub was just as dense and the track more difficult to follow as it twisted around thickets and rocky mounds. It would have been hard work for the terrorists, carrying big, heavy packs laden with weapons and explosives. Moments after having that thought, I spotted a Chinese-made stick grenade one of them had dropped.

I was already carrying fragmentation and phosphorous grenades, plus I had a 42Z rifle grenade on my web belt, so I didn't want any more. I turned to Jonny behind me, who nodded, so I left it on the track for him to pick up.

We moved silently forward, stopping every so often to look and listen. We had to be close now.

I ducked under a low, overhanging thorn bush and was just straightening up when a camouflaged figure popped up from behind a mound no more than ten paces in front of me.

What happened next was all a blur at the time, but as the pumping adrenalin subsided I clearly remembered the sequence of events.

I saw the camouflaged figure pop up like one of the targets on a shooting range.

There were two sharp cracks very close to my right ear as the AK-47 bullets flashed past.

I felt a stinging pain in my right arm from what turned out to be wood splinters off a tree hit by the rifle fire.

Then, all in the same moment, I realised he was firing on automatic and I knew that all rifles lift when firing an automatic burst.

He'd had his chance. He'd missed me by inches and now he was fucked.

The two-round double-tap from my NATO 7.62 FN hit him in the chest, lifted him off his feet and back-flipped him to the ground.

I ran forward to the cover of the mound where he had concealed himself, expecting to hear the deadly sound of the RPD machine gun opening fire at any moment.

Nothing happened.

I glanced at the body on the other side of the mound to make sure it needed no further attention – which it didn't – then I heard a whisper behind me.

It was Karate. 'You OK?' he asked.

Rex and Horse, meanwhile, had moved out and were now edging through the tangle to my right and ahead of me. On the left, Jonny was doing the same with Fish. The SAS had borrowed these tactics from the great Zulu armies of South Africa: 'the horns of the bull' they called it as the flanks moved forward to envelop the enemy.

Karate and I waited and watched while they moved ahead of us. Horse suddenly darted forward and dived into cover behind another mound. The RPD fire I had been expecting started up and I saw Rex and Pig Dog dive behind the mound where Horse had gone. By now he had the bipod down and was putting a series of short bursts back in the direction of the fire.

I glanced to my left: Jonny's group were in a good position and they too had opened fire. I realised from the conservative way Horse was firing that the terrorists must be well concealed or in good cover.

*Whoosh!* Fish let rip with a bazooka. There was a scream, and an AK cartwheeled through the air. Two down.

As the rocket shrapnel shrieked through the air, as the dust from the explosion was still rising, I dashed forward 5 or 6 metres. I dropped down and went into the aim as Karate followed and joined me.

Two or three moves later, we had reached the base of a large anthill. I squinted round the side and saw the movement of the RPD gunner and another terrorist as they returned fire at Horse, off to my right. I could see at once why Horse was not wasting ammunition. They were well positioned inside a small cave above us, and to get there we would have to cross broken, rocky ground with no cover.

It was time for plan B. Time for some technology.

I reached over behind my back and from my webbing pulled out the 42Z rifle grenade I was carrying. I signalled to Rex and Jonny what I had in mind and indicated I wanted covering fire when I was ready. They acknowledged.

Rifle fire, directed at Jonny, suddenly erupted from a new location. I heard the return fire then there was a loud explosion. Jonny had used the stick grenade to great effect. Another one down.

I took off the FN magazine, ejected the loaded cartridge and slotted it back into the top of the magazine. The 42Z grenades were propelled by a large, ballastite cartridge – a big blank – but they had powered up the charge so it went fast and low. That made it very accurate, but the downside was the rifle kicked like a mule.

I pulled off the tape I had used to secure the ballastite cartridge to the grenade and fed the cartridge into the breach. Our FN rifles had a grenade launcher built on to the end of the barrel and the 42Z fitted tightly over it. Finally, I removed the safety pin from the side of the grenade that prevented it from exploding if accidentally dropped.

I did all this lying on my back out of sight behind the anthill. To see the target and give myself a chance of hitting it, I now had the choice of standing up or crouching off to one side of our cover. I decided to stand up. Crouching would be safer, but there was too much risk of the grenade being deflected by the tangle of branches.

All ready. I signalled and the flanks put down some good fire. I stood up. It took a moment or two for me to find the cave again and then I pulled the rifle butt hard into my shoulder. As I squeezed the trigger, bullets cracked the air next to my head for the second time that afternoon.

The grenade hit the roof of the narrow cavern immediately above the RPD gunner. There was a brilliant crimson flash, a massive bang and a cloud of dark grey smoke. Rock fragments fizzed through the air around us. I returned the magazine to my rifle and started forward. While they were still reeling from the effect of the grenade, we would close in and finish them off.

The others were already on the move. Another camouflaged target popped up in front of Jonny's group on the left. His AK was slung over his shoulders and on his chest. As he moved his arms – maybe to surrender – maybe to fire at us – he took three, almost simultaneous double-taps from Jonny and the boys. A capture would have been interesting, but if surrendering was his intention he'd left it far too late.

Rex and Horse, meanwhile, had reached the edge of the cave and fired a couple of shots as they went inside. No chance of a capture there, either. The body of the RPD gunner lay slumped over his weapon, and to one side another body was sprawled across a rock – his AK–47 dangling from a punctured, bloody chest.

Inside the cave were six big packs and we had killed six terrorists.

We searched each terrorist for any form of identification then pulled out their packs to see what they were carrying. All were heavy with ammunition and grenades and in two we found TMH46 anti-tank mines.

I glanced back at the bodies and was glad we hadn't got a capture.

Rex found a spring with clean water. We topped up our bottles and took some extra to cook a decent meal that night as we hadn't eaten much all day.

We were to be picked up next morning by helicopter. As there was nowhere to land in the thick scrub of the contact area, we backtracked to the more open woodland where we'd find a landing zone.

Rex led the way down. I was happy to be in the middle where I could semi-switch off for a while and give my brain a rest. In this relaxed state I nearly bumped into Fish, who had stopped in front of me, acting on a signal from Rex. We all dropped down and shook off our packs.

Could this be a straggler from the first ambush, trying to catch up with the splinter group?

I watched for any signal from Rex, but he continued staring ahead, then slowly and deliberately came up into the aim. He fired and the bush erupted with the whirring of wings and raucous alarm cries.

I breathed out and laughed.

With dinner in mind, he'd shot one of my rare crested guinea fowl.

# The Spirit's Cave

Getting involved in weird and wonderful projects probably comes with the territory when you're in the SAS, and we certainly had our fair share.

I was summoned to a meeting with the brigadier and his operations staff. There was an air of friendly amusement as I greeted everyone and I immediately sensed they had something unusual for us.

'Mick, we want you and three of your team to escort a couple of VIPs who have been doing some good work on landmine detection for us. They will be conducting field trials on a road you know well near the Rekometjie River. You'll be away three or four days.'

The brigadier paused then asked, 'You did zoology at university, if I remember correctly?'

I nodded.

'Perfect,' he said, and that was the end of the meeting.

A couple of days later, we were at a rural police station where two Alouette helicopters were waiting to take us down to the test area. Two grey, police Land Rovers arrived in a cloud of dust, with a father and son team who ran a film studio in South Africa. They specialised in training captive animals for anyone who needed lions, tigers or elephants in their movies.

They opened the back of the Land Rover and out jumped the VIP. It was the biggest spotted hyena I had ever seen.

'Howzit. I'm Ollie.' The elder of the two South Africans thrust out a welcoming hand to me, just as the hyena arrived and inquisitively sniffed around my testicles.

'This is Four,' Ollie announced, while the animal did the hyena version of a cat purring then started to rub his neck against the front of my trousers.

I nervously stroked him as you would a dog.

'Hyenas don't smell too good,' said Ollie, 'but he obviously likes you.'

He went on to explain that he was the fourth born in the litter – hence his name – and that all hyenas were very cautious animals and never put a foot down without first sniffing the ground beneath it. It was this instinctive action on their part that Ollie had used to train Four to find landmines buried in a road.

Ollie and his son, Viv, let the hyena run around and mark his new territory, as all dogs do, and then it was time to get down to business.

Smelling of hyena, I got into the helicopter. Four jumped in next to me and Ollie wedged him in between us on the back seat. The big, hairy animal seemed to be enjoying himself, and started following the rotor blades with his head and eyes as the pilot powered up. Soon they were spinning too fast for him and he lost interest, but he had spotted something else.

I put on the headphones and spoke to the pilot: 'Pete, you're going to feel something funny on that bit of bare neck beneath your helmet. Nothing to worry about, mate – it's only a hyena.' As I said that, the animal leaned forward and with a long tongue started licking the sweat trickling over the exposed bare skin.

'The grandkids will never believe this one,' said Pete as he calmly lifted the aircraft off the ground.

Four was like a friendly Labrador dog, but twice the size and several times smellier. He'd chase after sticks and bring them back to you and soon we all lost our fear and petted him like the dog at home.

The trials went well and the hyena never failed to find the mines we laid. While that was impressive enough, I wondered what difference a single trained hyena could make in the conflicts of central Africa, where the use of landmines by the terrorist groups was both widespread and completely indiscriminate.

The answer was psy-ops – psychological warfare.

Ollie and Viv had brought film gear with them, and took much coverage of the hyena at work in the natural setting of the Zambezi Valley bush. The hyena was feared by most African tribes, who regarded the animal as the incarnation of evil spirits; the idea was to use this belief to discourage the use of landmines. The evil spirits, in the form of the hyena, would find the mines, dig them up and take them back to kill those responsible. The hyenas would feast on the blood of the victims.

I have no idea if the film and leaflets produced ever made any great difference. I doubt it. But forever etched in my memory are the sickening images of an overloaded bus that exploded a mine in an African tribal land. A young,

African schoolgirl lay dead in front of the bus. Her legs had been blown off her body. In a way she was lucky, because injured survivors would endure dreadful pain and suffering before either dying or condemned to a life of misery as a dependent invalid.

If Four's work stopped just one mine from being laid in the roads of Africa, then it was all worthwhile.

Not long after this, we were to have a much closer encounter with the spirits of Africa, in a setting film-makers Ollie and Viv would have marvelled at. But for us it was one that involved far more danger than working with a tame hyena.

Returning from operations in the Zambezi Valley, or beyond, often involved a long drive over difficult roads and it could take two or three days to get back to civilisation. We had found a good camp spot, in a sparsely populated tribal land, in which to break the journey and had used the site a number of times on these travels.

The first time there, we sought permission to camp on the land from the local headman. In appreciation, we gave him some surplus army rations and said he should let us know if there was anything else we could do for him. I told him we had a doctor with us, who could treat anyone in the five or six families living in the village who might need some medical help.

The headman's name was Witness Mukombe. He had two wives and seven children. He told us how they collected wild honey in the bush and sold it at a roadside store, along with the fruit and vegetables grown in the village gardens. The bus came through three times a week and the thatched shelter with the local produce became a popular stop for the travellers. They had made enough money from this enterprise to buy a new bicycle and a Singer sewing machine with a foot treadle for Mrs Mukombe, his first wife.

Later that first afternoon, Witness and one of the other men came across to our camp.

'Things are going well here but we have a problem,' he said after the usual polite greeting. 'There is a very large kudu bull that has found our vegetable garden and even though we have put up a string with tin cans to frighten it, the animal will not go away. It now believes it owns our gardens and has become aggressive towards anyone who approaches. Soon there will be no vegetables left.'

He pointed to my rifle and asked if we could help them.

In the fading light of that evening, Rex fixed the problem and the village had plenty of meat to eat while their vegetables recovered. We took home some wild honey and were always welcomed warmly whenever we returned.

Two years on and the briefing I had just been given would mean returning to see Witness Mukombe. But this time on more serious business.

The brigadier started with some history.

'In 1898 British troops martyred a female spirit medium called Nehanda, unaware of her powers and influence over the Mashona people. She was accused of inciting rebellion and in the harsh circumstances of the day, was duly hanged from a tree, in a pleasant place called Mazoe where now there are citrus orchards. Her people carried the body to a secret cave, where ceremonies took place to appease the spirits, before her shrivelled, naked form was laid down and covered with stones.

'For the terrorist groups, there could be no better psychological weapon than a link with Nehanda – a powerful, female spirit that epitomises rebellion. Their propaganda broadcasts already describe how Nehanda was now leading them in a great war of *Chimurenga* – freedom and liberation – and, remarkably, they said they had sent cadres to find her and seek her wisdom.

'Initially,' he explained, 'we just dismissed this as propaganda. But our views quickly changed when a long-distance truck driver let it be known that he had been paid to drop off three armed men from Lusaka at a big river close to Witness Mukombe's village.

'Mick, your mission is to find and eliminate the three terrorists. The local people have high regard for Nehanda, so this threat has serious cultural implications. We cannot allow her remains to be desecrated and used by terrorists, or anyone else for that matter. We can't change what happened in the past, but we can acknowledge her importance and demonstrate our respect to the local population by ensuring she is not molested in her final rest place.'

To do that we – like the three terrorists from Lusaka – would have to go in search of Nehanda's sacred shrine.

I knew we could never do it on our own. If the shrine was, in fact, in the general area of Witness Mukombe's village, we would need his help to at least point us in the right direction. Either way, it would be a sensitive issue with him and we would have to handle it carefully.

On the way up to meet Witness, Rex stopped us at a general store in what was the last major settlement before entering the remote tribal lands. We walked into the store and started proceedings by cleaning out the small fridge of cold Cokes. Refreshments in hand, Rex and I looked around at what might persuade Witness to help us on this unusual mission.

We settled on a bolt of bright blue cotton cloth and blue cotton thread to keep Mrs Mukombe's sewing machine busy. We bought a spare tube and a puncture repair kit for Witness' bicycle, two big pockets of oranges for the kids and for the men five gallons of *chibuku* – the traditional African beer made from fermented millet. We hoped it would be enough to loosen their tongues, because we wanted to talk about Nehanda.

We had an enjoyable evening with Witness and his extended family, sharing a meal around a big campfire in the centre of the village huts. As the fire died down that evening, I stood up and asked Nelson, with his exquisite linguistics skills, to stand next to me and translate.

'Headman Witness, we would like to thank you and your village for allowing us to stay here on your land. We have enjoyed being here and have always been willing to help you with any problems to the best of our ability.

'This visit has also been very enjoyable, but I am afraid our presence here this time could bring difficulties to you, and none of us want that to happen.'

I had their attention from the start, but now I could see Witness and his village people looking at me with apprehension. I didn't want to frighten them or, even worse, come across as threatening, but I had to somehow explain the gravity of the problem.

'Before my grandfather's time,' I explained, 'there was a great spirit medium called Nehanda. She was cruelly killed at a time when many were being killed in conflicts between Mashona, Matabele, and the new white tribe that arrived in 1896.

'The influence of Nehanda remains strong to this day, but there has already been enough killing in her name. We have heard there are evil people who have come looking for her remains which, if found, will be taken out of the country and used in the terrorist war.

'We cannot let that happen. Nehanda must be allowed to remain in dignity where she was enshrined by her followers nearly 100 years ago.'

Nelson interpreted in their language. It always seemed to take much longer than my English, no doubt because of the detailed descriptive channels they used to get to the point in question, and I admired their way. There were no hecklers, just simple, proud people weighing up their options as they were presented.

Eventually I reached the crunch point.

'Witness, have you ever heard stories about a sacred cave somewhere near here, containing the remains of the great spirit medium Nehanda?' The gathering around the fire went deadly silent.

Witness stared at the flickering embers for some time saying nothing, maybe trying to work out what he could say to me and how to say it in a way the spirits could not object to.

Eventually he spoke.

'We follow the Inyati River downstream hunting and looking for beehives. After three days, there is a large, flat expanse of rock where a smaller river joins the Inyati. This river always has clean, fresh water and the bush grows thick along it. If you follow that river upstream, you will come to some low hills and a place of many broken rocks. We do not venture further because strange noises come from the ground. This could be the place you are looking for.'

I thanked him, and was about to get up to check my maps, when he added that two of the villagers had been that way hunting and were expected back in the morning. They would know if any strangers had passed through the area.

I spread out the maps, followed the course of the Inyati River, and found what I was sure was the river junction Witness had described. On the map the side stream was not drawn as the usual twisting blue line. It was discontinuous – as if the cartographer's blue pen was running out of ink – a series of unconnected blue squiggles. What did it mean?

At the head of the stream, where the contours showed steeper, broken ground, in small print was the word 'Guano'. It was printed in the way mines are named on maps, but didn't have the pick and shovel symbol that usually goes with it. Why call a place hundreds of miles from the nearest coast Guano, the Spanish word for cormorant and seabird droppings?

Next morning we were packed up and ready to leave, when Witness came over with two men, each carrying a small-headed axe they used to open up beehives found in trees. They were the hunters he'd spoken of the previous night.

We sat down with them and made some tea, then went through the usual pleasantries that open all discussions in Africa. After establishing that we had all slept well, the two men described where they had been in much the same way as Witness had done the night before. Nelson questioned them about this in their own language to get more detail for us, and it was during that discussion when the younger of the two said he had found tracks of strangers.

There were three and all were wearing boots with a distinctive tread: he made a figure eight in the sand at my feet.

Chinese-issue boots. They were terrorist tracks.

I relayed the news back to base on the radio, while Rex and the others threw the camouflage nets over the Sabre Land Rovers and tied them down.

The hunters showed us a short cut to the river and we took off at a good pace, following the track used by the villagers.

As we went, I was thinking the terrorists could still be searching for Nehanda's burial place; on the other hand, they could already have found what they wanted and were possibly returning. We might meet them head on, so I put Jonny up front with his machine gun alongside Rex and Pig Dog, who led the way.

An uneventful day passed and as the night approached, we backed off the track into an ambush position.

Karate and I were on watch from midnight. As 02.00 approached, we heard movement on the track to the left of us. Somebody, or something, was approaching. We nudged the others awake and lay there in the aim, straining ears and eyes to get a target.

Moments later two bush pigs trotted into view. Somehow sensing they were not alone both stopped in the middle of our killing ground. They turned and stared intently in our direction. We were no more than ten metres away. Still they stared then, probably getting our scent, suddenly snorted, and tossing their heads rushed away.

We changed guards. I drifted off to sleep, smiling at the thought of a wild pig roasting over embers on the old Land Rover crank handle I'd kept as a spit for just such occasions. I was happy. We had just proved the quality of our ambush.

Late on the second day, Rex called a halt and signalled for me to go forward and join him.

'We're on to them, Mick,' he said, pointing to the sandy ground where the figure-eight boot patterns were still clearly visible.

Looking ahead, I could see some low hills and guessed we were close to the stream junction Witness had told us about. Another two hours and we would be well into the likely target area. Tomorrow could be a big day for us. We moved on a short distance. I chose another ambush position. Apart from once hearing a leopard calling, the second night passed without incident.

By 08.00 next morning, we had reached the sheet rock Witness had described and could see the smaller river course coming in from our left. As he said, the bush changed as the river course climbed towards a narrow gap in the surrounding low hills. The thorn trees were replaced by larger, green hardwoods and figs. Thick tangles of creepers shaded the scattered boulders. Great yellow spider webs spread across the stream that was narrow and rocky.

While I sent our position and a brief report back to base on the radio, Rex and Pig Dog moved forward to do a local recce. Would we find more recent tracks amongst the boulders? Which way had the terrorists gone?

The tracks Rex found were not new but led up the stream. It was rocky and difficult for tracking, but Rex and Pig Dog could follow them. They looked for upturned pebbles; bent clumps of the short, yellow, dry grass; a broken twig; a damaged spider web, all the while assessing where they would have walked if going in this direction.

We followed close behind, senses on high alert, looking forward beyond our trackers who were focused on the ground immediately in front of them.

We climbed up through a narrow gap between bush-covered boulders and suddenly broke cover into a small clearing.

A rock wall and tall trees blocked our path. And the river had gone.

Rex again called me over to where he had found a small hole. Kneeling down, we could hear the sound of running water deep underground. I realised then what the map was indicating with the discontinuous blue line. In this broken country, the stream would disappear underground into a rock fissure then reappear on the surface some distance further on.

Small comfort though, because this was dangerous country. The ground forced us into moving through narrow gaps that could easily be covered by an enemy watching from the safety of the large boulders above.

We moved across the clearing, looking for a way up or around it. Rex disappeared into a crack between two huge, rounded boulders. 'There's a track here. This way,' he signalled back to us.

We caught up with Rex after a steep climb and struggle through vines, stinging nettles and spider webs and found ourselves beneath a great rocky outcrop. The stream had reappeared from under the rock, but vanished again close to the crack between the boulders.

'Listen,' I said. 'What's that noise?'

From the rocks in front of us came a faint twittering that slowly became louder and then faded away.

I was crouched down listening, trying to work out what the sounds were, when Rex shouted in alarm.

I heard the hissing *whoosh* of an RPG7 bazooka as it passed close above my head, and I instinctively hugged the ground as the rocket smashed into a rock above and behind me and exploded in an ear-shattering blast.

My ears were ringing with the explosion and I felt a sharp pain on the side of my neck just below the jaw bone. Blood dripped on to my FN. I touched the affected area to assess the damage, but could feel nothing. Looked like I was OK.

I hugged the ground as another bazooka exploded. Rock fragments showered down on my back. We needed to do something fast. The first rocket took us all by surprise; in the rocky maze above us we had no idea where it came from. The tables turned with the second shot. Pig Dog spotted the terrorist as he aimed and fired the bazooka at me. He got the shot away, but was dead before the rocket exploded.

Karate, meanwhile, had somehow scrambled up one side of the rock face. Although dangerously exposed, he could see the ground behind the maze of boulders. A second terrorist appeared, carrying an RPD with the front bipod hanging down. A well placed machine-gunner would be a difficult proposition in this ground, but Karate cut him down and things went quiet.

There was one left and somewhere in there would be where he'd die.

We waited and watched for a while, then I signalled for Karate and Pig Dog to cover the rest of us while we scrambled up the rock face to join them before making our next move. My ears were still ringing from the bazooka explosions and I wasn't at my mental best, but the bleeding from the cut on my neck had stopped and we still had a job to do.

Between two huge, vertical slabs of rock was a narrow passage. As we approached, we felt a flow of cool air and following it down, unexpectedly found ourselves in a high-roofed cavern of great size. It was light inside, as part of the roof had collapsed, leaving a hole through which we could see daylight. There were three backpacks on the ground next to where a small fire had been made. The twittering sound we had heard earlier was now much louder.

We cautiously explored the cavern – nerves on edge – expecting deadly fire to open up at any moment. It was a cool, damp place with an earthy smell from what we now saw was a compacted mass of droppings. It was a strong odour but not unpleasant.

We were in a bat cave.

'So, where are all the bats?' asked Horse. 'There must be another cave deeper in than this one.'

We spread out on either side of the cavern. Nerves were on edge as we searched for the last terrorist. Would we be greeted with another bazooka?

Rex stopped and signalled: 'Over here.'

In a dark corner he had found a narrow tunnel; forever the tracker, he had seen the familiar figure-eight boot print leading into it.

We were closing in on the final act of this deadly drama and a scene worthy of the best horror movies.

The tunnel was like a mineshaft: just high enough for walking in a stooped manner and wide enough for one person at a time. We could see a few bats dangling from the roof at face level. Rex pointed to the ground. There were the fresh boot tracks leading into the tunnel, but it was pitch-black and it would be suicide to go further after an armed terrorist.

'Don't worry, Mick,' said Rex reading my thoughts. 'We'll flush him out.'

He gestured for us to position ourselves on either side of the entrance to the tunnel. Satisfied with our positions, he darted forward into the entrance of the tunnel and fired a sustained burst on automatic into the darkness.

He ducked back out of the way just in time, as the cave exploded with a wild cacophony of screeches, screams and wingbeats as the bats panicked.

At first there were thousands of bats screaming as they struggled to leave the narrow tunnel. But what we didn't know was that beyond this first tunnel were another three caves, all linked by narrow tunnels like the one Rex had fired into. The panic amongst the bats spread from the front tunnel to the first cave and then into the second and third caves as thousands, then tens of thousands, and finally hundreds of thousands of bats fled their roost in a shrieking, black wave.

Hugging the side of the wall at the cave entrance, we were engulfed by the animal mass and by the noise, droppings and urine. We covered our faces to protect ourselves from the beating wings, helpless to do anything except wait for all the bats to leave the cave.

After what seemed like an eternity, the noise suddenly stopped. I looked across at Rex. He cautiously opened his eyes. A bat dangled from the brim of his bush hat. He brushed it off and then in a flash dropped to his knees, his FN firing repeatedly at something I couldn't see from where I stood.

The third terrorist fell face down into the fresh *guano* dropped by a million frightened bats.

The bats would undoubtedly return, so before they did we got out our torches and explored the caves. The orange light of the torches picked out the weird shapes and flashing eyes of a few bats that had remained in the tunnel. We sidled past, trying not to disturb them. Stiff, dried-out bodies of dead bats crackled underfoot. It got noticeably warmer as we went deeper and deeper into the hillside.

The first tunnel led into a high, narrow cave. A few more bats twittered and fidgeted nervously above us and we felt a shower of droppings as we moved past.

There was another tunnel similar in size and shape to the first and seemingly darker still. It was getting warmer all the time. The tunnel eventually opened into the second cave. A small stream of running water crossed the floor then disappeared down a sinkhole.

The third passage took us deep into the bowels of the earth. It was by now very hot and I could feel the sweat running down my face and back. A startled bat fluttered away, hitting my neck with its wings, and I remembered I had been bleeding earlier. The bat screeched and struggled to find a new perching spot on the tunnel roof as we walked past.

Eventually this passage opened into the largest of all the caves, and it was there that we found Nehanda.

At the back of the cave a large, flat rock had fallen to the ground, leaving a hollow in the wall where it had previously been held. Sheltered from the bat droppings was a skeleton. Some of the bones had come adrift, but it was generally intact. Scattered on the ground with the bones were bronze spears, copper bangles and broken clay pots.

We carefully gathered up the loose bones and put them back in their proper place. We put the spears and the other items neatly alongside the skeleton then put what we could find of the rock mound back over the bones. It was hot work and we were glad when it was done, especially as by then some of the bats were returning to the cave.

We left the dead terrorists where they were, picked up their weapons and the three backpacks, then headed back to the sanity of the river junction. Fully clothed we submerged ourselves in a deep pool of deliciously cool water.

Fish called me over as I had started to bleed again from my neck. He cleaned up what was a thin but deep cut, then put on a dressing.

We all stripped off to let our clothes dry in the sun and made a start on cleaning up our weapons and webbing harnesses. As I picked up my harness, something pricked one of my fingers. There was a thin, razor-sharp piece of khaki brown-coloured metal, the size of a small coin, embedded in the shoulder padding. It was a piece of the RPG7 bazooka that had exploded above me and I realised that was what had cut my neck.

Several years later, I was at a social function with a group of medical people. One of the doctors noticed the 75-millimetre scar beneath my jawbone and commented that it was very neat work.

I couldn't help myself.

'Yes,' I said. 'The man was trained by the Chinese and this was the last operation he ever did.'

And I left it at that.

# The ZAPU Arms Cache

We were on the shooting range doing reflex training. Each of us had to position ourselves in the centre of the firing point and crouch as if stealthily advancing into contact. Behind us, the training officer had a device that could release hidden targets on the firing range twenty metres away. As the spring-loaded targets popped up, we would respond with immediate fire, then we'd drop into a kneeling position ready for more action.

The targets varied from head only to full body size and sometimes were partly side-on and difficult to hit. They were activated at completely random times and sometimes two would be released one after the other. We'd fire at the first, drop, roll, then engage the second target.

The training officer marked us according to how he judged our reaction speed, combined with the hit count on the targets. Karate and Pig Dog were like greased lightning. Rex and I were a little slower, but we were better shots and usually scored a few more hits. But Jonny, the big Fijian who carried the machine gun, blew us all away and the targets as well in the process.

The brigadier enjoyed this type of training and had joined us to observe our skill levels and to have some fun by participating himself. We joked we had no chance against him, given he would already have told the training officer what score he wanted.

After the shooting, we cleared the weapons then reviewed the results with the training officer and had a look for anything we could possibly improve.

'It's impressive,' said the brigadier, then he asked us to sit down on the firing point as he wanted to talk to us.

'I have another operation for you,' he began. 'I'll brief you this afternoon once I have the latest air photographs, but what I want to discuss with you now is an idea I have about the way you operate.

'I have heard you speak of how you like to be "invisible" on these operations; judging by what you have achieved that tactic is clearly working well. But as good as it has proved to be so far, it's my belief it has the potential to bring even bigger returns for us.

'Your operations may be against one terrorist group or another,' he continued, 'but the truth is you are part of a much bigger game being played out between superpowers.

'The political leaders, and those aspiring to be leaders, of these central African countries have, without exception, organised themselves along tribal lines and, as in other parts of the world, there are differences between tribes that go back a long way.

'The influence of the Europeans who originally colonised Africa is slowly but surely being replaced by Russian and Chinese interests, riding on the back of African nationalism and the tribal differences that go with it.

'So, on the one hand, the Russians chose to support the MPLA in Angola and, closer to home, the ZAPU terrorist group from the Matabele tribe of Rhodesia.

'On the other hand, the Chinese have put their weight behind Frelimo in Mozambique and the ZANU terrorist group from the rival Mashona tribe of Rhodesia.

'The two Communist nations are in a race to get their hands on the mineral wealth of Africa, and our real job is to make that as difficult as possible for them. Every time we inflict a blow against a terrorist organisation we, at the same time, damage the plans and hopes of the power backing them.'

He paused, giving us time to absorb what he had said and to wonder where he was taking us.

'It's my view we can optimise the return on your actions with some subtle deception. I have obtained a supply of both Chinese and Russian military clothing and we already have their weapons. So in future if we are up against a Chinese-backed faction, you will wear and carry Russian gear, and vice versa if we are taking on a Russian-sponsored group.

'In addition, on each operation you will be given "souvenirs" to leave behind that will suggest a rival terrorist faction was responsible for what happened. This will further protect your true identity, and it should also cause dissent between the different factions and their backers to a point, hopefully, where they will start killing each other.'

'Brilliant,' I said, on behalf of the team who all had broad grins on their faces.

We met the brigadier again later in the operations room, where he had projected an air photograph on to a big screen dropped down in front of the maps covering the wall.

The high-resolution camera in the nose cone of the aircraft had picked up a recently used bush track that led to a clearing. A truck was parked on one side and there were a number of thatched shelters. At the far end of the camp a path led to a big hole in the ground.

'It's an arms cache,' said the brigadier. 'They are building an arms cache from which they will supply gangs sent to infiltrate the country.'

He pushed a button, the white screen rolled back into its case and he turned to the maps. He'd put a red marker arrow on the Zambian map close to the Zambezi River, in an area marked as the 'lower Zambezi game area', not too far away from where we'd been with the elephants in Mupata Gorge.

'The group you ambushed on the Chewore River in January were all Chinese-backed ZANU. This time it's the rival faction, ZAPU. Your mission is to destroy the camp and the arms cache. I want you on your way before first light day after tomorrow. The arms cache isn't complete yet so we have some time, but it's going to take you three days to reach the river and another three to cross the Zambezi and get to the camp. Things should be happening by then.'

In the dead of night, four days later, we crossed the Zambezi River and hid the kayaks in thick cover on the Zambian side of the river.

We walked for another two nights through the thick, thorny bush of south-eastern Zambia, memorable for a million biting insects; a flock of the uncommon crested guinea fowl that wandered into one of our lay-up positions; a solitary lion that grunted and groaned as it walked alongside us throughout the second night of the infiltration.

In the early evening of the third day, Rex stopped and beckoned me forward.

'There's the track,' he said, referring to the bush track on the air photograph. We crept forward to have a closer look. There were fresh vehicle tracks that would have been made by the truck in the picture.

'Rex, we'll stay in cover here,' I whispered, 'while you, Nelson and Pig Dog take the light intensifiers and follow the road into the camp to see what's happening. We'll make a plan once you get back.'

Rex nodded and we returned to the others. We were already in good cover so the rest of us kept watch while Rex got his team ready for the recce.

As they reached the track, Pig Dog snapped a branch to mark where they would find us on the way back, then the three of them disappeared into the darkness.

Rex and his recce group returned much earlier than I expected. 'There's nobody home, Mick,' he reported. 'We walked right through the camp and the truck is parked pretty well in the same place as in the air photo. I thought there must be a caretaker group that would look after everything, but there is nobody there. Maybe they have gone off somewhere for a beer.'

I shook my head in disbelief. 'Let's go and have a good look,' I said.

A big moon gave us good vision as we advanced quietly and cautiously towards the camp. There was no sound. We moved in closer, concealed ourselves and watched and listened. Again there was no sound and no movement.

From our position we could see several low, A-frame thatched huts that made up the camp. In the centre, on the track leading into it, was the heavy, six-wheeled, Russian military truck.

We moved in closer. It was eerily quiet. We stood up then moved cautiously into the open cleared area of the camp. We were on high alert. Safety catches were off and we were ready to fire at any sign of life.

Moving in behind the truck, I looked up at the rear-view mirror.

'Stop!' I hissed in alarm and we all ducked down.

In the mirror I had seen the camouflage uniform of a terrorist, seemingly asleep in the cab of the truck.

Concealed behind the vehicle I briefed the team.

'We don't know what's going on here,' I whispered, 'so I don't want shots fired at this stage if we can avoid it. Better to stay invisible. Karate and I will move in on the cab and I'll take out the driver silently with my knife. The rest of you keep an eye on the general area. I don't want surprises.'

While we all carried the practical Swiss Army knives, Rex, Pig Dog and I also carried bigger blades on the back of our web belts.

Rex and Pig Dog carried big bowie knives they kept razor-sharp for skinning and butchering the game animals they hunted. They were also deadly weapons.

I had a smaller, American-made KA-BAR knife I'd found in an army surplus store in London. It was described as a 'fighting knife' with a 175 millimetre blade and was designed specifically for the US Marines. It was beautifully made and I treasured it.

And for the first time I was about to use it for what it had been designed. 'You ready, Karate?'

(*Above*) Author Mike Graham at
medal investiture ceremony.

(*Right*) Horse.

(*Above*) Fish with his beloved bazooka.

(*Left*) 'Harves' – helicopter pilot
extraordinaire.

Operational parachuting with equipment.

Ambush victims.

Headman Witness Mukombe
and his garden.

TMH-46 mines and other captured weapons.

Indiscriminate terrorist killing with land mines supplied by Russia and China.

The horror of a land mine attack.

The mines were sometimes boosted with the addition of explosives, mortar bombs or grenades.

# Uyai kumusha zvisina njodzi

# Come home in safety

**DZOKERA KURUNYARARO NEMHURI YAKO**

**UNOFIREI PASINA CHINHU UCHISIYA MIDZIMU YEKWENYU ISINA KUTEURWA**

Ukadzoka murunyararo, Mauto neMapurisa anochengetedza runyararo achaita kuti upenyu hwako husave munjodzi.

**UNOZOKWANISA KUGARA MURUNYARARO**

Izvo unofanira kuita kuviga zvombo nezvimwe zvekurwisa zvako panzvimbo yakavandika na:

(a) Takura chimuti chakasungirirwa jira obva waenda kukambe yeMapurisa iri pedyo newe kana kuti kamba yeMauto neMapurisa, kuhofisi yaMudzviti kana kune mushandi weHurumende. Kana wava pedyo neimwe yenzvimbo idzi, donhedza chimuti ichi, oisa maoko ako pamusoro wako kuratidza kuti wauya murunyararo;

**KANA KUTI**

(b) Zunguza-zunguza chimuti ichi mumhepo apo unoona Mapurisa kana Mauto anenge achifamba kana mushandi weHurumende. Kana wave pedyo nemumwe wevanhu ava, donhedza chimuti ichi oisa maoko ako pamusoro wako kuratidza kuti wauya murunyararo;

**KANA KUTI**

(c) Kana wakakuvara, tumira munhu wemusha kune imwe yenzvimbo idzi kuti azotitaurira uko murapi angauye kuzokutora.

**ITA KUTI USAVE NECHOMBO CHEKURWISISA KUTI USAPINDE MUNJODZI**

**DZOKA MURUNYARARO UGOZOCHENGETWA ZVAKANAKA UCHIPIHWA PEKUGARA, KUDYA KWAKANAKA, NEKURAPWA.**

**UKARAMBA UCHIRWA UNOFIRA PASINA CHIKONZERO UYE MIDZIMU YAKO IGOSHAYA ZORORO.**

**MHURI YAKO ICHARAMBA ICHITAMBUDZVA NENGOZI YE MWEYA WAKO.**

---

**RETURN TO PEACE AND YOUR FAMILY**

**WHY DIE FOR NOTHING AND LEAVE YOUR FAMILY SPIRITS UNAPPEASED?**

If you return in peace the Security Forces guarantee that your life will not be in danger.

**YOU WILL BE ABLE TO LIVE IN PEACE**

All you have to do is hide your weapons and equipment in a safe place and:

(a) Carry a stick with a piece of clothing tied to it and go in safety to the nearest Police Station, Security Forces base, DC's office or Government official. When you are close, drop the stick and put your hands on your head to show you come in peace;

OR

(b) Wave the stick in the air when you see the Police or a Security Force patrol or Government official. When they are close, drop the stick and put your hands on your head to show you come in peace;

OR

(c) If you are injured, send a tribesman to one of these places to tell us where a Medical Officer can come and fetch you.

**MAKE SURE YOU DO NOT HAVE A WEAPON AND YOU WILL BE SAFE**

**RETURN IN PEACE AND YOU WILL BE WELL LOOKED AFTER AND HAVE SHELTER, GOOD FOOD AND MEDICAL TREATMENT**

**IF YOU FIGHT ON, YOU WILL DIE FOR NO REASON AND YOUR SPIRITS WILL NEVER REST. YOUR FAMILY WILL CONTINUE TO BE TROUBLED BECAUSE OF YOUR WANDERING SPIRIT.**

Printed by the Government Printer, Salisbury.

Leaflets urging terrorists to surrender were widely used but to very little effect.

An RPG7 bazooka, boxes of ammunition and anti-personnel mines supplied by Mother Russia.

(*Above*) Carrying AK47s in the dense thorn scrub of the Zambezi Valley.

(*Left*) After our attacks we would leave 'souvenirs' suggesting the involvement of a rival terrorist faction. They fell for the ruse and turned on each other.

# The Rhodesia

*Incorporating The Nation*

ESTABLISHED 1891 ✶ ✶ ✶ SALISBURY, THURSDAY DECEMBER 22 1977

## SECOND GUN BATTLE AT NKOMO'S HQ IN LUSAKA

LUSAKA.

A FIVE-MINUTE gun battle with machine-guns and smallarms broke out at the head-quarters here of Mr Joshua Nkomo's ZAPU movement early Tuesday for the second day running. ZAPU is banned in Rhodesia.

A ZAPU spokesman blamed "Rhodesian agents" for the attack on "Zimbabwe House". But the ruling UNIP party-owned Times of Zambia quoted "informed sources" as saying the gun battle was a faction fight between Kalanga and Ndebele tribal groups in ZAPU.

## Fights as thousands are stranded

LONDON.

THOUSANDS of Irish Christmas travellers yesterday faced more delays — London's Heathrow...

## Over 8000 killed in five years of terrorist war

*Defence Reporter*
*Chris Reynolds*

COMBINED OPERATIONS Headquarters announced the deaths of 31 more victims of the war last night—the 46th anniversary of the start of the present terrorist offensive.

### Gunman holds hostages

SUBIC BAY (Philippines).

A FILIPINO gunman yesterday held 21 hostages in a tank on the huge U.S. Subic Bay naval base and said he wanted money and a getaway helicopter.

The gunman, believed to be a former employee at the base, hurled bomb employees and customers into a room of the bank just as it was closing, reports *Sata-Reuter*.

...angels need their hair doing

The Zambezi River that we crossed at night using our Zodiacs or the Klepper kayaks.

Recoilless Rifle and other weapons in the Russian backed ZAPU camp.

Shallow defensive trenches dug around the camp.

Assembling the Klepper kayaks at the start.

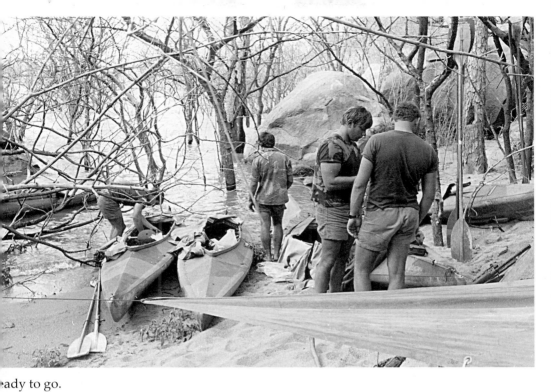

ady to go.

r photograph showing the terrorist boats and camp that were destroyed in the raid.

(*Left*) A skinny looking author after over 300kms of paddling.

(*Below*) During the Mague camp attack we picke up a camera and subsequently developed the fil This picture shows the Frelimo terrorists posing with one of the KPV 14.5 mm anti-aircraft guns that put on a big show for us during the night attack.

(*above*) Author with Rhodesian Minister
of Defence Pieter 'PK' van der Byl. 'Mick,
here are some interesting chaps I want
you to meet', he said. 'Let me know when
you are back in town.'

(*right*) Lord Richard Cecil parachute
training with the SAS in Rhodesia, 1978.

Many grateful
thanks to all friend
at P.TS (for
scanning the xxx
out of me)
R. Cecil

(*Left*) Bridge demolition rehearsal

(*Below*) Bridge demolition rehearsals. Inspecting the results.

(*above*) Bridge demolition rehearsals. The team
working on how we could lay charges under
a bridge while suspended 30–40m above
the ground.

(*right*) Sergeant Andy Chait. Fantastic soldier
originally from the South African Parachute
Battalion.

Static line parachute training jump with equipment. A full load inside the DC Dakota.

Frank Hales – ex 22 SAS and 2 I/C of the Parachute Training School – recovering from an eye infection joins the author for some fun on police horses during a training exercise in the Eastern Highlands.

He nodded. I put my AK on the ground and took out my knife, adrenalin pumping gallons and nerves on edge.

Crouching down we silently moved towards the door of the truck.

I took a deep breath as Karate reached up and wrenched open the door.

I leapt forward. My left arm encircled the neck and I thrust my knife deep into the Russian camouflage jacket.

Karate broke all the tactical rules by cracking up with howls of laughter as I stood there shaking, my knife blade sticking through the dark grey fabric of the jacket that now lay limp across my arm.

I'd just killed a coat hanger.

I sheathed the knife and picked up my AK. 'Put a fucking sock in it, Karate. We've still got a job to do here,' I growled. But my tone was more out of embarrassment than annoyance.

I signalled to the others and we started to move through the deserted camp. There were some ongoing sniggers but the team managed to get serious again as we moved tactically, checking each shelter cautiously as we had done in so many previous situations. I was alert as ever. But in the back of my mind were images of the boys re-enacting my magnificent knife attack in various bars in town on our return. This incident was not going to go away in a hurry.

In the centre of the camp, we found a well-worn path that led towards an anthill thicket and there we found the concealed entrance to the underground cache.

The slatted wooden lid, secured by a peg on the ground, was well camouflaged in spite of the obvious track leading towards it. This could be dangerous. Was the lid booby-trapped – especially since it had been left alone and unguarded?

Suddenly serious again, we deployed around the area in defensive mode while Rex went forward and carefully attached a nylon cord to the lid handle. With that done we hugged the ground as he slowly pulled on the rope to open the hatch.

As with my knife attack, nothing happened, but our reaction this time was relief not amusement. We stood up and went to the cache.

A rough ladder made from tree branches and twine rested beneath the entrance. Rex and I descended for a look while the others kept watch above us.

'Wow!' Rex exclaimed as we stood inside the cache and switched on our mini Maglite torches.

We'd never seen anything like it. A square hole, the size of a garage, had been dug into the ground. Without mechanical diggers it would have been a huge effort to excavate something of this size.

The walls of the cache were lined with wooden poles and in the centre were two stout posts that supported a low roof structure covered in thatch. On the outside the thatch was no more than a foot or two above ground level and had been well camouflaged with tree branches and raked-up leaf litter.

Against the walls were crude, but tidy wooden racks made from sawn timber, upon which were rows of AKM assault rifles, bazookas, rockets and mortars. On the ground beneath them – on timber poles to keep them dry – were dozens of TMH46 anti-tank mines and boxes and boxes of ammunition and explosives.

The cache had been organised into two parts. Most of the space was taken up by the munitions, but in the smaller second compartment were piles of cheap, metal plates, cups and saucers, cooking utensils and a selection of garden tools. In one corner we found a few boxes of notebooks and pencils sitting on top of boxes of candles and sacks of nails. On one shelf were two boxes of trinkets: cheap jewellery, toys and the silly prizes you win in Christmas crackers.

Their arms and these trinkets were what they hoped would gain the support and political allegiance of the people living in the remote African tribal lands, support the invading ZAPU terrorists knew would be critical to their survival.

'They have put a massive amount of work and energy into this,' I said to Rex in amazement. 'Then there is the cost and effort of bringing in all this gear. It's unbelievable.'

'And even more unbelievable is they have left it unguarded,' he replied with a grin.

It was decision time again and our course of action was obvious.

The risk of leaving this accumulation of arms and other materials was too great to ignore. We also needed to work fast. If a decent-sized terrorist group were to suddenly return we could have trouble holding them off.

We were carrying plastic explosive, Cordtex, and a number of TNT primers, so while machine-gun Jonny and the others kept watch, we got Karate to join us as we went to work inside the cache.

We moved mortar bombs, mines and boxes of grenades against the firearm stacks. We opened the boxes of yellow TNT explosive to supplement the small amount of PEA plastic explosive we had brought in. We arranged our charges and the connecting Cordtex ring main to create a simultaneous explosion that would destroy the cache, and the aspirations of ZAPU in this area.

With the charges laid, Rex left Karate and me to rig up the detonators and safety fuse while he dealt with the Russian truck.

Knowing his way around vehicles, Rex placed a lump of plastic explosive directly beneath the driver's seat, then threaded a length of Cordtex detonating cord back through the innards of the engine compartment, where he finally taped a detonator to the exhaust manifold. When the vehicle was recovered by the terrorist group they would drive happily away until the heat of the manifold warmed up sufficiently to activate the detonator. They wouldn't get far.

The terrorists were being terrorised and they would have no idea who was doing this to them, but we left a few clues in the form of opposition ZANU messages they were bound to find.

Once Rex was done with the vehicle, I climbed out of the cache and lit the safety fuse. I had British-made time pencils with me that could give us a delay time of an hour, but I didn't want to risk our charges being detected.

Safety fuse burned at a rate of 300 millimetres in thirty seconds. It was heavy, so I carried no more than a 3-metre roll that would give us five minutes to get away from what was going to be a huge explosion. We ran down the track past the booby-trapped vehicle, trying to get as far away as possible before the blast.

Using the vehicle track as an escape route helped us greatly because when the charges detonated we were at least 400 metres away, which was just as well.

There was a sound like a massive, overhead thunderclap, followed by the whizzing of metal particles propelled through the air at supersonic speeds. We felt the shock wave as it radiated outwards and shook the trees above us.

'Get down!' I ordered urgently.

We were still well within the range of deadly fragments. Just as I spoke, a garden spade cartwheeled over our heads and embedded itself into the ground close to us. We heard muted thuds as other solids smashed into the ground nearby.

The air calmed and we looked back. In the moonlight we could make out a dark cloud that spiralled upwards over the cache area. There would be nothing left for ZAPU. It would be a big blow for them and they would be wondering what to do next.

Rex set a fast pace, and we kept it up for two hours through what was easy bush before reaching the dense, thorn thickets that separated us from the Zambezi River. I was happy with what we had achieved. I didn't believe we were in any danger, but we kept going through the night to give us a good head start in the unlikely event of terrorists trying to follow our tracks.

Our exfiltration was without incident. Except for what we assumed was the same vocal lion that again walked parallel with us for a few hours on the last day as we approached the Zambezi River. We pulled out our concealed kayaks and paddled back across the Zambezi River to safety and the end of another successful operation.

On the way home, Horse and Jonny composed their own version of Louis Armstrong's famous *Mack the Knife* that was predictably altered to become Mick the Knife, but thankfully it didn't last long and I had an ally in Pig Dog, who had nothing but admiration for what I had tried to do.

Back in Lusaka, ZAPU were incensed at the loss of the cache, and absolutely seething over the death of the driver and the front-seat passenger in the truck as it exploded and burst into flames. They would somehow have to explain their failure to the Russians and await another arms shipment before trying again.

The first thing they did was to send a political commissar with an armed escort to deal with the caretaker group who had left the camp and cache unguarded. The leader and his two deputies were shot while the others were tied to trees and brutally beaten with sticks.

While this was happening, a second armed group was sent to exact revenge on the small ZANU contingent that operated a radio station in Lusaka, beaming propaganda across central and southern Africa.

They had picked up the ZANU notices we'd left for them and were certain the destruction was done by their rivals.

The newspaper reports that followed described how the radio station was smashed and how the charred bodies of five ZANU members were recovered from what remained of the burnt-out building.

The brigadier's hopes of the terrorists killing each other had started in grand style.

# The Big Bang Theory

ZANU military commander Josiah Tongogara spent much of his time moving between training camps in Mozambique and Zambia, planning operations and motivating the recruits. He was also a key player in negotiating with the international supporters and sponsors of his organisation, and to do that he needed to be in Lusaka.

ZANU purchased a spacious house on an acre of land in the southern suburb of Chilenje, and there Tongogara made his base. He could entertain important guests, and develop strategy with leaders of the exiled political wing of the party who lived nearby.

Cadre leader Rex Nyongo was a trusted lieutenant and had been summoned to the house. The guards let him onto the property and led him to the wide veranda where he was told to take a seat.

He stood up and braced as the towering figure of Tongogara stepped through the French doors a few minutes later.

'Sit down, Comrade Nyongo,' he ordered.

Tongogara took a seat opposite Nyongo. He knew Nyongo by reputation but they had never met. The small, scrawny figure with shifty eyes fidgeted nervously in his seat as the big man took some time to look him over.

Eventually, he spoke: 'You are a trusted member of our organisation, and for that reason you have been recommended for a special mission here in Lusaka.'

Nyongo nodded. He relaxed a little but stayed silent.

'Three weeks ago, our radio station was attacked by ZAPU freedom fighters, based with the Zambian Army in the Arakan Barracks not far from here. They killed five of our loyal comrades, they destroyed our radio station and then they burned the building and the bodies.

'We have no idea what provoked this attack,' he continued, 'but we cannot and will not allow them to do this to us. For generations the Ndebele have treated us like slaves. They have stolen our cattle and our land and they have taken our women.

'Perhaps they think we are too timid to oppose such aggression. If that is the case we shall soon convince them otherwise. Times have changed.

Now it is the time of the Mashona people to rid themselves of the colonial oppressors in our country. At the same time, we will end the dominance of these Ndebele tyrants.

'The attack against us would have been ordered by ZAPU leader Isaac Ndlovu. He lives at Number three Kalene Road in the suburb of Kalundu, near the University of Zambia. He must now pay for his actions.'

Tongogara stood up and went into his lounge. He returned moments later holding the fold-out carrying handle of a TMH46 anti-tank mine. He handed the mine to Rex Nyongo.

'Comrade Nyongo, you are to plant this mine in the gravel driveway of his house, at a time when you can be sure he will run over it in his car. Ndlovu is a regular visitor at the local hotel bar, he goes there most nights. My suggestion is you lay the mine while he is out drinking. On his return he is unlikely to notice any disturbance in the ground.

'You are to remain close to the house to witness the explosion, and I want you to check the vehicle to ensure there are no survivors. You have a Tokarev pistol?' he asked.

Rex Nyongo nodded and spoke for the first time. 'Thank you, Comrade Tongogara. I will not let you down. We will get even with the Ndebele.'

Just before midnight two days later, Ndlovu's blue, Isuzu pickup truck detonated the mine. Rex Nyongo ran forward and, braving the fire that had started beneath the vehicle, he peered inside. A prostitute was sprawled across the passenger seat, her neck hanging at a strange angle. Ndlovu was slumped over the steering wheel. They were both dead, but to be sure Rex Nyongo put a bullet into their heads then fled the scene.

The brigadier's ruse had scored again.

Friday night, three days later, twelve ZANU terrorists were enjoying millet beer and women in one of the illegal beer halls at the Kabwata Cultural Village markets. Eight of them sat outside, listening to traditional African music that blared out of a ghetto blaster. The other four were inside the building, propping up the rough bar that had been made from old oil drums and wooden pallets.

ZAPU had been tipped off and sent ten of their men to get even for the killing of their leader. Under cover of darkness they silently approached the beer hall.

They crept through the deserted market stalls and stopped within twenty metres of the ZANU terrorists. Some were sitting smoking and talking to the girls, a couple were on their feet and dancing.

'Now,' whispered the ZAPU leader. They darted out into the street and opened fire with their AKs. There were screams but they didn't last long. The leader lobbed a grenade into the beer hall, then they all dashed back into cover as the explosion rocked the night.

Satisfied with the attack, they walked without undue haste back towards the minibus they had left a block away.

The brigadier's score was mounting.

President Kenneth Kaunda paced up and down in front of the ZAPU and ZANU hierarchy who sat silent and uneasy facing his wrath. They had all been brought to his office by armed police who stood off to one side watching.

'First the radio station,' ranted the president, 'then the assassination of Ndlovu and now the attack at the markets. I don't care if you kill each other, but this time you have also killed Zambians!

'It's not acceptable!' he shouted and smashed his fist on to the tabletop in front of where they sat. His eyes blazed, burning in anger beneath the broad expanse of his receding hairline. Beads of sweat trickled down his cheeks.

He moved in front of Tongogara and pointed his finger at him. 'You are the cause of this.'

His finger was trembling slightly as he pointed and his voice moved another notch up the anger scale.

'Get out!' he shouted. 'Get out of Zambia and stay out. You will be taken by police escort to your house, you have twenty-four hours to pack up and get out of Zambia. The police will escort you to the border with Malawi. Now get out of my sight.'

Tongogara, who had sat expressionless throughout, stood up and left without a word.

Later at their headquarters ZAPU were elated. They had paid a local police inspector to report the market incident as being caused by drunken ZANU cadres fighting amongst themselves. There was nothing to link ZAPU with the incident and the explanation seemed plausible.

ZANU had been expelled from Zambia.

Theoretically, they could never again blow up a ZAPU arms cache. But in spite of this the ZAPU leaders decided to move their operations further west, closer to Victoria Falls. This part of Zambia was much closer to the Matabele tribal area of their origin and was well away from their ZANU rivals.

Over the next few months they began looking for suitable camp locations and eventually chose an area about 100 kilometres downstream of Victoria Falls. The area was remote and unpopulated, but they found an old mine track that was still passable for their six-wheeled Russian truck.

The track ended in a valley about thirty kilometres away from the Zambezi River. A series of shallow, prospectors' trenches had been dug amongst the scattered hardwood trees that provided shade and cover. There was water in a nearby stream. It would be a good campsite.

They sent out patrols to scout through the general area and to go as far as the Zambezi to look for suitable places where they could secretly cross the river and infiltrate into Rhodesia. The deep water swirled in the strong current but crossing would not be too difficult. There were sandbanks on both sides of the river where boats could be launched and landed.

It was ideal, and the camp known as *Kalomo* was soon under construction.

In the weeks that followed, ZAPU sent out regular patrols towards the Zambezi River where they would watch for any sign of activity on the opposite bank. One such patrol was given the task of finding the best crossing point. Its members had been to the river before and had never seen any sign of activity on the opposite side, which is what they expected given it was described as a wilderness hunting area.

They dropped down from the hills and went to the edge of the river. They moved with caution as they checked out the small bays and sandbanks to assess their suitability.

On the opposite side of the river, two hunters were following the blood trail of a wounded buffalo bull; for that reason they too were very cautious. They were on a low hill overlooking the river when they saw a man in camouflage gear carrying an AK assault rifle. The two hunters froze in cover and watched.

Four days later, the brigadier called Rex and me to the operations room. The report from the two hunters had been passed on by the police and he'd ordered a high-altitude photo-recce mission.

The pictures showed a camp complex and what we were sure was another cache being built. Both were at least twice the size of the eastern camp. One of the air photographs showed a small mechanical digger, presumably brought in to excavate the cache and possibly to make some defensive positions.

'This is a very different kettle of fish to your first ZAPU camp,' began the brigadier.

'For a start they will not be caught off-guard again. There will be guards around the camp and they will probably put others in elevated observation positions while daily clearance patrols will be looking for any threatening sign.

'On top of that, I want more from you this time. Blowing up their arms caches is good but eliminating their trained personnel is better. Taking out both at the same time is better still and that is what we will do.

'The critical issue is timing,' he continued, 'and the only way we can get that right is to have a recce team watching and reporting back to us. Once the terrorists arrive at the camp, they will be given arms from the cache and I'm sure they will start their infiltration not long after that. One or two days later at the most, I would think?'

We nodded in agreement.

'From the pictures it looks as if they have largely completed the excavation of the cache. I think we can safely assume they will line it and put in the rough shelving you described at the other site. Then they have to bring in all the munitions that will be in storage somewhere in Lusaka.

'On that basis I'd say we have ten to twelve days to play with, because once the cache is stocked they will start bringing through the terrorist groups who will infiltrate into Rhodesia, and at that point we must be ready to strike.

'The first priority is to get a recce team in there. Free-fall parachute entry tomorrow night. The air force has been briefed and is on standby. Rex, will you get that organised while the major and I look at what we'll need to get the job done?'

Rex stood up and glanced at me. 'Karate and Pig Dog,' I replied to the silent question. 'And Rex, tell Mack to come and join us. I can already see we will need some of his expertise.'

Rex left the room and a few minutes later Mack came in, saluted and sat down next to me.

The brigadier again turned to the air photographs.

'These pictures show fifty shelters, spread out over about 150 metres but contained within a narrow area between what looks like old earthworks. We can take two things from that,' he said. 'Firstly, it means we could be up against as many as fifty terrorists – possibly more if two of them share a bivvy – and secondly, in that narrow area we would require no more than twelve men for the assault group in a camp attack.'

He looked up and I nodded again in agreement.

'To cut off terrorists fleeing from the attack, I estimate we will need eight four-man teams in ambushing stop groups. They can subdivide into pairs once on the ground to achieve better coverage. That's forty-four men in total so far.'

'Yes, and in most cases that would be plenty for an attack of this nature,' I replied. 'But if they have made defensive positions, that could make things difficult for what is a small assault group. We need more firepower.'

'Take the mortars,' he said. 'Use them to initiate the attack and to deal with anything we don't know about. If you take four tubes, that's eight men to carry the tubes and baseplates, plus you'll need two fire controllers. If the members of the attack party carry one bomb each, you'll have ten bombs per tube. That's plenty.'

We discussed these attack plans a little longer and then the brigadier turned to Mack.

'Mack, we have to get fifty-four heavily laden men secretly across the Zambezi River in the middle of the night. You're the boatman. How are we going to do it?'

Mack stood up and walked to the large-scale map on the wall. He took the pointer and we listened intently as in his soft, Scottish accent he calmly described the plan we would adopt.

'It's not the actual crossing that poses the risk,' he said in opening. 'It's taking our vehicles into the target area and mucking around trying to get everything to the river – especially on the scale we plan. That's the problem. We would be inviting compromise. We need to keep well away from the target area.

'Thirty kilometres upstream is a road leading to a concrete landing, used by a white-water rafting company operating out of Victoria Falls. It's where they recover the rafts and customers after their trip and ferry them back to their base.

'My suggestion is we make camp somewhere out of sight near the landing. We'll assemble the Zodiacs and when we are ready to go we'll launch the boats from the concrete ramp.

'Up there – and at night – we will be well away from any unwelcome attention, and our Zodiacs will get us into the target area in about three and a half hours. A good moon phase would be useful, but we can always resort to infrared if we need help to navigate along the way.

'And why three and a half hours, you'll no doubt be thinking? Well, that's because we won't be using the engines – we can't risk the noise. We'll silently paddle down with the current and drop everybody off on one of the sandbanks in the target area.

'Once everybody is off, the boat parties will carry on paddling downstream until we reach the landing at Msuna, just before Devil's Gorge and the upper reaches of Lake Kariba. We'll base ourselves there and wait for your return. Obviously we'll use the engines for the extraction, but by then the noise won't matter.

'I'd recommend we take six Zodiacs. It means that in addition to the fifty-four men of the attack party we will need another twelve to man the boats, plus there are the truck drivers and their escorts.'

'Mack, you are a genius,' beamed the brigadier.

Just before midnight, Karate and Pig Dog leapt into space from a DC3 flying slowly at 12,000 feet. The two stayed close together during the long descent to 2,500 feet and at that point they tracked away from each other to deploy the free-fall parachutes.

In the moonlight, Karate saw what looked like a plateau between the hills with open spaces and scattered trees. He picked his spot and used the toggles to glide into the landing. Pig Dog followed him in and landed ten metres behind.

The two bundled up and hid the parachutes in a patch of long grass, checked their compasses and started the walk towards the camp.

They had been dropped about ten kilometres north of the camp. The plan was for them to find the rough vehicle track leading into the camp and monitor the road movement. Our thinking was that ZAPU would focus their attention on the area between their camp and the Zambezi River. That is where they would be planning to cross into Rhodesia and they'd want to know the coast was clear.

We hoped they wouldn't think of a threat possibly coming from the opposite direction – the way they routinely used to reach the campsite.

Karate and Pig Dog walked for three hours then bedded down in cover on a low, wooded ridge.

'We first need to find the vehicle track,' said Pig Dog, as they prepared to move again next morning, 'and then we need to find water.'

They moved carefully through the bush in the direction of the track. Pig Dog led the way, stopping frequently to watch and listen. Satisfied all was clear, he'd then move silently forward to the next place of his choosing and again he'd stop and watch.

It took them four hours to reach the track. There were tyre tracks but no human footprints.

In front of them the track wound past a low boulder-strewn ridge. On top there was good cover and a clear view of the track below. A line of darker trees ran behind the ridge and there, amongst the rocks, they found small pools of water. 'This will do us,' said Karate as they filled up their water bottles.

Karate and Pig Dog made themselves comfortable on top of the ridge, and their reports started to come in.

Day two: 'Six-wheeled Russian military truck passed at 10.23 hours heading north. Driver plus one passenger in the front. Truck empty.'

Day four: 'Same Russian truck returning towards the camp. Heavily laden with boxes in the back.'

Day five: 'Followed the track into the camp last night. Took two hours. Guard positioned at edge of camp.'

Day six: 'Truck passed again at 09.52 hours heading north. Empty.'

Day seven: 'Truck returned. Heavily laden with boxes in the back.'

ZAPU were stocking the cache. It was time for the rest of us to get moving.

In the late afternoon three days later, we turned off the narrow road to the white-water rafting landing and drove for some distance into the bush where we made camp. We'd cross the following night. After two days in the back of a truck, it was good to have a day where we could stretch our legs and get ourselves physically and mentally prepared for the operation.

Mack was brilliant. Instead of us having to struggle to the landing with the boats and the heavy engines, he got us firstly to inflate the Zodiacs then strap them onto the truck trailers. After attaching the big Evinrudes, the Mercedes trucks were reversed down the concrete ramp until the trailers were submerged. We then undid the webbing straps and launched our boats.

It was a great start.

In such fast-flowing water, we decided to travel down the river individually with five-minute intervals between boats. That had the added benefit of Mack and me, in the lead boat, getting to our drop–off point first where we could signal to the others to come in. It meant they had no need to navigate and could, instead, just focus on the tricky business of getting safely down the river.

There was still some lingering light in the sky as we pushed off. Mack controlled the paddlers with whispered commands to get us into the middle of the river. We spun around at first with the nose pointing the wrong way, but the paddlers and Mack eventually got us facing the right direction and we took off.

A combination of the current and paddle-power whisked us down the river, and my worries quickly disappeared. This was great fun. I had no problem navigating as in the moonlight I could easily follow the river bends and side re-entrants on my map.

We were making good time and as we approached the proposed landing area, I tapped Mack on the shoulder to let him know we were now close. He looked up and pointed to a sandbank 150 metres in front of us.

The paddlers helped us in towards the sandbank and Mack jumped ashore holding the bow rope. The Zodiac swung round and settled against the sand. We'd made it.

We all jumped out quickly and dragged our packs further up the sandbank and away from the river. Rex took control as Mack and I waited for the next Zodiac to arrive.

Using my binoculars, I spotted the second craft some distance away and Mack flashed a red-filtered torch signal in their direction. We pulled them ashore and pointed them towards Rex higher up the sandbank.

The remaining four boats arrived without problems; it had taken us less than three hours to cover the thirty kilometres.

While we got everyone organised on the ground, Mack jumped into the lead Zodiac with his paddler and, after giving him instructions, pushed off and disappeared into the night. The other boatmen followed. They had another thirty kilometres on the river before reaching Msuna.

The start of the operation had gone perfectly. We'd landed fifty-four men in complete silence.

The next three hours were difficult; with our heavy loads we struggled up the steep sides of the gorge to the high ground of the ridges we would follow towards the camp. Rex did a great job leading us up at a steady pace, but pausing frequently to let everyone get their breath. It didn't matter how long we took to get to the top of the ridges, because once we were up we would be safe and there would be little chance of being detected.

It was a bit after midnight, but the ground below us was illuminated by a full moon and the features were clearly visible. I called over the troop commanders and explained to them where we were and pointed out the direction we would be heading.

We'd continue for another four hours then call it quits for the night. I pointed out the dark patch on the horizon where there were big trees and where I was sure we would find water.

Two more nights walking and we'd be at the camp.

The walk in was hard work as we went up and down on the ridge lines, but that was the only way I was confident we could reach the target area undetected. Remaining invisible was absolutely essential to the success of our operation. The boys knew and appreciated this and I could sense a growing excitement as we closed in on the target.

At the end of the second night we met up with Karate and Pig Dog close to their observation point. It was a safe place and we were in good cover. ZAPU didn't have guards or observation points this far out and there had been no patrol activity.

During that day as we rested, we heard a vehicle heading towards the camp and the sound of singing. ZAPU were bringing in their cadres.

We stayed secure in our cover until midnight, then moved on to the vehicle track.

I'd put Pig Dog and Rex up front to lead us down the track towards the camp. Rex carried a light intensifier but the moon was still good.

Having already been down the track, Pig Dog recommended we move to a dispersal point in an open area he thought would be suitable for the mortars about 500 metres short of the camp. A little over two hours later he stopped and called me forward to inspect his site. It was ideal and we got to work.

The stop groups unloaded their packs and took out the mortar bombs they had been carrying. They placed them on the ground where the mortar team were busy setting up the baseplates and tubes. The two troop commanders checked their compasses.

Taking a wide detour to one side they would move around and behind the camp, along the way positioning the four-man groups in readiness for the attack. This was not an easy task but there was a good moon to help them and they made no mistakes.

There was also a fine line for them to judge. On the one hand, the closer in to the camp you could get would guarantee a bigger success, but the downside was the possibility of compromise and that you might also get caught up in the mortar barrage.

The groups silently advanced to within thirty metres of the camp perimeter. The trap was set.

Meanwhile, I'd sent Rex, Pig Dog, Karate and one of the mortar fire controllers forward towards the camp.

Pig Dog led the way – every sense alert, knowing there was a guard somewhere in front of them.

He suddenly stopped and signalled urgently to Rex. He'd heard something in front of them. They both crouched together watching and listening.

Fifty metres away, there was the flare of a lit match and the smell of burning marijuana drifted their way. They used the night scope. The guard was sitting on the ground leaning back against a tree trunk, enjoying the joint. They saw the outline of an AK propped against the side of the tree.

'Fifty metres from us to the guard,' Rex whispered to Pig Dog. 'And, what do you think, maybe another 75 metres to the centre of the camp?'

'Make that 100,' he replied.

Rex turned to the mortar fire controller. 'One hundred and fifty metres from here to the centre of the camp,' he whispered. 'We'll now count the paces back to the baseplate position and you'll have an accurate range.' He smiled at the bemused look he got back, and added, 'It's an old trick we learned in Mozambique and we know it works.'

Rex and Karate rejoined us with the news of the guard and an estimated range to the camp of 447 metres on a bearing of 155 degrees. The mortar team adjusted elevation and their sights. We were ready to attack.

Pig Dog and the mortar fire controller stayed where they were just fifty metres away from the joint-smoking sentry. Pig Dog's instructions were to eliminate the guard the moment he heard the first mortar bomb being fired, while the fire controller would adjust the mortar fire after we pounded the camp in the opening stanza.

They would join us in the assault so the controller could call on the mortars if we ran into difficulties.

As the sky above us lightened there was stirring in the camp. One man yawned and walked towards one of our stop groups behind the camp. He urinated into the grass, uncomfortably close, as they hugged the ground and tried to keep still and out of sight.

The man wandered back into the camp area as I gave the order to open fire.

Four 81-millimetre mortar bombs whistled through the air towards the camp. Seconds later, and having adjusted the elevation, another four bombs were airborne, and seconds after that a third salvo was on its way.

Hearing the mortars, Pig Dog shot the bemused guard in the head while his fire control companion rattled off orders back to the baseplate position. The mortar crew rapidly responded and another deadly barrage landed deeper into the camp.

We moved down the vehicle track to join Pig Dog. I heard the first bursts of fire from our stop groups. The mortar barrage continued to pound the camp. We closed in, watching and waiting as I ordered one final salvo from the mortars.

The bombardment stopped. We fanned out and started our move through the camp.

We advanced tactically as we always did. Nobody moved without some-body watching and ready to give covering fire. Firing continued intermit-tently from the stop groups as we crept forward.

We met little resistance until suddenly an explosion above us had us duck-ing for cover. Off to one side of the camp, the terrorists had built a defensive position for an 82-millimetre recoilless rifle. In panic, I guess it had been fired wildly in our direction. We were too far away to do much about it. But our mortars could, and in no time the fire controller was transmitting instructions. Another round from the anti-tank gun came much closer to us as we hugged the ground. I heard the scream of the incoming mortars and risked a glance at the terrorist fire position.

It erupted as a salvo of four bombs landed just short of the target. Our fire controller gave the corrections and the next salvo was right on target. One of the bombs hit their ammunition stockpile. There was a huge explo-sion. I saw the gun and a body thrown through the air. A crimson fireball surrounded by black smoke rolled up into the sky.

'Hold your fire!' the mortar man with us ordered, and we got up off the ground and continued our sweep through the camp.

There was no lingering resistance as we cautiously advanced. We took no chances and made sure there were no survivors. The mortar barrage had been sensational. Looking at the broken bodies caught up in the attack, I thought back to the devastation Frelimo had caused with its mortar attack on the Portuguese barracks at Furuncungo. As bad as that was, our own action here showed just how lucky they were that Regone Mwanza had not been properly trained.

With the stop group tally we had killed thirty-seven ZAPU terrorists. I called the stops in to sweep around the perimeter then to join us in the centre of the camp.

I kept the mortars on standby in case anything else happened. The fire controller with us rattled off more instructions: they'd shadow our movements ready to fire instantly if required.

With the action obviously over, we could relax and explore the camp. It wasn't long before we found the massive arms cache.

The underground structure was three times the size of the cache we had blown up in the north-eastern camp. It was filled with much the same material, although there were many more of the TMH46 landmines: a wicked weapon used unscrupulously in the African conflicts. I could never understand why it didn't seem to matter to the terrorists that the mines usually killed and maimed their own people.

Each mine contained 5.7 kilograms of TNT explosive and there were more than 100 of them. Over half a tonne of explosives in the mines would make a spectacular bang on its own, but in addition to that there were boxes of explosives, grenades, rockets, 50-millimetre mortar bombs and row after row of ammunition boxes.

In another part of the cache were racks of weapons: AKM assault rifles, RPD light machine guns, RPG bazookas, Tokarev pistols and 50-millimetre mortar tubes.

We had never seen anything like it. But we all knew that when we lit the fuses there would be an explosion bigger and more spectacular than anything we'd ever experienced.

We'd need to be well out of the way when this one blew.

We put out a defensive perimeter guard on the road leading into the camp with mortar support while the demolition parties went to work. Rex again took care of the vehicle, but this time we'd blow it at the same time as everything else.

It took us nearly two hours to get all our charges organised and the initiation set ready. With that done, I got everybody to pack up and move away down the vehicle track we had followed into the camp while Rex, Karate and I lit the fuses.

We doubled back to join the rest of the team and then made all haste to get out of the area. We had used a dual initiation set in case one failed and both were timed to explode fifteen minutes after lighting the fuses.

It's hard to describe in words the blast that followed, such was its magnitude.

We later received reports of it being heard over 100 kilometres away in Victoria Falls. Apparently, it was recorded as a tremor on scientific seismographs monitoring the Zambezi Valley along the fault line.

Fifteen minutes' walk away the explosion was a deafening, fearful sound that made our ears pop and our eyes water. We felt the shock wave in the ground beneath our feet as the trees thrashed wildly above us. The oxygen seemed to be sucked out of the air as a huge cloud of dust and smoke accelerated into the sky. We looked up in awe, overwhelmed by the frightening power of the blast.

We watched in wonder as the massive, black umbrella cloud rose into the air behind us. I thought of the brigadier and his SAS team directing nukes on to their targets. But lucky for us this wasn't radioactive. We walked away without a single injury, feeling pretty pleased with ourselves.

I called a halt and sent a signal through to the brigadier. A competent Morse code operator acknowledged our message.

We walked out in daylight. The need for invisibility was no longer important, although we did remind everyone of the remote possibility of Zambian Air Force activity. Indeed, we did see an Aermacchi cruising over the river the day before Mack roared up with his Zodiac fleet to take us home.

It was important now to get as far away from the area as fast as we could. The explosion would have been heard and reported in many places. I didn't want the SAS associated with any speculation as to what might have happened.

While we were returning to base, the brigadier tasked another air photo recce of the target. The pictures showed a massive crater where the cache had been and all the trees within a 200-metre radius had been flattened. Parts of the Russian truck we had blown up were scattered across the area and here and there were bodies of dead terrorists.

This would be yet another huge setback to ZAPU and their Russian support. They were being defeated before their cadres even reached the start line. Meanwhile, their Chinese-backed competitors were having better luck, successfully infiltrating the tribal lands on the eastern border of Rhodesia from Mozambique.

What would they do next?

The brigadier asked me that very question.

'You destroyed their effort in the north-east with a big bang, and now you've done it again in the north-west with an even bigger bang,' he said with a friendly twinkle in his eye. 'So, Mick, what's your Big Bang theory? Where is all this leading us with ZAPU?'

On the long drive back from Victoria Falls I had been mulling it over. We had pushed them out of the north-east and they had thought rival faction ZANU was responsible for that attack. But this latest operation was miles away from the nearest ZANU base, so they were unlikely to blame them this time round; and if anyone chose to investigate, they would find the tracks of fifty-four men heading south towards the Zambezi.

I didn't think they'd bother – or dare – to look too closely at what had happened at the north-west camp. But for sure they would be rethinking strategy.

I explained this to the brigadier and said, 'I think there are two options and both may happen.

'The soft option would be to try to get into the country through Botswana to the south. But there are many difficulties with that. Botswana is increasingly prosperous these days. Politically I can't see them being overenthusiastic about Russian-backed guerrilla groups roaming through their country and inviting retaliation from the armed forces of their neighbours.

'They might try it,' I said, 'but the Botswana police would surely get on to that pretty quickly?'

There was a silent nod of agreement and I continued.

'So, in reality they only have one option. An option that is frightening but one Mother Russia will both applaud and support. I can't see them bringing in the Cubans again, but one thing they can do is supply any amount of heavy weaponry. We've all seen the "Iron Fist" pictures of the Eastern bloc military might, and that's what they will try next. They will bring in tanks, artillery, armoured personnel carriers and the mobile rocket launchers they call the "Stalin Organs".

'To hell with guerrilla warfare, they will be saying. It doesn't work for us. Instead, we will smash the opposition with our power and they have nothing that can stop us.'

I paused.

'But they don't know they are up against the SAS. Sure, we won't be destroying ZAPU camps and arms caches any more – we've done that and it's finished. The next phase for us will be destroying their arms build-up. We'll take out the ships as they bring in the tanks and guns. We'll blow the bridges and destroy the trains as they transport them in towards the border, and they can't stop us. The country is too big and we can strike anywhere.'

I'd given him my Big Bang theory. As events unfolded later, it turned out my predictions were right on the money. We were about to enter a new phase fighting ZAPU and Mother Russia.

# Chaos by Kayak

By 1977, the nature of the second scramble for Africa changed quite suddenly.

The Russians and the Chinese may have been global allies but locally, in our patch of central Africa, there was plenty of competition between them.

For some time we had been fomenting trouble between the different factions they supported. So far there was nothing to suggest they knew what we were up to.

Our recent attacks on Russian-backed ZAPU had curtailed their activity while they recovered from the setbacks and redefined their approach.

In contrast, the Chinese-backed ZANU faction was thriving.

The military coup in Lisbon resulted in an immediate withdrawal of all Portuguese forces from Africa, and in Mozambique that meant ZANU now had unopposed access to the vast expanse of the Rhodesian eastern border. It was no longer restricted to the high-risk infiltration routes through the Zambezi Valley where cadre leaders, such as Rex Nyongo, had struggled for success, and where ZAPU efforts had so far failed completely.

ZANU now had an 800 kilometre border to work with. And in many places the international boundary – no more than a line on the map – bisected tribal lands where the locals continued to work their land and live their lives as they had for decades before the white men had made them people of one country or another.

For a guerrilla warfare campaign, conditions could not get much better.

Small groups of terrorists could now move with impunity right up to the Rhodesian border and quietly infiltrate and occupy one tribal area after another. Small-scale operations in these conditions would stretch military and police resources to breaking point.

But before anything like this could happen ZANU had to establish supply lines. And that's where we came in. There was nothing like a Special Forces unit for causing chaos on communication and supply lines. We had multiple options of reaching them, and in the African bush we knew more about operating as invisible, small groups than anything taught at the School of Mao.

'Just as I thought,' said the brigadier, showing us pictures of the huge lake created by the damming of the Zambezi River at Caora-Bassa Gorge in Mozambique. It extended nearly 300 kilometres back towards the Rhodesian and Zambian borders; in some places it was no more than twenty kilometres from what were remote and undefended parts of the Rhodesian border.

The air photographs revealed eight boats moored near the hydro dam wall with a military camp close by. There were a couple of vehicles and a pile of fuel drums visible in the picture.

Further west and roughly halfway up the lake was the old Portuguese missionary settlement known as *Mague*. It was partially obscured by cloud, but the images showed a large camp where civilians had been rounded up to work and provide food for the terrorists. Off to one side of this civilian camp was a parade ground and barracks, and on a small hill overlooking every-thing was a KPV 14.5-millimetre anti-aircraft gun battery with mortars and defensive trenches. There were no vehicles.

An inlet from the lake reached in towards the camp with a well-used track leading to a clearing on the edge of it.

'It's plain to see,' said the brigadier. 'ZANU are driving up to the Cahora-Bassa Dam wall, then using the boats to bring in supplies and newly trained terrorist groups that are deployed from *Mague* on to what is now a much extended eastern front.'

My orders were simple.

'Mick, your first objective and the priority of the operation is to destroy the boats. There are pockets of population alongside the lake, especially to the north, so the only way of reaching the target undetected is by kayak and by paddling at night.

'On your return journey you are to attack the *Mague* base. I have no spe-cific instructions about the attack, except to say I expect you to put the fear of God into them.'

I glanced up at the back bench where heavyweights Horse, Jonny and Nelson sat alongside Rex.

'With the team I've got that should not be a problem,' I replied with a smile.

We stood up and saluted, then headed for the stores where we'd talk about what we'd need to do the job the brigadier had ordered.

The Klepper kayaks allowed us to carry enough food and munitions for prolonged operations. They were silent and fast, if there was trouble around we could quickly disappear into the covered, shallow waters or amongst the many small islands on the lake.

We would be out for at least three weeks.

'Mack, you're in charge of the boats, and I want you in the driving seat behind me in the lead kayak. I suggest we have one of the big boys at the back of the other four. We'll be carrying a lot of weight,' I said.

'Rex, you and I will work out what explosives we'll need.

'Fish, you organise the medical gear.

'Simmo, you and Pig Dog work out what rations we will take and how we will supplement them to extend our stay without resupply.

'Karate, you take care of the radio equipment. Don't go overboard with HF, but don't skimp on VHF batteries.

'Horse, you, Jonny and Nelson take care of weapons. We'll use Russian gear and Fish, as usual, should carry a bazooka.'

The only special equipment we requested was clothing and footwear. No good wearing boots inside a canoe, but we'd need some foot protection getting in and out when launching and landing, so I ordered ten pairs of sandals and opted for zip-up, navy blue overalls as our paddling dress.

I'd just organised the air transport to get us to our start point when Mack came into the office with a list.

'Mick, this is what we have organised so far,' he said handing me the sheet of paper. 'Just want to be sure there is nothing we have missed.'

'Good job, Mack,' I replied. 'Let's have a look.'

Personnel:

- kayak one: the major and Mack
- kayak two: Rex and Pig Dog
- kayak three: Horse and Fish
- kayak four: Jonny and Karate
- kayak five: Nelson and Simmo

Kit and Equipment:

- five Klepper kayaks with spare paddles, splash sheets and repair kit
- ten buoyancy jackets

- fourteen days ration packs per man plus additional energy bars and brew kit
- two RPD light machine guns – Russian
- eight AKM assault rifles – Russian
- one Tokarev 7.62 millimetre pistol with silencer – Russian – carried by the major
- one RPG7 bazooka with six rockets – Russian – carried by Fish
- two TMH46 anti-tank mines – Russian
- sixteen limpet mines – 2 kilograms TNT explosive – Russian
- 50 kilograms plastic PE4A explosive in 5-kilogram slabs
- five 100-metre rolls of Cordtex detonating cord plus safety fuse, detonators and fusee matches
- six white phosphorous incendiary grenades
- three Icarus parachute illuminating rockets
- two mini flare projectors with twenty magnesium capsules
- three A60 Phillips VHF radios and one T27 HF radio plus spare batteries for both
- two infrared spotlights, battery packs and IR goggles

## Day one: Saturday, 7 May 1977

We packed all the gear into the DC3 Dakota at the airbase and eventually arrived at the military and police outpost of Mukumbura on the north-east border of Rhodesia at 14.00 hours.

We put the canvas bags holding the kayaks and the explosives onto the escorting gunship helicopter, and somehow managed to squeeze the rest of the gear and ourselves into the four Alouette troop carriers. The choppers had just enough fuel needed for the return trip to a landing zone on the lake edge selected from the air photo.

As a deception ploy, we initially flew due west from Mukumbura for a time then banked sharply to the north, flying just above treetop level. The landing zone was OK for the choppers, but not so good for us as it turned out to be a patch of stinging nettles. We found a better place to assemble the canoes and started paddling at 18.05 hours.

It wasn't a lot of fun at the start. The water in that part of the lake was dirty, full of algae and the whole place reeked of rotting vegetation. On top of that, it was difficult working the heavy kayaks through shallow water infested with weed and flooded trees.

The moon rose at 22.00 and then we could vaguely see what we were doing. We eventually hit open water and fortunately the lake was calm. We paddled until quarter past midnight when we reached a slightly elevated promontory and made camp.

## Day two: Sunday, 8 May 1977

I sent out a clearance patrol at first light to be sure we were not camping in somebody's backyard, but the patrol had nothing to report except lots of game spoor. We spread the camp out tactically, then from back bearings established our position. In a little over six hours paddling we had covered no more than thirteen kilometres the previous night.

We would be better organised henceforth; now we were clear of the shallow, flooded forests we should be able to push up the pace.

I reported our position at 08.15. Not long after that Simmo, who had brought along a small, telescopic fishing rod, caught two fair-sized fish. We were hoping he'd do OK with the rod, as any fresh provisions would be both welcome as food and would extend the time we could spend out there without resupply.

The wind got up mid-morning and persisted into the night when we set out again. It was seriously hard work paddling the heavy kayaks into the wind; the waves were relentless. We were all soaking wet, but the splash-sheets did a great job keeping water out of the boats.

Around 22.30 the wind suddenly stopped, as if controlled by a button, and it wasn't long before the waves on the lake settled down as well. We pushed on with renewed vigour. Although I thought Mack, in the cockpit behind me, was a little disappointed as he'd clearly enjoyed every minute in the rough, spray-soaked conditions.

The moon came up at 23.55 and we tried for a landfall.

It was a bad mistake as we ended up in thick, flooded bush and shallow water. We struggled back into the deeper channel and headed for some silhouetted high ground. At 02.15 we eventually found a good beach and landed.

Throughout the night, we paddled close to brilliant white flares and eerie lines of light that flashed and danced over the surface of the water around us. We presumed this was the ignition of methane gas, created by all the rotting vegetation recently submerged in the rising water level of the dam. We had been very close to some of the flares and there was no sound.

## Day four: Tuesday, 10 May 1977

I overconfidently got the show on the road at 17.30 when it was still daylight. We soon found ourselves close to the north bank and in deep water with only a few trees offering any cover. Not wishing to be seen, should there be fishing camps in the area, we found a thick patch of trees and rafted up for half an hour until it got dark.

The wind had gone completely and the lake was mirror calm. We paddled at a fair pace; it was one of the darkest nights imaginable and there was no horizon. The sky merged with the dark water of the lake, so it was like paddling into a black void in outer space. We were floating now both figuratively and literally.

Mack, with his sea experience, was brilliant, and in the conditions I would have struggled with the navigation without him. We'd pick a star close to our required bearing and for the next spell use it as our marker.

After a bit over an hour and a half paddling we'd stop, close up and rest for a short while. We'd try and stretch our legs and adjust our seating and back supports, which you couldn't do while you were moving. It was a chance to make sure everyone was travelling OK and that the boats were all good. We'd check each other's rudders and clear any weed we may have picked up. It was hard enough work as it was without dragging a few kilos of weed behind the kayak. Mack and I would then pick another star or planet, we'd let everyone else know, and off we'd go again.

We had to stay close together. I didn't want anyone getting lost, and as wonderfully stable as the Kleppers were in the rough water we had experienced, capsizing remained a distinct possibility. If the worst happened, we needed to be close together to help the boat in trouble as quickly as possible.

In the event nothing untoward happened, except that one of the kayaks was rammed by a big tiger fish and a second was pursued by a huge eel for a short time. Pig Dog was keen to take it on, as smoked eel was a delicacy in New Zealand. But he soon backed off when I told him there were electric eels in these waters and that grabbing it might just charge his batteries a bit more than he'd enjoy.

We did five 100-minute, non-stop paddling sessions then spent another hour or so searching for a suitable camp, eventually bedding down at 03.47 hours. It was a good night on the water.

## Day six: Thursday, 12 May 1977

For the third night in a row it was incredibly dark, but the lake conditions continued to be mirror smooth and we were making great time towards our target. We paddled due east for three kilometres, then swung north through the Munheriere Gap, which was the old Zambezi River course.

It was deep water and would be miserable in rough weather as the wind would be channelled through the narrows, but that night the gods were on our side and we cruised through at good speed.

We had aimed to hit the north bank near the Muangwa River, but as we approached we could see the campfires of local habitation, so we changed course to a dark area where we could see no fires. It turned out to be the foulest smelling, flooded bush and its tangled and shallow waters seemed to be quite endless.

Next morning we established it to be the Sangere River. Although it was truly dreadful, on the credit side the chance of compromise was minimal as no sane human would go in there by choice.

After dodging a family group of hippo, we eventually rafted up around a huge, old tree and tried to sleep in the boats. So far we had paddled 184 kilometres.

## Day seven: Friday, 13 May 1977

If long-haul jet travellers think getting a good night's sleep in economy class is difficult, they should try doing the same in the cockpit of a Klepper kayak, floating in shallow water with methane gas flares lighting up around them. It wasn't a good night, and during the day we had little respite from the sun and biting mosquitoes.

We had closed in on the target of the terrorist boats, but our position was dangerous. It was clear to us there was considerable local movement around the area; mainly fishermen, who were no physical threat, but if we were compromised by them our mission would be in serious jeopardy.

There were two or three small islands close to the harbour with the boats. I decided we'd take our chances hiding on one of these during the day before the attack. It didn't take long to get there and the conditions were good. After concealing and camouflaging our kayaks we got a welcome early night fully stretched out on firm ground.

## Day eight: Saturday, 14 May 1977

There were a few local boat movements around us but nobody came close. As the sun dropped over the horizon I breathed a sigh of relief. We had managed to reach the target undetected. They couldn't stop us now.

Immediately after dark, I called everyone together to explain my plan for blowing the boats and harbour facilities. I opted for going straight in with the attack, without a preliminary reconnaissance, as there were so many locals close to us that compromise was more than a distinct possibility.

Nobody disagreed, so we sorted out the explosives amongst the kayaks and left for the job at 19.45 hours.

It was another very black night.

We reached our dispersal point on the peninsula north of the harbour and the party split. Rex, Pig Dog, Horse and Fish headed towards the western side and the terrorist base on the edge of the harbour. They would take the heat off should we be compromised while laying the charges on the boats.

Mack and I and the other two kayaks, meanwhile, headed for the boats in the harbour. In the impenetrable darkness we initially failed to find them. We surmised we had hit the wrong inlet and wasted some time checking bays to the east and west, but eventually Mack led us back towards where we had started and we found the harbour. In the dark and cover of trees it had been obscured from view on the angle of our original approach. It was a tense time as we closed in on the targets.

I had fitted the silencer to my Tokarev, just in case we found crew on board any of the boats. We paddled silently from one to another and thankfully it wasn't required. Undetected we set about our work.

We firstly put Jonny and Karate on the open deck of the 42-metre barge that was conveniently located in the centre of all the boats. I'd given them responsibility for making up the demolition initiation set, so as we laid our charges on the different boats, we'd paddle back to the barge, unwinding the yellow Cordtex detonating cord as we went. Karate would then cut the cord and attach it to a primer. We'd then go to the next boat and repeat the process, until we had done all seven boats and completed our deadly explosive web.

While Karate gathered in the lengths of Cordtex and taped them together, Jonny was busy laying charges to sink the barge. It took us nearly an hour to have everything in place. Finally, Karate attached two detonators to the bundle of Cordtex and primers lying on the deck of the barge.

We had laid our charges as follows:

- 42-metre steel barge with twin-engine diesel: three limpets on the hull; 5 kilograms PE4A on the steerage; and 2 x 5 kilograms PE4A on the engines.
- 22-metre steel ferry with wheelhouse: two limpets on the hull beneath the engines; 5 kilograms PE4A on steerage.
- 18-metre wooden ferry: 5 kilograms PE4A on the engine; three limpets on the inside of the hull.
- 12-metre barge – a beautiful, brand new vessel with twin 150hp Mercury outboards: three limpets on the hull; 5 kilograms PE4A on each outboard.
- 9-metre barge: two limpets on the hull; 5 kilograms PE4A over the engine.
- 9-metre cabin cruiser: one limpet on the hull; 5 kilograms PE4A over the engine.
- 5-metre glass fibre dingy: one limpet.
- 5-metre glass fibre banana boat: one limpet.

We were ready to go.

Jonny got into the kayak tied alongside the barge while Karate lit the fuses. He jumped into the front cockpit. Seeing that, we all paddled like hell to get out of the area.

We were still too close for comfort when the charges blew.

The explosive force lifted the boats out of the water and blew them apart. After the initial thunder crack, we could hear a strange hissing noise as what was left of the boats sank into the depths of the harbour. Large pieces of wood from the old ferry and bits of engine parts peppered the water around us as we continued to paddle away as fast as we could.

Rex and Pig Dog, meanwhile, had laid a TMH46 mine on a road they found leading into the base, then closed in and were waiting for the blast.

On hearing the explosions on the water, they attacked the camp using the RPG7 bazooka and tracer bullets, initially aiming at the fuel dump. They threw white phosphorous grenades into the area and poured fire at likely targets. The camp was soon ablaze: two vehicles were on fire, a fuel tank exploded and then there was a big explosion and a metal-clad building disintegrated. It would have been their weapons store.

In the dark they could not be sure of human casualties, apart from two guards killed at the initiation of the attack. Judging from the activity and noise around the camp, Rex guessed there were ten or twelve terrorists present at the time of the attack.

With the damage done and the first part of our mission accomplished, it was time to disappear into the night.

Rex joined us at about 03.45. Then we paddled as hard as we could for the cover of a group of small islands we'd seen on the way in. We landed just on first light.

The islands were deserted. There was little shade, and we spent a hot day waiting for darkness and the opportunity to get even further away from the target area.

At 16.23 hours we heard a loud explosion in the distance. Somebody had driven over the TMH46 mine.

For the next four nights, we put as much distance as possible between us and the target area. We were helped by the weather. The wind had got up again, but this time it was behind us and the kayaks were now a lot lighter. We surfed along and made great progress.

The first and main part of the mission had been accomplished to perfection. Could we now add the icing on the cake?

## Day thirteen: Thursday, 19 May 1977

We were now about halfway to the *Mague* camp and in a great place to rest.

We had found another small island with tall shade trees, separated from the mainland by a flooded gully no more than fifty metres wide. Our camp would be invisible to anyone passing, and with a convenient lookout on a high spot we could not be surprised.

We spent the first day washing clothes, cleaning our weapons, checking the Kleppers and generally sorting out our gear. Simmo again did good work with his fishing rod, catching enough for all of us to enjoy fresh food.

First thing in the morning, Rex and Pig Dog had been on to the mainland to make sure there was nobody around. They found nothing but game spoor, which was good news because I was keen to venture further afield. On the way back to camp Rex had shot a klipspringer – a small antelope.

I watched in awe as the two practised bushmen hung the small animal from a tree and expertly butchered the carcass. Once skinned, Rex cut out the heart, liver and kidneys and put them to one side. He then cut out the

Chaos by Kayak    119

small intestine and the rectum tube and went down to the lake edge where he squeezed water through the tubes to clean them of the waste matter. From his pack he produced a large garlic clove and some dried herbs. After chopping it all up he sprinkled it over the offal that Pig Dog had cut into small pieces. The two of them then squeezed the offal into the intestine and rectum tube, triumphantly tying a knot at each end. The SAS Master Chef team had made a sausage. It was delicious.

## Day fourteen: Friday, 20 May 1977

On the air photographs there was a track that looked as if it had once been used by vehicles running parallel with the lake that headed towards *Mague* camp. I estimated it to be about four hours walking from where we were located. I wanted to check it out; if it was being used by the terrorists we might get another crack at them.

Seven of us would do this mission. I left Karate in charge of the camp with instructions to have everything ready for a rapid departure on our return.

## Day fifteen: Saturday, 21 May 1977

We left camp at 02.00 hours on a cool, still night. A new moon gave us good visibility and the going through open woodland and across the low, stony ridges was easy. I didn't use my compass; instead I just followed the Southern Cross, knowing it would unerringly lead me to our target area.

We startled small herds of antelope along the way, but there were no predators – lion or hyena – and the only sounds we heard were the calls of night birds.

The morning light arrived and I called a halt on top of a low ridge. As the sun came up we could see the track no more than 300 metres ahead of us. We cautiously approached to look at the signs. There were no vehicle tracks so we didn't need the TMH46 mine we had carried with us, but there were fresh boot prints: the popular figure-eight track of the Chinese-made army boot. This was clearly a terrorist patrol route.

'Rex, down here next to the track our visibility is limited,' I pointed out, 'but back on that low ridge you can see for a long way in either direction. How about you and Fish going up there to keep watch and give us early warning of anyone approaching while the rest of us wait here in ambush?'

We moved into position and settled down for a long and quite possibly fruitless wait.

I would spring the ambush with a shot at the middle member of any group that came along. The boys on my right and left would take out as many as possible on either side. We had good concealment and fire positions no more than thirty metres from the track.

We were in the shade, but it was still very hot and we lay there and sweated. We took turns having a doze. We had been up since 02.00 hours.

This time of year it got dark around 18.30, at which point we would move back to join Rex and Fish, where we would spend the night before returning to the ambush before first light next morning. Water was a problem. We didn't have much and hadn't found any since leaving the lake.

With such thoughts worrying me, I was jolted back to reality when suddenly the muted radio gave three blips: it was Rex, signalling that terrorists were coming along the track from the left.

I gave the thumbs up to the others as we nervously checked the safety catch position again on our weapons.

There were five of them and they were all talking loudly as they approached us. I risked a quick glimpse and saw they were all carrying AKs.

We hugged the ground as they came closer and closer.

My heart was pounding. I took a deep breath to try and control the nerves raging in my belly. In my head there were voices shouting: shoot now, shoot now, but I knew I had to wait.

I looked down the barrel and over the foresight of my rifle; I imagined I was on a rifle range and that calmed me. With both eyes open, I slightly increased pressure on the trigger as the first terrorist passed through my sight. Then the second. My target suddenly appeared and I fired. He dropped, but instantly there was a second target. I fired again and he too dropped. I fired again into both targets now on the ground. They were already still, but I couldn't help myself and I gave them both another two rounds just to be sure. The bodies jumped as the bullets hit them.

I don't recall hearing the shots from Horse, Pig Dog, Jonny and Nelson on either side of me, but they too had hit the targets. Five dead terrorists lay sprawled across the track in front of us.

I waited a few minutes for no reason other than for all of us to regain our composure.

We didn't bother to check the bodies. But with the empty cases of our Russian-made ammunition strewn on the ground around our ambush position, I wedged a photocopy of a Zambian newspaper article under a rock. It reported the assassination of a ZAPU leader in a Lusaka suburb.

We joined Rex and were soon on the move at a good pace. We would have an hour and a half of daylight to help us cover the ground. It was good knowing we didn't have to conserve water any more.

Rex pushed it along and eventually called a halt two hours later. We had made good progress, but needed a rest and some food before the final leg to our lakeside camp. Our eyes would get used to the dark, and although the moon came up much later, the starlight was brilliant enough to help us through the open woodland.

During the break we set up the radio and I called Karate who, to conserve our precious batteries, would be listening for five minutes every hour. Comms were good and I told him to expect us in about two hours. I wanted the kayaks packed and ready to go when we got there. We were too close to the ambush area and we'd left tracks. It was again time to silently disappear into the night.

On the way to the ambush position, I'd taken a little time to look back across the lake from one of the higher ridges with my binoculars. There seemed to be good cover all the way along the edge of the lake. However, what caught my attention was a group of small islands in the distance way out in deep water.

It was perfect. We'd go there for some rest and make our plans for the attack on *Mague* base.

We were paddling before 20.00. The lake was like glass, the moon came up and we made the islands three and a half hours later. We found a good beach and landed.

I was suddenly exhausted. Without needing to say anything, Karate just took over.

It had been a long day.

## Day sixteen: Sunday, 22 May 1977

I woke briefly not long after first light, when a brown hornbill landed in the tree above me and started feeding on clusters of small berries. Some of them dropped down and bounced off the brown, parachute silk of my sleeping bag. I smiled to myself as the bird called: a beautiful, musical piping that had a touch of sadness about it. I dug deeper into the warmth of the silk and nodded off again.

The sun was well up when Rex tapped me on the shoulder. 'Mick, we've got company,' he whispered.

I sat up startled and grabbed my AK.

'No panic,' he said. 'But there are two dugouts with four fishermen working the shallows around one of the neighbouring islands.'

I went up to the lookout on the high point of the island and had a good look with binoculars. The four men were not armed and were certainly no physical threat to us, but I was not happy at the prospect of being detected and compromised; and if they came over to fish around our island, that was a certainty.

Irrespective of the reality that sometimes people just suddenly turn up, as was the case here, I regarded compromise as an operational failure.

We built our operations around surprise and stealth. We would launch our deadly strikes at places and times nobody expected. With the business done we would then simply disappear. Nobody knew who we were and nobody knew where we had come from.

That was the way to run these sorts of covert operations, but it only worked in areas that were unpopulated or very sparsely populated.

So what to do here?

Rex and I watched them for a while and could see the fishing was going well. They were using cast nets; every time they hauled them back in we could see the small, silver fish frantically trying to escape.

I thought about it. If a compromise situation seriously threatened our safety, I would have no hesitation in killing to remove the threat. I had a silencer for my pistol and I'd done it once before. The fishermen were only a threat to us if they found us, and if they were then able to report our presence and numbers back to the local rebel base.

They had paddled out a long way into the centre of the lake, in boats that would not fare well in the waves if the wind came up, as it did late afternoon on most days. Given the fishing was going well, there was a good chance they would pack up early and paddle back to the shore before the weather changed.

They were about 300 metres away from us, and we were camped on the opposite side of the island from them. With any luck they would stay where they were, but if they started to come our way we would send out two of our kayaks to intercept them. We would put them ashore on the island where they were fishing and bring their boats back to our camp. We would have to move that night, but before disappearing we would moor the two dugouts in the shallows of the fishermen's island so they could get back home.

Around midday the fishermen headed for home.

I breathed a sigh of relief and Simmo got his rod out.

## Day seventeen: Monday, 23 May 1977

The fishermen didn't return. We spent a relaxing day cleaning equipment and generally getting ourselves organised for the operational finale – the attack on *Mague* base.

In Mozambique it was common for the terrorist groups to round up any civilians in the area of a base and make them live in a camp right next to them. The subjugated locals were then responsible for feeding the terrorists and acting as porters, carrying heavy munitions into their active operational areas, the women were molested at will, and anyone showing dissent would be severely beaten then shot.

The air photos showed a large civilian camp off to one side of the shallow basin where the *Mague* base was located. This camp was no impediment to our attack plans, but it did mean that locals were likely to be active in the wider area around the base, fishing, checking snares and hunting, looking for beehives with honey and anything else that could be eaten.

The risk of compromise would be high anywhere within a 10-kilometre radius of the camp.

The problem this created for us was finding enough time to reach and attack the camp then return to our kayaks and paddle away before daylight.

The air photography showed some islands in a good location for us with deep water all round that would be a good launch point. There was an inlet we could follow that would position us about two kilometres from the base, and in the kayaks we would get there quickly. But even so time was going to be tight.

Looking again at the photography of the top end of the lake, and remembering the struggles we'd had on the first couple of nights in shallow water under recently flooded woodland, I realised that so long as we had an hour of darkness to clear the immediate target area, paddling in daylight was actually a good option.

We didn't think the terrorists had boats at *Mague* but even if they did, a boat could not follow our escape route. They would never find us.

With that critical detail out of the way I turned my focus to the attack itself.

I knew full well that with the limited resources we had there was no way we were going to raze the place to the ground as we had done with other camps like this, but then we didn't need to. Sure, we wanted to inflict as much damage as possible, but the extent of it didn't matter in the context of what else we had done.

We had destroyed all the boats used to resupply the base and bring through new terrorist cadres, and we had destroyed the base camp that organised and provisioned it all and had inflicted casualties in the process.

We had killed five of their men in an ambush on a track that was the only other way into this remote part of Africa.

And now we were going to kill a few more of them and put the fear of God into the survivors.

They didn't know who we were, or where we had come from, and we would again show them we could strike anywhere.

Altogether, it could be enough to close down this supply line.

Late afternoon, I called everyone together and went over my plans for the attack. We all had a good look at the photographs to get an imprint in our minds of the ground we would be crossing in the dark.

I finished by saying that while taking on a 14.5-millimetre anti-aircraft gun emplacement sounded scary, the fact was the guns were pointing towards the sky. They could not be depressed sufficiently to be fired at us on the slope beneath them.

The disbelieving looks I got told me I'd impressed nobody with that little gem.

'Business as usual?' questioned Horse with a raised eyebrow.

So far we had paddled 353 kilometres.

## Day nineteen: Wednesday, 25 May 1977

We left camp at twilight time. There was just enough light to give us a horizon and help with direction as we paddled in towards the *Mague* base.

Simmo and Mack had drawn the short straws and were to remain at the beachhead to look after the boats.

The pictures showed what looked like a mortar emplacement on the north side of the camp. Rex, with Horse carrying an RPD and Fish with his RPG7, would take care of this target. I suggested the bazooka might be a good way of introducing themselves.

That left five of us to take on the main part of the camp. To do this we would firstly take the high ground with the guns and mortar positions. From that vantage point we would then pour fire into the camp complex below.

The going was easy and as we reached the edge of the gun emplacement, we could hear voices above us.

Covering the next 120 metres was the most dangerous part of the mission. I did not want to get involved in an uphill firefight.

We paused for a brief rest and a swig of water before the final assault. For once I was thankful there was no moon. We were still in the cover of light woodland as the boys spread out on either side of me. I took a deep breath to try and calm my nerves then started the slow advance.

'Take your time, Michael,' I whispered, trying to reassure myself. 'We have to get this right.'

I moved silently forward ten metres then went down into a crouch. I saw the shadowy forms of Jonny and Pig Dog move up alongside then drop down. My turn again. Another ten metres up the hill that was steeper than it looked on the air photographs. So far so good.

The voices on top of the hill were getting louder. We were making good progress and closing in.

When we were no more than twenty-five metres away from the top, I paused for a minute or two to get my breath and steel myself for what was to come. They had cleared away the bush to get a clear view from the guns and between where I crouched and the top there was about as much cover as you'd get on a bowling green. I could see the 14.5-millimetre gun barrels ominously silhouetted against the night sky. Our next move could not be missed by the guards.

Another deep breath and I doubled forward, crouched and weaving, waiting for the burst of fire I knew could come.

Nothing happened. The boys were alongside.

One last move. I stood up cautiously, listened to the voices. They were off to one side of our position and at least twenty metres away. A guard at the guns would have seen us by now.

It was looking good.

We reached the top and crouched down between the guns. On both sides of us were 60-millimetre mortars, and we could see the boxes of bombs on the ground behind them. Beyond the mortars the terrorists had built a low, thatched hut as a shelter. Seven or eight of them sat in a group, talking and smoking. There was the pungent smell of marijuana – they'd be going out on a high.

Seconds later they lay sprawled on top of each other, torn apart by a hail of bullets from our RPD and the AKs.

In the distance I heard an explosion and more gunfire. That would be Rex introducing himself.

There were shouts on the hill slope below us. Shots came our way. With the advantage of the high ground, we lobbed fragmentation grenades down on top of them, followed by a couple of white phosphorous canisters.

We heard screams as the chemical burned into flesh. Dry grass caught fire. We fired mercilessly at the sounds and movement below.

From the civilian camp we could hear shouts of confusion and terror. I felt for those poor people. We would do them no harm that night. If we did succeed in driving away the terrorists, they would get back their freedom. They wouldn't know it, but we were their best option.

Only sporadic rifle fire was coming our way from the camp below, but I could hear shouting as they organised some form of retaliation. I left two of the boys to return fire at any flashes they could see while the rest of us turned our attention to the mortars and guns.

We'd use their weapons against them.

The mortars were easy and we got them firing in no time. We picked up the front bipods and turned the barrels round to face the camp area below. Karate and Jonny took over, adjusting the elevation and sights while the rest of us opened the steel boxes with the bombs. As the first salvo was fired, I launched one of the Icarus illuminating rockets over the camp. It was time to see what was there. And allow Karate to adjust his mortar fire.

We laughed as we saw tracer bullets following the slow descent of the parachute flare, and the boys fired back.

*Crump*! *Crump*! *Crump*! The mortar bombs exploded behind the camp. Something caught fire. Karate adjusted the elevation and fired again, and again and again.

The rest of us, meanwhile, were struggling with the two big anti-aircraft guns. The mountings each weighed over 150 kilograms and they were dug in, but we eventually managed to turn one of them around and were in the process of lowering the barrel towards the camp, when suddenly all hell broke out.

On the air photographs, cloud had obscured four other gun positions also on higher ground around the camp. And now they showed themselves. Opposite us and about 1,000 metres away was another 14.5-millimetre gun position. Another, closer to Rex, was firing 122-millimetre rockets that whistled through the air. At yet another position we could hear the deeper *boom* of a 75-millimetre recoilless rifle. The *thump* and *crump* of mortars was all around.

But none of them were firing at us. The recoilless rifle actually looked as if it was firing at one of the other gun positions, but mostly the fire went in big, harmless arcs across the empty night sky.

After a few minutes the fireworks show ended and silence returned to the African night. Not for long. We had all stopped to watch the show, but Karate still had plenty of mortar bombs and started firing again. Not to be outdone so did everyone else, moments later the sky was again lit up with speeding tracer bullets.

Karate's mortars were having an effect in the camp area. He'd hit a building that was now well ablaze. Some fire came our way from the camp, but I was happy to contain that with our RPD for the time being.

Meanwhile, we had got back on to the 14.5-millimetre. But instead of trying to lower the gun to shoot at the camp, I told Pig Dog to have a crack at the other gun emplacement about a kilometre away on the opposite side of the camp. No problem with range – these guns were effective up to at least 2,000 metres. We took a guess with the sights and Pig Dog opened fire. His first salvo was short, but after adjusting the aim the tracer was suddenly on target. 'Empty the magazine at them!' I shouted, and the big gun blazed away.

The magazines on the anti-aircraft gun were big, heavy boxes that clipped on the front of the gun mounting. I couldn't see another, and we were starting to outstay our welcome. Small arms and mortar fire at our position was now intensifying and Karate had fired off all the mortar bombs.

It was time to pull out.

We had taken what remained of our explosives and, before leaving, placed charges on the mountings and barrels of the two big guns.

The other gun positions opened fire yet again – the fireworks show was far from over.

We lit the fuse of the explosive charges and left the scene.

It had suddenly gone quiet.

Three minutes later our charges blew and that started everything up again.

The *screech* of a 120 millimetre rocket passed above our heads and it exploded in front of us.

Tracer bullets flashed over us, glowing bright then suddenly dying as the magnesium light was spent.

We increased our pace. *Mague* was clearly a much bigger base than we had expected. We had done considerable damage but there were still good numbers of terrorists manning the guns. They would not risk coming after us that night, but morning was less than two hours away.

I was pleased to see Rex already back at the boats and Mack had everything ready to roll. We stashed our weapons and headed out of the inlet towards deep water.

It had been a big night out.

## Epilogue

The remaining few days after the camp attack were uneventful, we stayed under cover in shallower water and only paddled during the day.

My diary notes recorded one incident that I put at the back of the book with the bird observations I had made during the operation. In all, I recorded ninety-seven different bird species. The best of these was a three-nest colony of the rare and large goliath heron, found on the second last day.

As I was the major, I got to stop the boats for a few minutes while I checked the nests. They were large structures of sticks, about 1.5 metres across, in the remains of a very old acacia thorn tree semi-submerged by the lake.

I somehow scrambled out of the kayak and pulled myself up on to the first branch of the tree. I looked down and saw everyone grinning. I knew exactly what was going through their minds.

'Don't you bastards even think of paddling off without me!' I threatened.

One of the nests had two pale blue eggs and I took their measurements. The other two nests both had a couple of young chicks. I later forwarded the records to the curator of the natural history museum. He was very pleased and professional enough not to question what I was doing there to get them.

Later that afternoon as we were paddling towards our pickup spot, I heard singing, followed by howls of laughter from Nelson and Simmo in the lead kayak.

Karate and Jonny, Horse and Fish, then Rex and Pig Dog drew alongside them and joined in – the song again collapsed amidst uncontrolled laughter.

Mack and I were some distance behind, but as we got closer I recognised the song. It was *The Twelve Days of Christmas*: '... Five mortars crumping. Four rockets whistling. Three tracers burning. Two bombs a blowing. And the major up a thorn tree!'

# Sinking the Hopes of Mother Russia

After the Big Bang, there was very little terrorist activity along the northern border between Rhodesia and Zambia. A small group crossed into Botswana upstream of Victoria Falls, but was intercepted by Botswana police and taken back to Zambia. We didn't think peaceful and prosperous Botswana would want to get dragged into these bloody conflicts. Thankfully it wasn't.

It was my belief that ZAPU and their Russian supporters would have had enough of these small-scale operations that so far had been complete failures. I was sure they would now be giving serious thought to a new, bolder approach because the Russians had more armour and heavy weaponry than anyone on earth. If they could put a force together in Zambia, they could take the 'iron fist' approach and simply smash the opposition.

The Rhodesian army and air force would be the first casualties. They had no genuine anti-tank capability and no missile defence systems. They had no chance and the country would capitulate as soon as the capital city, Salisbury, was taken.

Then the fun would start: the focus would move to rivals ZANU and the majority Mashona tribe they represented. They would once again be brutally subjugated, just as Chief Lobengula had done a hundred years earlier.

Time passed without contact or conflict with ZAPU and we focused on the ever-expanding operations of their rivals, ZANU. Then, nine months later, we received information of a big Russian freighter that had docked at the Frelimo-controlled port of Beira, in Mozambique.

Air photography showed tanks, mobile artillery and rocket-firing vehicles, as well as armoured personnel carriers and six-wheel military trucks being unloaded. The ship was identified as the *Vladivostok*. Tracking that back we learned it was part of the Black Sea Fleet operating out of Odessa.

It all looked like my prediction was on the money. And we couldn't let this happen.

A few months later, we received information from friendly intelligence that the same ship was heading for the Suez Canal and was again destined for the Port of Beira. We assumed it would be carrying a similar load to what had been photographed by the Canberras on its first voyage.

We had prepared for this and were ready to go.

The big, silver C130 of the South African Air Force started its descent into Ysterplaat Air Force Base, on the west side of Cape Town. The flight engineer poked his head through the cockpit door and told us to return to our seats and do up our seat belts.

We complied with grateful relief.

The C130 may well be the best freight plane ever made, but for passengers on a 2,000-kilometre flight it was an absolute nightmare.

The seating consisted of a fold-down, saggy canvas fitting divided into less than generous individual sitting spaces. As the aircraft was carrying freight, we had no more than a 600-millimetre space in front of us so it was impossible to stretch our legs. We folded the seats back and fastened them against the side of the plane as soon as we were airborne and instead found various places where we could lie down, or at least stretch out for the long flight.

The other discomfort was the constant hissing and wheezing of the hydraulics that operated the stabilising wing flaps and which made sleep impossible. Midway through the flight, I went forward to the flight deck and was chatting to the flight engineer whose space, in comparison, was first-class travel. He grinned at me: 'It's all deliberate, Major,' he said. 'If we made it too comfortable you paratroopers wouldn't want to jump out.'

Our ears clicked with the pressure change. The aircraft bounced around a bit in the fresh sea breeze of the Cape then touched down smoothly. We taxied towards a hangar where a dark blue covered truck marked 'Navy' was waiting for us.

We loaded all the gear into the truck and jumped in.

Simonstown was the headquarters of the South African Navy. It took us the best part of an hour to get there. I joked with the guys: 'We've just flown 2,000 kilometres across Africa in a plane with no windows, and here we are in a covered truck going through one of the most scenic parts of the world and we still can't see anything.'

'They are getting you used to it, Mick,' said Mack with a laugh. 'There're no windows in a submarine, either.'

The navy truck drove into a hangar and the sliding doors closed behind us. We still couldn't see South Africa.

A lieutenant commander was waiting for us with a squad of sailors who would unload our gear: the boats, the weapons and the explosives we had brought with us. They would take it all to their magazine until we had finished our briefings and then the submarine commander would decide where he wanted everything.

'We are putting you in a training wing in a quiet corner of the base,' he said, 'where you'll spend the night and prepare for the operation. The submarine sails tomorrow, late afternoon. The plan is to have you waiting off the Port of Beira as the *Vladivostok* arrives.'

We had agreed with the South Africans that the best time for us to attack the ship was on that first night after its arrival. The crew would be keen to get ashore and into the bars and the local women, and we didn't want to give them time to unload anything.

The *Vladivostok*'s time of arrival was estimated at between 19.00 and 21.00 hours in five days' time.

'We'll be sending down lunch to you in about half an hour,' he continued. 'You will then have time to sort yourselves out and get a bit of rest. The meeting with the base commandant and the submarine commander will be at 16.00 hours. We will come and pick you up, all of you, and take you to our operations room for the final planning session.'

'Perfect,' I replied. 'Thank you, Commander. We are looking forward to the meeting. I'd also ask if you could let the staff officers know that as part of the operational briefing, I'd like thirty minutes to update you all on the latest ground intelligence I have from the countries to the north of you.'

'No problem, Major, that will be appreciated,' he said, and left us to select a bed space and unpack our personal equipment and clothing.

The ten of us that made up our Special Ops call sign, Sierra One Seven, were together and excited about the operation. It would be unlike anything we had ever done before.

Well, true up to a point.

I told the team we had blown up plenty of bridges, buildings and vehicles before, the only difference this time was that a submarine was going to take us within range of our target. Blowing up a ship was basically not much different to what we had already done to the ZANU boats on Cahora-Bassa.

'This operation will certainly involve more danger and a lot more explosive,' I said, 'but that aside it's just business as usual.'

'Business as usual – sinking a Russian ship?' laughed Horse in his loud and musical Cornish accent.

We all laughed with him.

This was going to be fun.

The caterers brought down trays of delicious food; iced fruit juice from Ceres, on the other side of Table Mountain; and two pots of earthy, black coffee. It had already been a long day for us and, with the exception of Mack and I, the team stretched out and was soon asleep.

I wanted to go over the intelligence briefing I knew would be of much interest to the South African High Command and then review our operational plans before the presentation. A vital part of the plans involved our boats. I had left that entirely up to Mack because this was new to us: we had never deployed from a submarine before and we were pretty sure the South Africans had never done anything like this before, either.

Coming from a Scottish fishing family, Mack knew the sea. He had already come up with contingency plans if the weather was bad and it was too rough for our kayaks when we went in for the attack. In addition to the five Klepper kayaks, he had also brought along two small Zodiacs, each with a 25hp Evinrude outboard.

Mack had also pointed out that the most critical part of the operation would be launching the kayaks. With the amount of explosive and weapons we needed to carry, they were going to be very heavy. The Kleppers were incredibly stable, we knew they had been successfully paddled across the Atlantic, but for bush warfare specialists like us, paddling at sea was going to be a brand new experience.

Mack had no doubt we would be fine once we were on the water, and if conditions were reasonable. Loading, getting into the boats ourselves and then launching would not be easy, but Mack had thought of a way to fix the problem.

'There should be enough space to assemble and pack the kayaks on the deck of the submarine,' he explained. 'Once assembled and loaded, we can get into the boats ourselves without any risk of tipping over while still on the deck. When we are ready, we'll ask the submarine to gently submerge and as it goes down we'll be left floating on the water and on our way.'

On the return journey, the procedure didn't matter so much because the boats would be light. We could use a rope to pull ourselves up on to the deck of the submarine and then simply haul up the kayaks after us.

If the sea was too rough for our Kleppers, we could do exactly the same with the two small Zodiacs.

It all made sense to me. I liked it. But the decision would be with the submarine commander. He might have a completely different way of getting us safely on and off his vessel, so we left it at that for the moment.

The one thing about which there would be no debate was how we were going to sink the Russian freighter. We were going to use magnetic limpet mines.

The limpet mine had been used to great effect in the Second World War. We could see no reason why it would not do the job again. In 1943, fourteen of our Special Forces forebears had sunk seven Japanese ships in Singapore Harbour using limpets. Those limpets had no more than two kilograms of what was now regarded as a very basic explosive.

Our limpets, in contrast, each had five kilograms of one of the most powerful plastic explosives ever made, and our magnets were better. The mines could also be linked together into a Cordtex ring main, which would produce a simultaneous detonation of all twenty mines we planned on attaching to the hull of the Russian ship. It would sink into twenty metres of water at high tide and would clog up the Port of Beira indefinitely.

In Singapore, the commandos had used poles to lower the magnetic mines onto the ships' hulls as far below the waterline as possible. It was a good tip for us: we'd use the kayak paddles to do the same.

The wharf at the Port of Beira was built out from the land on concrete pillars. Our plan was to take the kayaks beneath the wharf structure, where we would be invisible, and attach the limpets to the side of the moored Russian ship facing the dock. We would link all the mines together and attach the initiation set to somewhere convenient under the wharf, activate the fuse timers, then paddle away as fast as we could.

We would then move to the secondary target: the fuel tank farm at the harbour.

There were ten large fuel and oil storage tanks on the edge of a breakwater bank of rocks some 200 metres away from where the Russian ship would dock. A long jetty extended some 500 metres out into the harbour and it was here the fuel tankers berthed.

Once we had initiated the limpets, we would paddle under cover beneath the jetty, secure our kayaks and go ashore. We would all be carrying RPG bazookas and each of us would have three rockets. As the charges blew on the ship, we would let fly with the rockets at the fuel storage tanks.

So, we all knew what we would be doing at the target. What we didn't know was the detail of getting there and getting back.

Dressed in the light coloured, very comfortable South African camouflage gear, without rank or unit embellishments, we presented ourselves to the staff assembled in the base operations room. The boys stiffened up behind me as I saluted and introduced myself. I stood to one side and introduced the team individually as they filed past and were guided to our seating area by a staff officer.

I went forward to personally greet the base commander, Rear Admiral Peter Squires. He shook my hand warmly and told me how much they had been looking forward to meeting us and helping make this operation a total success. He said they regarded it as something of a dress rehearsal for what they were sure would happen again, in the not too distant future, with their own Special Forces.

He introduced me to his deputy, various staff and intelligence officers, including one from the army, and finally he stopped in front of a small group led by one of the biggest men I had ever seen. 'Major, this is Etienne Swart,' he said, 'commander of the South African submarine *Maria van Riebeeck*. Captain Swart's mission is to get you safely to your target area in the time frame requested, and to get you back again without compromise or mishap.'

I shook his huge hand and grinned at him and the admiral. Pointing at Rex, Jonny and Horse, I said that one of my serious concerns had been firstly getting men that size down the hatch and into a submarine and secondly, finding space for them if we did somehow manage to squeeze them inside. But that clearly was not going to be a problem.

It was a good start. After the admiral's introduction, and emphasis on the secrecy of the operation, I was given centre stage. A large-scale map of southern and central Africa was projected onto the white wall. To this I attached red and yellow stick-on markers, as I recounted our experiences and current knowledge of Russian (red) and Chinese (yellow) sponsored terrorist activity.

I finished off by describing in detail our 'Big Bang' operations – in which we destroyed the ZAPU camps and arms caches – that led to my belief the Russian-backed terrorist faction would turn to heavy weapons and a more conventional assault as future strategy. It looked like my predictions were now happening. And this operation was just the first step in making that as difficult as possible for them.

I gave them a chance to ask questions. There were several. Then, responding to a glance by the admiral, I moved on to outlining our attack plans at the Port of Beira and the contingencies for which we had prepared. I told them our plans were not etched in concrete. If a better idea was tabled we would have no hesitation in adopting it. I explained to them how we operated with our group, and how members of the team were encouraged to contribute to the planning detail.

The admiral stood up and congratulated me on my briefing, then called for a tea break. I looked at the audience and saw heads nodding in agreement and friendly smiles. I'd got their attention, they had not had a briefing of this nature before, they were amazed at the things we had done, but most importantly I could see I'd got their respect.

The tea break was a good move. I guessed the admiral recognised the mental exertion that went with presentations like that and wanted me fully focused for the next phase when they would do the talking. I had one of their strong coffees with a warm sausage roll. A quarter of an hour later I was all set to go.

Returning to the Ops room, I saw Captain Swart at the lectern fiddling around with the slide projector. A picture of a submarine appeared on the wall.

'Thank you, Major, for sharing your knowledge and remarkable experiences with us,' he said in opening. 'The reputation of your team preceded your arrival, but in this short space of time we can already see for ourselves that we are working with true professionals. It has given us great confidence in you, and we will try to match your standards with a professionalism we claim for ourselves. We are now greatly looking forward to being part of this operation.'

He was looking directly at me as he spoke, and I nodded my head and waved my hand slightly in acknowledgement.

In truth, I was a bit stunned by his words. Then I suddenly realised the main reason for calling the tea break. It had never occurred to me that the South Africans might turn us away if our credibility didn't stack up. I just assumed they had agreed to get us to the target and that was that. But I could now see their point of view. They were, after all, participating in an operation that would sink a Russian ship, and if the Russians somehow found out then goodness knows what the consequences might be for them.

'First of all, some facts and figures about our submarine,' the commander said.

'The *Maria van Riebeeck* is a Daphne class submarine built at the French Dubigeon-Normandie shipyard in Nantes. Displacement is 860 tonnes on the surface; it is 57.8 metres in length with a beam of 6.75 metres. It is capable of 13.5 knots on the surface and 16 knots submerged and has a range of up to 4,300 nautical miles in optimum circumstances.

'The ship has two Jeumont-Schneider electrical propulsion motors supported by two eighty-cell batteries and two SEMT Pielstick 450-kilowatt diesel generators. It is designed to be quiet because its prime purpose is to ambush and destroy nuclear-powered attack submarines, and to do that we carry twelve 550-millimetre torpedoes – eight forward and four aft.

'Currently we are fully charged and ready to go. Weather conditions are forecast to be ideal for the operation, so our plan is to sail tomorrow afternoon at 16.00 hours. We will stay on the surface initially and head towards our normal surveillance area south of Cape Town, but as it gets dark we will submerge and change course for the Mozambique Channel. We will reach the entrance to the Port of Beira twenty-four hours before the estimated arrival time of the *Vladivostok*. Conditions are good and we think she will be in early,' he said.

'We will wait submerged as the ship approaches and will then monitor her arrival at the port. After dark we will move in towards the harbour, stopping roughly 6 or 7 kilometres offshore where we will surface. Once your boats are launched, we will submerge to periscope level and await your return on completion of the operation later that same night. There are numerous details to be worked through, but that is the general idea.'

The captain looked at me. I stood up, thanked him and said it couldn't be better.

The admiral said he wanted to see us both before sailing the following day, and if there were any snags between now and then we were to contact him immediately. We made the appointment for 15.00 hours. Then he and the staff officers filed out, leaving Captain Swart and his team to introduce us to the *Maria van Riebeeck*.

My first impression was that this black monster was much bigger than I had expected. The conning tower rose to a considerable height above the wide deck. I saw at once there would be plenty of space for Mack's idea of assembling and loading the Kleppers.

We were guided down the hatch and into what would be the bridge on a surface ship. There were sophisticated electronics and screens mounted in consoles in a semicircle around the periscope, exactly like what you saw in the war movies.

They had made space for us in the aft torpedo room where ten camp stretchers, each with a pillow and blanket, were already assembled. They had put a camp table with ten folding chairs up against the launch tubes. It was a good time to bring up the subject we had been most worried about. I outlined our concerns and told him what Mack had suggested about assembling the Kleppers and launching.

'We too were concerned about that,' said Captain Swart, 'especially since we don't know much about your equipment. Discussing it with my team, we came up with much the same idea, except we don't want ropes on the side of our submarine. For the recovery, we want you to paddle up to the conning tower and hold there above the deck as we slowly bring her up to the surface. You won't even get your feet wet,' he laughed.

'That's brilliant, but there is one more thing. I realise the less time we spend up on your deck the better, so I was thinking we could partly assemble the kayaks down here. We could do the front and back nose cones of the kayaks that involves most of the ribbing and struts. It will be quicker getting everything on deck and quicker to complete the assembly once we are outside, but are there any issues with that from your side?'

'Far from it,' he replied. 'That suits us too, and we'll give you a hand getting everything on deck.'

We met the rest of the crew, who clearly were as excited about this mission as we were. We listened, captivated, as they described the role they each had on the submarine. It was soon obvious they had had some experiences that made our work seem as safe as crossing a road, so we were looking forward to swapping a few war stories in the days ahead.

That night the caterers again excelled themselves, especially since two dozen cold Amstel lagers and a couple of bottles of Nederburg red wine were included in the fare. We slept well and couldn't wait to get on board the submarine.

A magnificent breakfast awaited our return next morning, after completing a few rounds of the assault course next to our accommodation block. We had time for a long and leisurely shower before getting into clean, new clothes. It would be our last body clean-up for eight or nine days so we all made a good job of it.

We met the submarine crew back in the operations room and listened to orders. We would get to the target area on the fourth day of sailing, and coastal air reconnaissance would meanwhile keep us advised of the progress of the *Vladivostok*. It was expected we would have to wait most of the day offshore at Beira before the ship's arrival, and they would monitor its movement as soon as it was within their acoustic range.

After the briefing, we went aboard the submarine and organised our equipment in the aft torpedo room as it was lowered through the hatch on pallets by a dockside crane.

The meeting with the admiral went well. He gave us the latest information on shipping movements in the Mozambique Channel. Another of their submarines was stationed in the channel and would be there throughout our operation. The South Africans had occasionally detected Russian nuclear submarines well out towards Madagascar. While there was no activity at present, it was nice knowing we had a friend out there keeping an eye on things.

The crew cast off at 16.00 hours, and the submarine slowly moved away from the dock and into the harbour channel. We stayed below and out of sight. We could feel the movement of the boat, but it was eerily quiet, just a low-pitched humming coming from the propulsion unit. The submarine increased speed and we could feel the boat's motion as it ploughed through the chop induced by the late afternoon sea breezes. It didn't last long. We heard the signal, there was a soft hissing and the movement stopped. We were submerged and turning gently north-east away from Cape Town. The engine hum increased as the submarine went up to full power.

Half an hour later, the captain came down to see us with Petty Officer Piet Vermulen, who would take us through the emergency drills, and who was assigned to look after us in the unlikely event of an accident or some sort of emergency situation.

Apart from visiting the heads and going to the galley for meals, we were now very much 'confined to barracks'. There wasn't room to wander around the submarine and, understandably, they didn't want us disturbing crew resting between shifts.

Rex appointed Jonny, Horse and Pig Dog in charge of exercise and entertainment. It didn't take them long to design a physical exercise circuit involving push-ups, sit-ups, chin-ups on an overhead pipe, and repeated lifts of one of the Zodiac outboard motors. They made charts for each of us and we would be timed on the four circuits we had to do each day.

The poker school started after the evening meal. We were carrying folding-butt AKs with us so, for currency, we each unloaded a magazine and used the ammunition as our chips. Each round was worth a million dollars. We were high rollers playing poker where it had never been played before.

I lost my first $30 million after about twenty minutes, bowed out of the game and went to my stretcher to read one of the thick paperbacks I'd brought along. There would be plenty of time for cards. Maybe the following night I'd get my $30 million back.

By the time the submarine stopped at periscope depth twenty kilometres off the Port of Beira, I'd lost $120 million and was near the end of my second Wilbur Smith novel.

The captain called me to the bridge. He took me to a screen showing the outline of the coast as far north as where the great Zambezi River flowed into the sea. He pointed to a blinking red light at the top – the northern end of the screen. 'The *Vladivostok*,' he said. 'She has made good time, as we expected, and will dock in about four hours. It's time for you to start getting organised.'

Suddenly feeling the nervousness in my stomach, I returned to the torpedo room and gave the news to the team. There were a couple of muted 'Woohoos!' but the mood quickly became serious as we started to prepare for the operation.

Piet Vermulen came down to see how we were getting on. He had with him a device that looked like a small underwater camera. Attached to the waterproof rubber housing was a metre length of nylon cord. He gave it to Mack.

'On your way back, paddle out to sea on a bearing of 120 degrees – the normal tidal currents around here will help push you in that direction anyway. After an hour and a half attach the loop on the cord to your wrist, press what looks like the shutter button and lower the device into the water.

It's a low-frequency homing beacon. We will receive the signal and come in to pick you up. We will be in the conning tower, watching. We don't want lights and we don't want noise. Once we have you on the deck, some of the crew will help with the unloading process. We want to spend as little time on the surface as possible. The less time we are up the less chance there is of compromise.'

We all nodded in agreement and understanding. The beacon was a great idea. It wouldn't matter now if we were a bit behind time or if we were pushed off course by tidal currents.

We folded up the camp stretchers and put them to one side, giving us more floor space to start assembling the Kleppers. We each had our own space: I would be in the first kayak with Mack behind me doing the steering. Rex and Pig Dog were in number two, Jonny and Fish in number three, Simmo and Nelson in number four and Horse and Karate were in the fifth boat.

Mack had organised things so that we would assemble the front part of the kayaks in the space nearest the exit hatch. Behind that he'd placed the folded skins of the kayaks and behind that were the rear parts. Then he lined up the kayak accessories: the seats, rudder assemblies, paddles, splash sheets and the foot pump we used to inflate the floatation tube that was built into the kayak skin. Behind that were the four limpet mines each kayak would carry. Karate would carry and organise the explosives initiation set while Jonny would have a spare that we hoped wouldn't be needed. Behind the limpets were our web belts and weapons: two folding butt AK-47s and two RPG7 bazookas with six rockets for each kayak.

We would be wearing the same dark blue overalls we had used on Cahora-Bassa, beneath a floatation jacket in which we had four chocolate-coated energy bars in plastic wrapping. We each had a water bottle we would secure under a bungee in front of us on top of the kayak.

Fish carried a medical pack and Rex had a canvas stretcher. If one of us took a hit, we sure as hell were not going to leave him behind.

With five neat rows of gear in place, we went down to the galley for a final feed, before blacking up and getting into it. The cook did us proud with sizzling *boerewors* sausage and mashed pumpkin. My God, we'd eaten well with the South Africans.

I stayed on the bridge as the *Vladivostok* pinged past us on the screen. Then as the sky darkened the submarine moved slowly forward to our departure position, about five kilometres offshore and slightly north of the harbour.

The submarine surfaced and we got the order to proceed with our launch. I led the way, ducking through the hatches en route to the conning tower, carrying the light timber struts and ribs that made up the front of the first kayak. Mack followed carrying the much heavier weight of the rubberised canvas skin, and behind him came Rex with the back part of the kayak, then Pig Dog with all the accessories. The others followed with the explosives and our weapons.

Piet Vermulen led me to a short ladder where a hatch had been opened. He took my load and told me to climb up, then he would pass up the front part of the kayak for me to lift out onto the deck. It went like clockwork. As Mack followed with the skin, I had time to look around. It was a perfect night for us. Gentle swells rocked the submarine, but the sea was flat and there was no wind. It was also very dark, but I could see the glow of lights on the horizon that would be the Port of Beira.

Mack joined me and together we unrolled the kayak skin. Mack lifted up the middle and I pushed in the front framework and forced it as far forward as I could. Rex appeared with the tail end and we shoved that into the skin in the same way. We took the seating and centre ribs from Pig Dog and forced everything into place. Rex used the foot pump to inflate the floatation tube while Mack assembled the rudder and attached the steering wires to the foot pedals where he would sit.

Pig Dog, meanwhile, went back to the hatch and hauled up our explosives that the others had brought forward. We stashed two limpets in the centre of the Klepper behind my backrest and put the other two in the bow, where they would be between my outstretched legs. Finally our weapons arrived. We put the bazooka rockets aft behind Mack's backrest and for the moment left the RPGs and the AKs in the open cockpit.

Kayak number one was ready to go. Mack and I turned our attention to helping Rex and Pig Dog put number two together. We hauled up the gear out of the submarine hatch while Mack supervised the assembly of the next kayak on the deck.

And so it continued until all five Kleppers were assembled and ready. It had taken just over an hour.

The kayaks were lined up on the deck. While everyone took their seats, Mack and I passed in their weapons and helped them secure the all-important splash sheets. With that done I got in the front of our kayak, stashed the RPG and AK on either side of me, then adjusted my backrest for comfort as Mack fixed my splash sheet. He got in behind me and after a short time tapped me on the shoulder and said, 'OK, Mick. We're ready to go.'

Piet Vermulen had been on the deck throughout the preparations. He came over and shook hands with all of us, then disappeared down the hatch.

Rex and Pig Dog were parallel with us on the deck, so we extended and held our paddles across both boats to create a catamaran effect that Mack said would be very stable in the wave swirl as the submarine submerged. We signalled to the others to do the same.

The massive form of Captain Swart was visible above the conning tower as slowly the submarine began to sink.

It was superb seamanship. The water slowly lapped over the deck and I felt the front of the kayak move, then suddenly we were floating. We paddled away from the conning tower as the captain backed off the submarine, then with a wave he closed the hatch and went below. Sixty seconds later the *Maria van Riebeeck* had disappeared without a sound or ripple on the water.

We were elated. The launch had been perfect and the sea conditions could not have been better for us. Mack worked the rudder and we led the way towards the lights on the horizon.

The submarine had given us the perfect launch position for the sea conditions: the tidal current washed down from the north and as there was no wind, the swells were low and pushed us forward towards our target as we paddled at an angle across them. I could see the wisdom, now, in the submarine picking us up some distance to the south, as the current would again help push us in the right direction.

Such thoughts quickly passed as we headed in towards the light glow. We had a lot of paddling to do that night so I kept a medium-paced rhythm that would be comfortable for everyone. We would be alert and ready for a quick countermove if another vessel came anywhere near us. Thankfully nothing did, and after just over an hour we reached the flashing green, port-side marker buoy on the approach into the harbour.

The red light of a starboard marker buoy flashed 200 metres ahead of us and we headed for that. I wanted to hug the pile of rocks that made up the breakwater on the north side of the harbour and follow that in towards our target. We paused to make sure nothing was coming in or out, then we crossed the channel at a good speed and headed towards the breakwater bank.

We paddled within two metres of the breakwater as we followed it into the harbour area. There was some swell deflection that rocked the kayaks a bit, but it was no real problem and we were safe there. We went forward slowly, aware there was a possibility of Frelimo defensive positions, but we saw nothing. Twenty minutes later we were under the wharf structure and alongside the berthed *Vladivostok*.

As we paddled alongside, I soon realised the ship was way bigger than we had envisaged. I was happy we had brought along as much explosive as we had.

We rafted up under the wharf. Firstly, to listen for any activity above us – there was none – and secondly, to fine tune the general plan we had made for sinking the ship. I thought we should try to place the limpets on the hull plating between ribs, and nobody disagreed with that. But how could we identify where the ribs were located from the outside of the ship?

Mack had been to the Glasgow shipyards and seen ships being built. This was neither the time nor the place for a detailed explanation, so he simply told us to leave the positioning of the mines to him. We all dug out the limpets we were carrying and placed them close to hand on top of the splash sheets. We were ready to roll.

We started at the stern of the ship. Mack paddled and steered, then as we reached a point of his choosing, he tapped me on the shoulder and indicated where he wanted the mine. We had attached a nylon loop to the mine casing that I fitted over the end of my paddle. Each mine also had a 10-metre length of Cordtex attached to it; I gave Mack the loose end to hold while I lowered the first mine into the water. I felt the weight disappear as the magnets silently attached to the hull, then I twisted the paddle to get the nylon loop off the blade.

With the first mine in place, Mack gave the Cordtex tail back to me while he carefully paddled another 5 or 6 metres forward. I unrolled the Cordtex loop as we went until he again tapped me on the shoulder. I picked up the second limpet and threaded the end of the Cordtex tail from the first mine through a plastic clip attached to the Cordtex on the second mine. I tied a knot so it couldn't pull out then lowered it into the water and onto the hull of the ship.

The plastic clips were a product used in quarry or opencast mining work, to connect the leads between multiple charges for a simultaneous detonation.

They were perfect for what we were trying to achieve. With the first two mines connected we continued slowly down the hull.

Once our four limpets were in place, Rex came alongside and put his mines on my splash sheet. One by one I linked his together with ours, placing them on the hull where Mack indicated as we moved slowly towards the front of the ship.

We took our time. There was no risk of being seen underneath the wharf structure and the water was flat calm. We were nervous but we were not under any pressure, and after all the effort involving a submarine to get us here the job had to be well done.

Eventually, all twenty mines were in place at regular intervals on the hull, a little more than two metres below the water level. I handed the Cordtex tail of the last limpet to Karate, who had come alongside to attach the initiation set. He used another clip to fix it and, as we had done with the others, tied a knot in the end so it couldn't come loose.

His initiation set was already assembled in a zip-up, plastic dry bag and consisted of two detonators each crimped to a British Army time pencil. The detonators were taped to a short length of Cordtex that extended through a sealed hole in the bag, and to which the Cordtex lead from the limpets was attached with the clip.

Karate found a good place on one of the wharf piles to attach the initiation set. All we had to do now was to pull the pins on the two time pencils.

With everything in place, we sorted ourselves out ready for paddling back the way we had come, then took out the folding-butt AKs and slung them over our shoulders.

Throughout all of this not a sound came from the wharf or from the ship.

The British Army time pencils we would use to initiate the mines were simple but effective delay devices we had used before on other operations. We had learned that in the tropical conditions where we usually operated, the time delay was generally much less than the official rating given to the device. It made sense because the time pencil consisted of a high-tension spring which, when activated, would exert pressure on a restraining piece of soft solder wire. This would slowly stretch with the pressure and eventually break, releasing the spring-loaded striker pin to hit the detonating cap beneath it. The time delay depended on the ambient temperature. If it was hot, the wire would be softer so would stretch and break more quickly.

Although it was a warm night, under the wharf it was cool and damp; Karate and I agreed the one-hour rating of the time pencils we were using would give us at least forty-five minutes to clear the area.

It was enough time.

Karate pulled the pins on the two timing devices, and we paddled quietly away from beneath the wharf and back out into open water alongside the breakwater.

Halfway along, we left the cover of the breakwater and paddled swiftly across the harbour entrance towards the oil terminal jetty. We reached it without incident and then, in a single file, we paddled beneath the piles in towards land and our second target.

We left the cover of the jetty and paddled in front of the tank farm. We found a small beach amongst the rocks where a storm-water outfall pipe protruded. There was just enough space to secure our boats; it would be easy getting in and out of the kayaks.

We pulled the boats together and made doubly sure they were well secured. We slung the RPG bazookas over our shoulders, put the propellant capsules in the pockets of our overalls and tucked the three rockets we each had into our belts. With the AKs in our hands, we clambered up the rocks of the sea wall and onto the oil terminal.

Pig Dog had been leading the way. As he reached the top he turned round and urgently signalled stop!

Rex and I moved up to him while the others silently moved into covering fire positions. Pig Dog put a finger to his lips demanding absolute silence. I adjusted the rockets on my belt so they wouldn't bump together and moved in next to him. Rex silently ducked down on his opposite side.

Twenty metres away, silhouetted against the harbour lighting, was the barrel of a 14.5-millimetre anti-aircraft gun. Behind the gun, we could hear the voices of the Frelimo guards coming from a small tin shelter where they would sleep and eat.

From this position we could also see three large fuel storage tanks.

We huddled together. I whispered, 'I'll get Nelson and Simmo to join you. Stay here. When you hear the limpets explode, put two rockets into these guys then another two into the gun. Use the rest on the storage tanks. We'll go off to the left; unless we find more guns we'll concentrate on blowing the other tanks.'

I took a rocket out of my belt and gave it to Rex, then dug around in my pocket to find the propellant.

'Take this, Rex,' I said. 'This can be your reserve in case something happens while we are on our way back to join you.'

He nodded with approval as I backed off to rejoin the others.

We clambered over the rocks for about 100 metres, away from the gun position, and then I went up to ground level to look around. All I could see was the white-painted fuel storage tanks. I signalled for the others to come up and we crouched down together within fifty metres of the nearest tank. I left Horse and Karate at that point and gave them their targets.

Walking in the open now, on a gravel perimeter track, we moved a further 100 metres away. Here I left Fish and Jonny, pointing out their targets. Mack and I went on for another 100 metres, stopping in front of the tanks we would hit. We screwed the propellant capsules onto the tail of the rockets, put the spares on the ground next to us, then loaded our bazookas.

We were in position and ready. All we had to do now was wait for the limpets to blow, and hope like hell that nothing happened in the interim to screw our well-laid plan.

The time pencil delay seemed to take forever.

From the forty-five-minute mark I looked at my watch every thirty seconds, mentally working hard to dispel the negative thoughts that wanted to take over at times like that. No. The time pencils will work, I told myself as fifty-five minutes passed.

Fifty-nine minutes and still no explosion. I thought with increasing anxiety: we've put two of them on the initiation set, surely they can't both fail?

Sixty minutes, sixty-one minutes, sixty-two minutes. Just as my Omega was ticking over for sixty-three minutes, the limpets exploded.

I stood up and could see the Russian ship. The front mooring rope had snapped and the bow had moved away from the wharf. The demons in my mind had suddenly disappeared. As I heard the *whoosh* of rocket fire, from Rex, it was back to business.

Rex and Pig Dog took out the Frelimo guards with their rockets while Nelson and Simmo blew apart the anti-aircraft gun. Pig Dog's second rocket hit the middle of the nearest tank, which ruptured. Dark liquid gushed out but didn't ignite. Rex put his third rocket into the middle of the neighbouring tank, it exploded with flaming liquid pouring onto the ground, and that ignited the product from Pig Dog's hit. Nelson and Simmo followed up with two more rockets into the tanks, which exploded again. A spiralling tongue of flame twisted violently into the air above them.

The flames billowed into the sky as our rockets hit one tank after another. Blazing fireballs roared uncontrollably within the shells of the tanks, others erupted into the air producing fountains of fire.

We were too close. It was time to get out before we became victims of our own firestorm.

Mack and I ran back along the gravel road on the perimeter of the tank farm, met up with Fish and Jonny and together we ran to link up with Horse and Karate.

As the fire intensified, we could feel the heat on our faces and the air was heavy with the acrid smells of burning petrol, diesel and bitumen. Tanks were still exploding as we ran past.

Rex and Pig Dog stood up to meet us. Rex had my third rocket loaded. He told us to get down to the kayaks where he'd already sent Simmo and Nelson to organise our escape. He and Pig Dog, meanwhile, would cover our descent over the rocks of the breakwater.

We were halfway down, picking our way over the jumbled boulders, when the lights of a truck appeared heading towards the shattered gun position. A Frelimo patrol was coming to see what was happening.

Rex waited for the vehicle to slow down as it approached the broken gun. Then fired. The rocket exploded in the cab, killing the driver and the squad leader who had the privilege of sitting in the front.

As Rex fired the RPG, Pig Dog opened up with his AK. He fired rapid double-taps into the canvas behind the cab where the Frelimo terrorists would be sitting. Rex dropped his RPG and did the same. In the light of the blazing fires, they could see men jumping off the back of the truck, trying to escape. But there was to be no escape for any of them.

Pig Dog changed magazines while Rex kept firing, then Rex did the same as Pig Dog dropped another two men at the back of the truck.

There was no more movement and the truck had caught fire. It was time to get the hell out of there.

At the small beach, we had already got the Kleppers turned round and ready to go when Rex and Pig Dog eventually joined us. We secured their splash sheets as they stashed their Bazookas and took their paddles. We pushed away and headed towards the long jetty as fast as we could.

We reached the jetty without incident then paddled slowly underneath it, aware there could be other big guns we didn't know about looking for a target. We paused beneath the end of the jetty, then, paddling as fast as we could, headed towards a green flashing buoy at the channel edge and from there out of the harbour.

I resisted the temptation to look back at the mayhem in the Port of Beira; to my mind the job wasn't over until we were back on the submarine heading for Cape Town. But the light glow behind me was a lot brighter than when we went in.

Out on the open water a light sea breeze had come up that chopped the surface. But it was behind us, and with the kayaks a lot lighter we were being pushed along by the wind and the ocean. Now and then we did some surfing as a bigger swell picked us up and took us with it for a few boat lengths.

We kept paddling hard for an hour and forty minutes, then Mack got out the magic beacon Piet had given us. We all hoped it worked. It was now just after 02.50 hours and we were way out at sea in our flimsy kayaks. The adrenalin rush that came with the attacks had long since gone; we were all looking forward to getting back aboard and going to sleep.

Mack pressed the shutter on the beacon and lowered it into the water. We sat in the kayaks, paddling only to keep the swells behind us. We waited, everyone looking around searching the sea for a big, black whale.

'My God, that's scary,' said Fish, who was the first to see the big, black conning tower rise silently above the water and head towards us. We all turned to look. As it got closer, the top hatch opened and we could see the unmistakable outline of the big commander homing in on his target.

We turned the Kleppers towards the approaching submarine and paddled slowly, trying to keep in line with the conning tower. As the nose of our kayaks approached the tower, he gently lifted the bow to put us safely on deck.

It was now very important to get everything below as fast as possible. This was the danger time for the submarine.

To be seen sitting on the surface, a few kilometres off a burning Beira, would be total compromise.

Piet joined us on deck, as before, and immediately started shovelling our gear down the hatch to a waiting crew who ferried it back to the torpedo room. It had taken us over an hour to assemble everything before the operation. We had everything below deck on our return in less than twenty minutes, then the captain lost no time in taking the submarine down to a safe depth and at maximum speed heading on a course for home.

We were ushered into the small galley, where the cook had a big pot of steaming, black coffee for us and a plateful of South African rusks. The captain came down to join us and listened intently as I described what had happened. I finished by expressing our thanks for their part in it all and said what a pleasure it had been working with the naval Special Forces. Which it had been.

With that, I put a 'Do Not Disturb' sign outside the torpedo room. I told them I had lost $120 million in the poker game on the way up there and I badly needed rest to give me a chance of winning it back on the homeward leg.

The latter was a vain hope.

By the time we approached Cape Town, my losses were up to $210 million and I'd run out of ammunition.

At the debrief, the senior Intelligence officer showed air photographs of the Port of Beira, taken while we were submerged and on our way home. The force of the simultaneous explosions had made the *Vladivostok* 'jump' in the water and the front mooring rope had snapped as if it were cotton thread. Released from the wharf, the bow had drifted out several metres while water poured through twenty gaping holes in the hull. The ship had listed slightly towards the wharf before settling on the harbour bed twenty metres below. The top structures and masts were above water, but the holds with the tanks and heavy weaponry were submerged.

Frelimo had no way of dealing with this. The ship would remain there indefinitely, unless the Russians committed to what would be a very expensive and complicated salvage operation given the weight and nature of the cargo. The feeling was they would simply abandon the ship and leave the fixing of Beira to Frelimo.

The pictures showed a still smoking tank farm, and without fuel for vehicles and power generators that would, in turn, create extreme difficulties for Frelimo and its terrorist allies.

It was a major setback for Frelimo.

To further complicate matters, we had left behind a few ZANU souvenirs to suggest its involvement.

Radio intercepts suggested ZANU, or possibly dissident anti-Frelimo, Mozambique-based rebels, were thought to be responsible for the attack after the discovery of tail fins of a Chinese RPG rocket.

The admiral congratulated us on our efforts, and told us the captain had made a detailed report on our organisation and preparation for the operation. He had commented that it could not be faulted.

He asked if I had any comments to make. I expressed the view that if sea conditions were difficult the use of kayaks would be impossible. One capsize and the whole operation could be jeopardised. We had taken along the small Zodiacs as a bad weather contingency, and that would have worked in terms of getting into the general target area, but not for the close-in work of laying the limpets.

We had used our big Zodiacs before as 'mother ships' and had launched attacks by kayak from them once close to the target. Future operations should be prepared for that contingency, and I thought it would be useful to see if a full-sized Zodiac was a practical proposition in terms of assembly and inflation on the deck of the submarine. They were big boats and ours were propelled by twin 40-horsepower Evinrudes that were big, heavy engines, but I thought it was probably manageable.

There were nods of agreement, and I could see the captain making notes; I was sure he'd give it a try before too long.

After the debriefing, I presented the admiral and the captain with hand-crafted SAS plaques featuring a silver-winged dagger mounted on our 'pompadour blue' felt. As we left, the admiral shook my hand warmly, and holding the grip told me he'd heard I wasn't the greatest poker player.

'Can't argue with that, Sir.' I replied with a laugh. 'I managed to lose $210 million on either side of the operation.'

'That's what I heard,' he said. 'Poker's obviously the wrong game for you, Mick, but I'd suggest that when it comes to Russian roulette there would be nobody better.'

# The Last Rites for ZAPU

After the sinking of the *Vladivostok* in Beira harbour, we expected the Russian sponsors of terrorist group ZAPU to be seriously unhappy with yet another failure.

They would persist with the intent to bring in enough heavy weapons – and probably MiG fighter aircraft like they had in Angola – to eventually take control of Rhodesia. Once they had taken the country they would consolidate, bring in more armour and air power, and quietly wait for the right time to strike south. With the ANC leading the way they would ultimately win the massive prize of South Africa.

In the SAS, meanwhile, we were busy trying to stem the ever-increasing flow of rival faction ZANU terrorists who, with Frelimo assistance, were making serious inroads into Rhodesia via an eastern border that was simply too big and in many places too difficult to control by the armed forces.

We mounted several attacks on their base camps along the border, culminating in a joint operation with the Rhodesian Light Infantry commandos at a camp in the Manica province of Mozambique known as *Chimoio*. The surprise attack was followed up the next day with another on a feeder camp much deeper into Mozambique known as *Tembue*, not too far away from Furuncungo where we had eliminated Regone Mwanza and his Frelimo group.

In the space of just two days well over 1,000 terrorists and trainees were killed. ZANU was reeling at the unexpected ferocity of the attacks and the fact that we were able to destroy two of their main camps, separated by hundreds of kilometres, in consecutive days.

We learned later that Mugabe was in despair at the loss and ready to give in. But his Chinese supporters were quick to point out that while it was a massive blow he still had many groups successfully operating within the country; more importantly, his rivals ZAPU had so far achieved nothing.

'Make smaller camps,' they told him, 'and spread them out all along the border. It is clearly stated in Mao's *Little Red Book* that by doing this you will stretch the resources of the enemy to breaking point.'

It was good advice, especially as at that point we turned our attention again to ZAPU.

Intelligence reports and subsequent high altitude photo-reconnaissance flights confirmed a steady accumulation of Russian-made armour and artillery at a location twenty kilometres south of the Zambian capital, Lusaka. They had found another way in.

The weeks passed and more hardware arrived in Zambia. The longer we let it happen the bigger the problem would ultimately be for us, so we requested a meeting with the Rhodesian military high command, ComOps.

The organisation was led by a general, himself an SAS man who had commanded the regiment during the Malayan Emergency. We didn't expect any preferential treatment, but it was good knowing we were dealing with someone who knew what Special Forces operations were about.

The general had the unenviable task of dealing with politicians and intelligence agencies, both locally as well as in a number of other countries. His position and experience would be invaluable to us because what we were proposing would undoubtedly generate some serious opposition.

We had looked at the maps. It wasn't hard to work out that ZAPU only had two options for bringing in the hardware: the Tan–Zam rail link from Dar es Salaam – ironically built by the Chinese and the most likely option – or via a road and rail link that went through Malawi. Cut those links and the build-up of heavy weapons and equipment would come to a grinding halt.

But while that made perfect sense in the military context, the political ramifications were another story.

By destroying these road and rail links, landlocked Zambia would then have just one option left for the imports and exports the country depended on: the rail link across Victoria Falls that went through Rhodesia and down to the South African ports in Natal and the Cape. Given the enmity towards the Smith-led regime in Rhodesia, it would be an untenable position for them.

Personally, I didn't care. Kaunda, to me, was just another tinpot African dictator who ten minutes after his election declared Zambia a one-party state. It said he cared more for himself than his people. If we made things tough for him, the country could perhaps get a better deal.

The general agreed that strategically our proposal to blow up selected bridges along both routes was sound. But he had doubts about getting the political clearances to do that, especially at a time when international diplomacy was working hard to bring all parties involved in these central African conflicts to a Kissinger peace and reconciliation summit.

I stood up as the meeting approached closure. 'General,' I said. 'Based on what you have told us, it looks like our current plans may be on hold for some time. I understand and accept that. The fact remains, however, that while this detente goes on ZAPU will continue to amass heavy weaponry and progress their plans for a conventional warfare attack into Rhodesia. If the peace process fails, and if we can't destroy the supply lines, we should at least be looking at ways of halting any ZAPU advance before it reaches the border.

'There are only a few ways of crossing the Zambezi River from Zambia into Rhodesia,' I continued. 'It's likely there are bridges along these routes that if destroyed would stop, or at least seriously delay, their assault.

'General, I'd like your permission to start making contingency plans. We'll need some air photography, and it's possible the public works department may have useful information on the roads and bridges from the days when Rhodesia, Zambia and Malawi were united as a federation.

'Once we have established all the possibilities and options, we'll arrange another meeting with you and your staff, because the next step would be to do some ground recce work with a demolition team so we know exactly what is required if the worst happens.'

'I want to make it clear that your plans for attacking the supply lines have not yet been rejected,' the general replied. 'Even if they are, we may need to resurrect them at short notice if the security situation deteriorates further. So stay prepared. Meanwhile, Mick, your contingency planning makes good sense and you've got my total support. I'll let my staff know and will organise things for you with the PWD.'

We didn't get what we wanted from the meeting – which was an immediate green light to bring Zambia and ZAPU to their knees – but at least we got something.

Once we had escorted the VIPs off site, the brigadier asked Rex to keep everyone in the presentation area while he and I went to his office for a talk.

'Good work, Mick,' he said. 'But we need to think about how we will handle this. The general said our plans to blow the Tan-Zam and Malawi bridges were definitely not rejected, and rumours from my contacts are the politicians are looking for ways of putting pressure on Zambia to join the team trying to negotiate a peace.

'No better way of doing that,' he continued, 'than by cutting the supply lines the Zambian economy relies on. Kaunda would then come under internal pressure that may threaten his regime. Mick, I think we have just given the politicians a way forward they had never contemplated.

'I'll prepare the regiment for blowing the bridges. I'm certain that will be ordered sooner rather than later. Meanwhile, you and Rex focus on how we might stop a ZAPU advance. Let's go and tell the boys.'

The three weeks that followed were really enjoyable. For a start, it was some time since we'd had that long back at home base. Although we were all very busy with different forms of preparation there was time for some overdue socialising, and doing other things you missed when on operations – like showering every day and wearing your own clothes. For me that meant blue Levis, a tee shirt and my blue and white Adidas track shoes – sans socks.

During the second week, at 04.00 each morning, I took our Sierra One Seven team and three other groups out to the parachute training school. It was some time since we had done free-fall and the night HALO entry we used to reach target areas undetected. So for the next six days we would do two jumps each morning to perfect our skills in rehearsal for the real thing.

HALO is the military abbreviation for 'High Altitude Low Opening', a parachuting technique designed to covertly infiltrate Special Forces on to or close to their targets. If you did it at night, as we did, the chance of detection was minimal.

The Rhodesian Air Force didn't have C130s, but still operated a fleet of DC3 Dakota aircraft that were an ideal low-speed plane perfectly suited to parachute operations.

On these HALO operations, we would jump at around 12,000 feet above the ground. The aircraft could fly higher than this but the problem then was cold and a lack of oxygen. It was possible to counter these issues, but there were health risks and it was fiddly so we opted for 12,000 feet, where it was not so cold and just on the edge of the oxygen zone.

For the first two days we did nothing more than a regulation drop: the groups of five exiting the aircraft in quick succession and once stabilised closing in and free-falling 9,500 feet in relatively close proximity to each other. I didn't want link-ups because when you were descending at terminal velocity at night it brought risks we didn't need.

At 2,500 feet on the altimeter we'd hit the ripcord. The pilot chute would spring open and drag out the main canopy. As the air was forced into the parachute there would be a rippling sound like distant thunder as it fully opened. There followed a jerk on the shoulders that brought our legs swinging up above waist level as we decelerated from terminal velocity to the gentle speed of the descent all in the space of a few of seconds and while dropping another 250 feet.

We used 'Para-Commanders', a joint American-French design made from low-porosity nylon with stabilising side panels and multiple vents at the rear. The material and stabilisers provided a slow, non-oscillating descent rate while the rear vents increased glide by directing the airflow rearward instead of upward. With steering toggles we could control our direction to reach the drop zone. More importantly, we could, on approach to landing, turn the chute into the wind to give us a soft, often stand-up landing.

They were great parachutes and had some useful safety features, including what were known as 'Capewell releases' – there was one on each shoulder webbing strap. It was thankfully not common, but for a variety of reasons a free-fall parachute sometimes would not open cleanly. The rigging lines would become entangled with the canopy and as a result the parachute would corkscrew rapidly downwards. In those conditions you couldn't deploy the reserve parachute because it would simply wind itself around the cabbage of the tangled main canopy and you'd plummet helplessly to the ground. The Capewell releases on each shoulder strap had steel wire loops that were pulled to release the canopy from the harness. By dropping free of the over-head tangle, the reserve parachute could then be deployed in clear air and you would descend safely to the ground.

Well, that was the theory. But doing something like that after a 10,000-foot drop at night over hostile territory called for a very cool head. And the only way to develop that was through experience.

After the second day jumps, I had a private chat with Squadron Leader Derek de Kok and Frank Hales, his 2IC. I told them I wanted the team to experience cutting away and using the reserve parachute. I explained my logic and pointed to the coat of arms above the door with their parachute school motto: 'Knowledge Dispels Fear'.

They liked the idea. 'Tomorrow we'll do both jumps that way, Mick,' said Derek. 'The first will be a novelty, but the second you will remember forever.

'Weather conditions are good. With the recent rains, the ground is nice and soft for the faster landings you'll get with the reserve chutes. We'll go through the drills and then we'll put you through some conventional landings off the ramp before we go up in the morning. We've never done this before, it's not something we can simulate on the training swings and harnesses, but you guys are experienced parachutists and I like your logic.'

We went out to the parachute school in the early morning for one main reason: the wind – or lack of it in this case – because calm conditions were best for parachuting and the last thing we needed was injuries.

On arrival next day, Derek and Frank were already organised. I hadn't told the boys what we had planned, but as soon as Frank invited us to get a coffee and take a seat in the lecture room, they all knew something was afoot.

Derek started by explaining that the Para-Commander free-fall parachute had a number of in-built safety features, then went on to describe what happened if it had a rare malfunction. He didn't spare the detail on what was likely to happen if the reserve parachute was deployed too early. While we were still absorbing his chilling descriptions, he announced that this was the day we were going to learn what it was like to experience a malfunction – we would cut away from the main canopy and descend using the reserve parachute.

'How many of you have used a reserve parachute before?' he asked.

No hands were put up.

'Just as I thought. So, you'll all agree it would be much better we give you that experience here, instead of having to learn it in the dark over some godforsaken place in Mozambique.'

Frank took over. 'Mick, your group will go first. On the first run we'll just go up to 5,000 feet and I want you to deploy the Para-Commander at 3,000 feet. I want the rest of you to keep an eye on Mick and as soon as he deploys, you do the same. OK so far?' he asked.

We all nodded.

'Mick, once you are sorted out, turn the parachute and head upwind. The rest of you do the same, and again, keep your eyes on Mick who will then turn in towards the drop zone. Once on course, Mick, you release the Capewells and drop free of the Para-Commander.

'Keep your feet and knees together and lift them up close to waist level when you let go. That will give you a stable drop position while you find and pull the reserve parachute ripcord. It will take a little time to deploy, and don't be afraid to help it on its way if it's slow getting out of the pack. You will descend between 200 and 300 feet while all this happens, but the important thing is to ignore the drop and just focus on making sure the reserve is out and flying beautifully for you. Nothing else matters.

'After that, there is nothing to do except to pull down on the back rigging lines to vent the air pressure from the flat canopy, which will keep you stable and slow you down for what will be a faster than usual forward landing.

'As soon as the rest of you see Mick cut away, you do the same and follow him in. Now, I want you all behind the ramp and we'll do a few fast forward landing rolls. Let's go!'

For the next half-hour we ran up the big ramp and leapt out onto the mats, feet and knees together with our ankles angled left or right for whichever landing Frank called for. On landing we'd collapse the thighs and roll forward and over our hips and shoulders, spreading the force of ground impact across the length of our body while avoiding any dangerous whiplash effect to the neck and head. It was hard work but essential to ensure we walked away intact after the parachute landing.

Mastering the 'cut-away' was next on the agenda.

I have always enjoyed the deep-throated roar of the big rotary engines that drive the DC3, but as we powered up for take-off my mind was not as appreciative as usual because in my belly butterflies were line dancing.

I was scared. Scared of the unknown.

I took a deep breath as the red light came on above the door in the aircraft. We stood up and moved forward towards the exit. Standing in the open door of the aircraft I turned to look at Horse, Pig Dog, Karate and Fish standing behind me.

Shouting to be heard above the wind noise, I asked Horse if he remembered what I'd said before we got into the submarine in Cape Town.

'Business as usual!' Horse shouted back immediately, and turning to the others behind him, laughed out loud. 'Don't worry, guys, the major says it's just business as usual. Business as fucking usual!' He was still laughing and shaking his head as he followed me out of the door.

I leapt from the aircraft and twisted in to face the direction we were going: arms out, legs apart and bent at the knees. It was a good exit and I was immediately stable. I dropped my right arm slightly to induce a turn where I could better see the others, then back into position to retain that all-important stability.

I watched the others stabilise and adjust their flight positions so they could see me. They'd all made great exits and were solid and stable as we rapidly headed towards a terminal velocity descent rate of over 200 kilometres an hour. At that rate we were going down at between 150 and 200 feet a second so it didn't take long to reach the 3,000-feet mark.

As my altimeter hit 3,000 feet, I reached over and pulled the ripcord located on my left shoulder. There was an immediate deceleration as the pilot chute slowed down the descent. The opening noise followed, I felt a tug on my shoulders and my feet were involuntarily swung up towards my waist as the canopy deployed in all its splendour.

Twisting around to get my bearings, and a feel for the wind drift, took a few moments, then I found the steering toggles and turned the parachute into what little breeze there was on a beautifully still morning.

I enjoyed a moment or two wafting along as I waited for the others to get organised and follow my lead.

The good feeling didn't last long.

I used the toggles to turn the parachute and headed towards the landing zone.

I glanced down at my altimeter.

My God. I was already below 2,000 feet. I put my thumbs into the loops of the Capewell releases on each shoulder; I took up the tension and, with a deep breath, pulled hard.

As I dropped free, I remembered what Frank had said about lifting my legs up to waist level; I did that while addressing the more urgent business of finding and pulling the ripcord of the reserve parachute attached to steel D-rings on the webbing over my belly.

The white nylon of the reserve chute popped out of the canvas enclosure and, after a nervous moment of fluttering, opened cleanly.

I breathed a sigh of relief. All I had to do now was to slow down the descent rate by pulling hard on the back rigging lines and prepare myself for landing.

It wasn't bad. I had experienced faster landings with bigger, static line parachutes, and came in with a perfect forward right roll just like we'd been doing off the ramp an hour or two earlier.

The rest of the team followed and they too were untroubled.

While the ground staff rushed around gathering in all the parachutes, we were taken back to the school for a coffee and a bacon and egg sandwich before a debriefing and preparation for the second jump.

The elderly DC3 again rumbled down the runway and into the air. This time we were much more relaxed as the plane droned round in wide circles to get us to our more usual altitude of 12,000 feet. We would again do the cut-away, but this time after a free fall of 10,000 feet.

I leapt into space on the green light, turned as I did before so I could see the team following me.

Conditions were perfect. With small arm and leg movements I positioned myself within three metres of Pig Dog and Horse. I could see the big Cornish grin as Horse signalled to Fish to come in and join us. As Fish closed in, Karate, who was above us, saw what was happening; never one to be excluded from a party, he initially tracked away then came in on a fast delta with arms back before spreading out and joining the unconnected link-up.

It was a lot of fun and we were enjoying ourselves, but I kept an eye on my altimeter and as the 4,000-feet mark flashed past I signalled to the others and cut away. They followed suit, bombshelling away from me.

I deployed the chute at 2,500 feet and the Para-Commander obliged by opening perfectly.

I pulled on the toggles to check on the others. As I turned I saw Karate shoot past, a tangle of olive green nylon rattling noisily above him. My God, he's had a real malfunction.

Twisting and turning in the air, Karate dropped like a stone.

I pulled on the toggles of my chute and turned to follow his flight.

I glanced at my altimeter. Eighteen hundred feet. 'For Christ's sake, Karate, cut away now!' I shouted.

He wouldn't have heard me. But at that instant the parachute suddenly broke free and drifted away as Karate dropped lower and lower.

I looked at my altimeter again in relief as the white nylon reserve chute finally opened. The three of us were now just 1,100 feet above the ground. Karate was 500 feet or more below us.

It was too late to cut away ourselves so I signalled to the others to follow me. I pulled on the toggles and at full speed we headed towards Karate.

I watched him land, roll then stand up. I flew over his position then turned the chute 180 degrees into the wind and towards him. I landed gently about twenty metres short. Looking back I saw Pig Dog, Horse and Fish following me in, ultimately landing even closer on either side of Karate.

I didn't know what to say, in the relief of seeing my crooked-toothed, right-hand man standing there grinning sheepishly.

Horse had no such problems. 'Bloody brilliant!' he exclaimed, patting Karate enthusiastically on top of his helmet. 'We got to ride the Para-Commanders all the way down. No silly little white chutes you can't steer. Great move, Karate, pulling that stunt.'

The only other words worth mentioning after that came from a smiling Derek, who reminded us he'd said we'd never forget the second drop. He left us with a slightly smug look on his face and with some justification feeling even more omnipotent than usual.

We did our final jump a couple of nights later with a special pallet built by the air supply team, because sometimes we needed more equipment than we could fit in our packs. On the pallet we could take extra rations, water, ammunition, explosives and anything else we needed to prolong our stay in hostile country without resupply and the possibility of compromise that went with it.

A reserve parachute was strapped onto the pallet with an automatic opening device known as a 'sentinel' that we could programme to open the chute at an altitude of our choosing.

The final touch was two small, battery-powered red lights on top of the pallet, which would be switched on just before despatch. As the pallet was pushed out of the aircraft we'd dive after it and follow the red lights. We'd try to delay our own opening until the sentinel fired and then we'd all drift in and run with it to landing.

Remarkably, it usually worked without a hitch. Satisfyingly, we added to that record on our final night training exercise.

While the parachute training was going on, our demolition experts, with some help from the engineers, were busy studying plans of bridges and visiting local sites to look at similar structures to those we would encounter on the Tan-Zam rail link and main roads in Zambia.

They were looking for the weak points. The best places to locate the explosives that would bring down the bridges. After our morning jumps, we'd join these teams to keep up with their developments.

On the last morning of our free-fall training, we were driving back to base from the parachute school when we were held up at a roundabout near the international airport. Several tourists in Avis and Hertz rental cars were starting out on their African safaris. We waved to them as they passed our open Sabre Land Rovers, they waved back enjoying the friendly gesture, clearly excited at the start of their adventures.

It got me thinking.

What we were planning was dramatic, both from an operational point of view and in terms of political impact. We had to get it right. But as time went by, I could see we were unlikely to get the detailed intelligence we needed to put the odds fully in our favour.

I requested a meeting with the brigadier and expressed my concern.

'Sir, there are only three routes ZAPU could use to launch an attack on Rhodesia.' I pointed to the map. 'To the west there is the road between Lusaka and Victoria Falls. In the centre there is the road from Lusaka to the Kariba hydro dam, and slightly east of that is a road that goes to the bridge across the Zambezi at Chirundu.

'Looking at the map, there are several bridges that appear to have the potential to block these routes if blown. But it's guesswork and that's not good enough. We need to know exactly which of these bridges will do the job for us, and to get that information we need to have a look at them.

'Conventional reconnaissance isn't a practical proposition, but I have another idea.'

His eyes widened then lit up as I explained the thoughts I'd had while waiting at the airport roundabout earlier that morning. 'We need to keep this strictly in-house,' he said. 'What the generals don't know about, the generals won't worry about. Go ahead, Mick. I'll get the money for you.'

I called a meeting with the team behind the Sabres in the vehicle yard. I told them I was worried we might be going into what was both a critical military and political situation without accurate intelligence. It wasn't a good way to operate, but we had time and a plan to tip the balance back in our favour.

'Horse, Mack and Fish, I'm going to approve ten days leave for you.' That immediately got their undivided attention.

'Tomorrow, we'll take you to the international airport where you will pick up a rental car. Acting as tourists, you will then drive up to Victoria Falls where you will stay in the hotel and enjoy a day marvelling at the sights.

'Take pictures. Keep all the tickets and receipts along the way to prove you are tourists, because your next move will be to cross the Victoria Falls Bridge and continue your tour through Zambia.'

They all looked at me in disbelief as I continued.

'Once across the bridge you are to stay for a night at Livingstone, on the Zambian side, where you will again take tourist trips to the falls and surrounds, then your real work starts in earnest.' I said with some emphasis.

'From Victoria Falls, your tourist plan is to drive through southern Zambia towards Lusaka, before heading south to Chirundu, in the Zambezi Valley, where you are going to see the river and the big game. From Chirundu, you will backtrack north until you pick up the road to Kariba. You are to cross back into Rhodesia over the dam wall then drive back to the airport to return the rental vehicle.

'Mack and Horse, I have chosen you because you are from the British Isles and your accents, passports and personal records authenticate that, so going into Zambia as a tourist is a legitimate right for you both.

'Fish, you were born in Zambia. Your father is held in high regard for his work with the copper mines, so there is no good reason why you cannot show off your home country to friends from the UK.

'Your mission is to obtain specific – that's measured and photographic – information of a number of bridges along the roads between Victoria Falls and Lusaka, between Lusaka and Chirundu and finally between Lusaka and Kariba.

'This information will be invaluable as we prepare to blow these bridges. The more we know about them the easier and safer it will ultimately be for us all.'

Horse responded without hesitation. 'It's brilliant, Mick.' Then turning to the boys his big face opened with a massive grin. He extended his arms in an evangelical way and looking down on everyone he laughingly exclaimed, 'It's just more business as usual, guys.'

We dropped them off two days later. As their dress code they had decided to adopt a football supporters theme. Horse wore his bright red Manchester United jersey. Mack wore the green and white of his home Celtic team while Fish was dressed in the black and white stripes of Newcastle.

Horse went to the rental car counter and said he had a booking in the name of Granger. Thirty minutes later, they were driving a well-worn Ford Cortina towards Bulawayo.

Along the way they took photographs of themselves posing at strategic places as evidence of their journey. It was a Saturday when they reached Bulawayo. Horse had the inspiration of going to a local soccer match where they joined in with the locals, and again they took pictures. Next day, at Victoria Falls, they tagged on to a tourist party and spent the day with them sightseeing and socialising, enjoying the holiday and the spectacle. They found a pharmacy with a film-developing machine and had their first batch of pictures printed.

Now firmly in the tourist mode, they crossed the border into Zambia with little apprehension and, showing their reservation at the Livingstone hotel, had no trouble at the customs and immigration station on the north side of the bridge. Another day playing tourist followed and then it was time for business as usual.

Horse was in his element.

The next afternoon at a police roadblock, he jumped out of the Cortina and went straight up to the sergeant, who was armed with an AK-47 that was pointing at him. Pointing in turn to the badge on his Manchester United jersey, he demanded to know which team they supported.

The sergeant looked at the black and white stripes of the jersey Fish was wearing: 'Newcastle United – same as him,' he replied with enthusiasm. 'And we have Gazza.'

Horse dropped to his knees and put his hands over his ears. 'Oh my God, how did this nonsense reach the middle of Africa?' he cried out, and for effect moaned and groaned as if in pain. The police sergeant looked on bemused.

Horse stood up. 'Where are you based, Sergeant? Is there a hotel in the same place we can stay?'

'We are based at Mazabuka,' he replied. 'There is a motel where you can stay.'

'And does the motel serve dinner and have a bar?'

'It does and the food is very good.'

Raising himself to his full height, and with his infectious laugh, Horse announced they would stay there that night, and he expected the sergeant and his patrol to join them for dinner when he could educate them on football matters.

'Where is this place Mazabuka?' Horse asked.

The sergeant explained that about 20 kilometres further on there was a high bridge over the steep-sided Kaleya River, and Mazabuka was the first settlement after that about another 35 kilometres further on.

The four Zambian policemen later joined the three SAS tourists for an enjoyable evening. Horse and the team picked up some useful information on routine police patrols, but more important was what they had seen at the Kaleya River.

On approaching the river, after the roadblock, it was immediately obvious there would be no short-term, alternative route west towards Victoria Falls if this bridge was destroyed. It was not a big bridge, but it spanned a deep gorge where a fast flowing Kaleya River was over thirty metres below.

They pulled the Cortina off the road onto a rough side track that led to a gravel pit and walked back towards the bridge. While Fish kept watch, Horse and Mack took pictures and measurements of the bridge, which had two supporting concrete piers built into the steep sides of the gorge. Serious damage to either of these piers would probably destroy the bridge, but reaching the underside to place explosives would be a challenge.

Next day, they turned off the main road to Lusaka and dropped down into the low-lying rift valley on the Zambian side of the mighty Zambezi River. They were heading towards Chirundu, where a suspension bridge had been built to link the two countries in the happier days of colonialism. Two bridges attracted their attention on this road, and they again took pictures and measurements.

After another night talking football with the Zambians at a motel near Chirundu, they backtracked to pick up the road leading to Kariba Dam – the third possible route for an armour-led invasion into Rhodesia.

On this road, they determined that if the Lufua River Bridge was dropped there would be no way round. And thus they progressed with this priceless information, supported by photographs and in most cases measurements, of the supporting spans and piers.

They crossed back into Rhodesia over the Kariba Dam wall and booked into the best of the resort hotels overlooking the vast lake. Horse led them to a bar with great views out towards the islands with Bumi Hills in the distance.

It was a great ending to what had been a fantastic SAS recce job.

We developed the pictures the team had taken of the bridges and enlarged them. We had measurements and we had people who had been there and seen the ground with their own eyes. We gave all this information to the engineers and our own specialist demolition experts, with copies to a brilliant, but somewhat eccentric, scientist friend of the brigadier's, who worked at the South African CSIR research establishment in Pretoria.

All the demolition teams – including Karate and I – had been trained by structural engineers and had practical experience in blowing up bridges, but we'd only ever done it in completely controlled situations where time was not an issue.

What we now contemplated was very different. We would be in hostile territory, it was likely there would be serious time constraints, and we had to do the job with the minimum amount of explosives because an SAS team on foot would have to carry it to the target.

The brigadier had invited the professor from Pretoria to join us in the planning phase of our operations. He helped us immensely.

He firstly explained how bridges could tolerate the greatest weight-loadings from above because the design ensured such forces were shared between the bridge span and the piers that supported the structure. Breaking the back of a bridge was, therefore, much more difficult if explosive charges were placed on top of the bridge because of the inherent resistance in the design. It wasn't impossible, but would require a lot of explosives.

A much better option, he went on to explain, was to place the explosive charges on the underside of the bridge. It would take far less explosive pressure to lift, or dislodge, part of the structure off the supporting ledges of the piers, and then a combination of weight and momentum would almost certainly result in a collapse.

All very well in theory. But how were we meant to reach the underside of a bridge that in some cases were dozens of metres above the ground? And secondly, if we did somehow manage to get there, how could we then secure the explosives to the underside of the structure?

The professor didn't have all the answers. But he had the one that really mattered.

He dismissed the first point by saying that was our problem. 'Of all people, the SAS should be able to work out how to reach the underside of a bridge,' he admonished, and I was instantly sorry I'd asked the question.

'But your second question is a good one.' Which made me feel a little bit better.

'I was considering a variety of options then realised that some industrial work I have just completed may be the answer,' said the professor. 'I was tasked by the mining industry to develop a super superglue. They wanted something for repairing pit props in mineshafts that was strong and fast-curing. I believe what we made will be ideal for your purpose.

'Before leaving Pretoria, I did a quick test with a wooden pallet and sandbags – in all, a little over 150 kilograms in weight – and the glue successfully held the pallet upside down on our test rig without any sign of stress.

'It will do the job for you under the bridges, but you need to be careful, he warned. 'It's a dangerous substance and must be handled with great care. Don't touch it without wearing these.' He held up a pair of thick rubber gloves.

It was a great solution. On the ground we would have the free-fall pallets and after gluing them to the underside of the bridges we could stuff them full of explosives – enough to bring down the bridge.

We gave it a try next day. As the professor suggested, it didn't take us long to work out how to reach the underside of a bridge. We used a rope loop to which we suspended a swing seat as a work platform.

While we honed our skills and reviewed our plans for destroying the bridges, the political situation in central Africa fluctuated between hopeful and hopeless. At the same time, air reconnaissance showed a steady accumulation of armour and heavy weapons at the ZAPU camp close to Lusaka.

It was 11 November – Armistice Day. I was thinking about my grandfather, who had somehow managed to survive the horrors of Ypres and other battles, but he wasn't well these days. I reflected on happy times with him at Morecambe Bay in Lancashire where he lived. The two of us had wandered way out onto the wet sands when the tide was out. A strong, cold wind was blowing off the Irish Sea. My nose was running and my eyes were streaming as I struggled to focus my binoculars on the curlews whose magical, haunting calls filled the air.

I felt a hand on my shoulder. 'You OK, Mick?'

It was Rex.

'The general wants to see you and the brigadier urgently at ComOps. The brigadier's waiting for you in his car outside the office.

'I'll have everybody assembled when you get back.'

The general with accompanying staff officers met us in their large operations room. We stood up and saluted.

'Don't sit down,' he said and pointing to the huge wall with the maps, added, 'we need to know what your plans are to blow the bridges in Zambia.'

I stood to one side while the brigadier detailed how we would firstly cripple the Tan-Zam rail link that would isolate Zambia from the north and prevent further heavy weaponry reaching ZAPU. We would, on the same night, destroy three bridges on the road link between Lusaka and Malawi, and next day we would demolish another two bridges that would cut the links between Lusaka and Victoria Falls and Lusaka and Lake Kariba.

'General, our actions will physically isolate Zambia. But we have deliberately left one option open for ZAPU should they choose to start their invasion, which in the circumstances we think will happen. Your intelligence services suggest their preferred attack route is across the Zambezi Valley via the bridge at Chirundu. To encourage them we will leave that road intact – at least until Mick does his business. I'll let him explain.'

The brigadier handed me the pointer. I went up to the wall with the map coverage.

'While the brigadier and the rest of the regiment are causing their mayhem, we will night-parachute onto the two bridges our recce team identified on the road between Lusaka and Chirundu.'

I pointed at the map to show their locations: 'I'll take the northern bridge on the Lusaka side. Rex will look after the other, which is forty-two kilometres away on the edge of the escarpment before the road drops down into the Zambezi Valley. We will fix explosive charges to the underside of the bridges, keeping the Cordtex detonating cord well concealed beneath the structures. From above nothing will be obvious, and even if ZAPU or the Zambians lean over the side of the bridge they still won't see anything.

'If they decide to inspect beneath the bridges, it is possible our charges may be detected. For this contingency we have electrical detonators. If it looks like we have been compromised we will immediately blow the bridges.

'That would stop any ZAPU advance, but in our opinion it's very much a second prize and we want more than that.

'With our charges in place we'll sit tight and wait. We know there is a regular Zambian Police patrol along the road to Chirundu and they will undoubtedly report their road is clear after the daily runs. We think this will trigger the threatened advance by ZAPU and possibly some elements of the Zambian Army.

'Any column would have passed over numerous bridges before reaching our position, and I am confident they will simply roll on over our bridge like all the others before it. If this happens, we will warn Rex and watch from concealment as they advance towards the border.

'Rex will wait until the lead ZAPU vehicles are on his bridge and then he'll blow it using electrical detonators. That will bring the column to a grinding halt. I'll then make sure it has nowhere to go by dropping our bridge behind it.

'Once they are trapped between the two blown bridges we then propose asking 1 Squadron – the Hawker Hunter ground-attack fighters – to come in for a turkey shoot.

'They will undoubtedly have anti-aircraft missiles,' I continued, 'but we'll not give them any chance to use them.'

The general had a smile on his face. Next to him the air marshal could hardly contain himself. Turning to the general: 'How can we say no?' he asked.

And with that, we were told to go ahead with our plans as soon as sensibly possible.

We'd had plenty of time to prepare for this operation and were ready to go at short notice, but the weather intervened and we had to wait while the first front of the inter-tropical convergent zone brought heavy rain to the countries of central Africa.

On 18 November the rain stopped and that night, by helicopter and parachute, the brigadier took his teams into action.

On 19 November, they cut the Tan-Zam rail link by blowing two bridges close to the border with the Congo Republic. Concurrently, another three teams blew three bridges on the Lusaka-Malawi road, including the bridge over the Chongwe River where Zambian police later shot dead an unfortunate Swiss tourist and a TV journalist investigating the incident.

On 20 November, helicopters took teams to the Kaleya River Bridge near Mazabuka – the first of Horse's recce sites – and on to the Lufua River Bridge on the road to Kariba Dam. The bridges were totally destroyed. Kaunda was in an uproar, calling for a general mobilisation.

Kaunda had no idea what to do about the bridges. But the call for a general mobilisation had the desired effect on ZAPU who immediately pledged to lead the counter-attack south into Rhodesia.

Rex and I, meanwhile, had dropped onto our targets not long after dark on the night of 18 November. We followed the red lights of the pallets laden with plastic explosive from 12,000 feet, and both teams landed close to their respective bridges with everything intact. On landing we firstly established communications with each other and back to base. We were on a high plateau above the Zambezi Valley so both HF and VHF reception was excellent.

There was no time to lose. We had a lot of explosive to carry and it took two trips to the bridge and four hours to get everything where we wanted it. I wasn't unhappy about that. Horse had said a Zambian police patrol would routinely return to base around 20.00 hours, so we should keep off the bridge until after that time.

We heard the noise of a vehicle approaching and then the distinctive, narrow headlights of a Land Rover appeared. We watched in the shadows as they slowed down to go over the bridge, then accelerated as they saw the structure was intact. They would know about the other bridges being destroyed in Zambia; once back at the police station at Chirundu they would report the bridges along their road were intact.

Karate tapped out a warning on the radio to Rex at his bridge forty-two kilometres further down the road, alerting him to the police patrol heading his way.

With no more traffic expected on the road that night we immediately got into action. We rigged up the ropes beneath the bridge and ran them out to the first pier where I had decided we would put the charges. Our bridge had concrete side barriers and every few metres there was a small drainage hole at the base. We threaded the ropes through these gaps and secured them.

Our first priority then was to secure the pallet to the underside of the bridge. I positioned Jonny with his machine gun on the far side of the bridge to cover us if things suddenly turned pear-shaped while we were exposed out there in the middle of the road.

With our insurance policy in place, we took the pallet out to the rope and hitched up Karate who, being the lightest and one of our explosive experts, was the obvious choice as operator. He took hold of the rope and gradually lowered himself beneath the bridge. He took some time to position the swing seat where he wanted it, then came back to the edge and told us he was ready.

Karate had the superglue bottle and his latex gloves in his trouser map pocket. He sat down in the swing seat and with his legs pushing against the concrete bridge pier had a stable platform to do his work. We lowered the pallet down on a rope, which he was able to reach and pull in towards him. He rested it on his knees and against the pier while he dug out his gloves and the superglue.

With the glue bottle in hand, he lifted his legs to bring the pallet level with where he was sitting so it could be applied without dripping off onto his legs. We didn't know what would happen if that eventuated and we didn't want to find out.

In his typically calm way Karate, dangling from a rope thirty metres above the ground, applied the glue to the top of the pallet as if it was something he did every day. He secured the top of the glue bottle and put it back in his pocket.

With his hands now free, he lifted the pallet and positioned it where a pre-cast concrete beam sat on top of the massive vertical pier. He held it against the beam with as much pressure as he could exert and counted out one long minute, then another long thirty seconds before letting go.

Karate let go tentatively and the pallet remained in place. So far so good.

He moved to the edge of the bridge and told us the pallet was in position.

I leaned over the side of the bridge: 'You OK, Karate?' I asked, and without waiting for his reply, suggested he had a little rest in the swing seat while we started to bring out all the explosives that he would stuff into the pallet.

'All good here, Mick,' he replied.

We had decided to do it this way because it reduced our exposure if a vehicle came along while we were busy. But also, we all knew that the more time we gave the superglue to cure, the stronger it would be by the time we started loading it up with our explosives.

With tanks likely to be rumbling across the bridge, we had to give it every chance of holding firm.

We ran back to the edge of the bridge where we had stashed everything and carried back the first few 10-kilogram bags of plastic explosive. We put three bags into a pack and lowered it over the side. Karate took out one bag at a time and stuffed them through a zip opening we'd sewn into the side netting of the pallet. It was laborious work but eventually the pallet bulged with the twelve bags we'd carried. He attached the primer and the end of a Cordtex roll that I held above him on top of the bridge.

With the charges in place, we helped Karate haul himself back up on top of the bridge. Then we carefully ran out the Cordtex roll as we walked back to the roadside where we would rig up the initiation set. We kept the yellow Cordtex out of sight beneath the bridge and tightened it up over an expansion joint where the bridge joined the road. Here, we taped on another primer with the electrical detonator that with small crimps was attached to the two leads of our 100-metre wire coil, which would initiate the charge with a radio battery.

Returning to the centre of the bridge, we untied then recovered the ropes, called Jonny back in to join us and set ourselves up in an ambush position off to one side of the bridge, no further away than our 100-metre reel of electrical wire would allow.

We had done all this through the night, so at first light I was anxious to see how it all looked. And it wasn't bad at all. Nothing was visible from the top of the bridge, even when you looked over the side. Even under the bridge only a very sharp eye would spot the Cordtex, and our pallet was invisible from the approach side because it was behind the first pier. We couldn't do anything more to improve things so we retreated to our ambush position and waited.

I gave Rex a call. He too was organised and ready.

All we had to do now was wait and see if anything happened.

We watched and we waited.

Mid-morning on 19 November, I sent Fish and Pig Dog away to the river to fill up our water bottles while we watched and sweated it out.

There was very little traffic on the road. Rex warned us of a Zambian police patrol heading our way mid-morning and later a blue and white five-tonne truck, heading towards Rex, passed us at midday. We warned him and a few hours later Rex reported it was heading back our way, laden with sacks of maize from the local farmers working the Zambezi River flats. The police patrol vehicle crossed the bridge heading back to base at 16.00 that afternoon, and that was the sum total of action for the day.

We sat expectantly through the night. Nothing happened.

We sat through the day of 20 November, while the clouds built up with the promise of some serious rain that in our current position we were not prepared for. It was quiet with no traffic on the road apart from the daily police patrol.

For some unknown reason I was dreaming of elephants, with a smile on my face, when a tug on my shoulders broke the illusions. It was Jonny. It was dark; looking at my Omega I saw it was 03.00 and our turn to be night guard.

I stood up to stretch my legs and look around. An eagle owl was calling from the riverine forest below the bridge – no doubt his territory and breeding ground. It was one of those nights when the stars were so bright and close you felt as if you could reach out and grab a handful.

At 04.00, I was looking at Jupiter through my binoculars and could just make out some of the moons that orbited around it. The eagle owl suddenly stopped calling.

I gently tapped Jonny on the shoulder. In the distance I had heard a strange noise, a rumbling as sometimes happens with an earthquake.

We stood up, listening intently as the noise got slightly louder, and at exactly the same time we both realised what it was. We shouted an alarm to the others.

ZAPU were advancing towards the Zambezi River and into our trap.

Karate tapped out a signal back to ComOps to alert the Hunter crews and I used VHF to alert Rex.

We hugged the ground in cover as the rumbling intensified.

Our plan was simple. If the ZAPU advance crossed the bridge without detecting the charges, or our presence, we would stay where we were and observe and report. When Rex blew his bridge we, in turn, would initiate our charges.

If ZAPU put ground troops out to survey the bridge ahead of the advancing column, I would immediately blow the bridge using the electrical detonators, then we'd run like hell to get out of the area.

We sat and waited as the noise increased. All of us were tense and nervous because we didn't really know what to expect.

At 04.23 hours a tank appeared with a powerful searchlight scanning the road ahead and surrounds. It slowed down on the approach to the bridge. A 12.7-millimetre cannon followed the searchlight as it swept the area ahead. We pushed our heads into the ground as the light came in our direction.

Detecting no apparent danger the tank advanced onto and over the bridge. A second tank moved up to cover the move. It too had a searchlight and again we hugged the ground as the light scanned over our position.

Once the first tank was safely on the opposite side of the bridge, those behind followed suit and the advance continued. We breathed a sigh of relief then watched in wonder as the invading column passed us.

Six tanks led the way. Immediately behind them came a dozen armoured personnel carriers, also handily equipped with 12.7-millimetre cannons. Five six-wheeler trucks followed with rockets on the back – the anti-aircraft defence missiles. Six low-loader vehicles, each carrying a tank, were next in line, followed by another dozen armoured personnel carriers. Mobile artillery vehicles came next, then a steady procession of fuel tankers and covered six-wheel military vehicles we presumed would be carrying more troops, communication equipment and supplies.

As they disappeared into the night, towards Rex, our first priority was to let everybody know.

Karate unwound the HF antenna and sent a signal in Morse code back to ComOps. We didn't bother with encryption because there wasn't time. And on the subject of timings, we could now work out that the ZAPU column would reach Rex's bridge on, or just before, first light.

The timing was perfect for the Hunters. In Japanese-fashion they could come in undetected out of the sun.

We recommended the first strike be aimed at the five rocket vehicles, eighteen vehicles back from the front, as these carried the anti-aircraft missile defences. There would also be some shoulder-fired SAM7 Strela missiles in amongst the troops on the front armoured personnel carriers, so we recommended they be the second priority.

With the air defence capability eliminated, there would be plenty of low-risk time to take out the tanks and the remainder of the column.

With the advancing column upon us I didn't want to risk VHF radio traffic to Rex, whom we had already alerted, like us he would hear the advance heading his way long before its arrival.

We packed up ready to go, except for the VHF radio and the spare battery we had kept out to initiate the electrical detonators. We'd keep all that in place until the final moment. It now looked like we could use safety fuse to detonate the charges, which was good news for us because we would then be a much safer distance away from the bridge when it blew.

It took the ZAPU advance column an hour and forty minutes to cover the forty-two kilometres to Rex's bridge. By that time there was light in the sky.

Rex watched as the first tank appeared at the edge of his bridge. Still operating the searchlights, they scanned the ground ahead and around them. Like we had done, Rex hugged the ground.

Satisfied there were no obstacles on or around the bridge the lead tank advanced. At that point, Rex touched the wire leads to the battery terminals and fired the detonators.

Within 100 metres of the bridge, Rex had found a wide concrete culvert pipe, built under the road to channel water from a side stream off the road into the river below. No better or safer place to hide when blowing the bridge. They blocked their ears as 120 kilograms of one of the most powerful plastic explosives on earth unleashed its power on the bridge.

The first tank didn't survive the blast. It rolled over the edge of the collapsed structure and plummeted into the river below.

The second tank opened fire immediately with both the main gun and the 12.7-millimetre cannon mounted on the turret. The gunners had no specific target but knew that somewhere close an adversary had just struck.

The fire was intense, but didn't threaten Rex and his team inside the culvert pipe. As the fire pounded the embankments above them they crept out of the pipe; undetected they dropped into the cover of the riverine woodland below. They made haste away from the area.

From the safety of a deep gully, a few minutes later, Rex used our VHF frequency to report the bridge was now impassable and the ZAPU advance had been halted.

He had used VHF because he knew that I would be listening and so would the 'Top Guns' of the Rhodesian Hunter squadron.

I acknowledged the call briefly then asked, 'Cyclone One, you copy?'

The laconic voice of Squadron Leader Richard Christian replied, 'Cyclone One, Red Leader, we copied that, Mick, thank you. Rex, you get the hell out of there. We are less than five minutes out.'

'Good hunting, Red Leader,' I replied. 'I'm dropping the back door now.'

And with that I lit the safety fuse, giving us five minutes to get away from our bridge.

We headed fairly cautiously down the steep-sided bank to the river, which offered us good protection from the blast that was about to happen. We reached a position on the edge of the river where, looking back, we could see our bridge in the distance. And at that moment the charges blew.

There was a deep crimson fireball, which only lasted an instant before being enveloped in a black, then brown, explosive cloud of dust, debris and energy. We watched in wonder as the explosives lifted one side of the precast concrete slab by a metre or so, and we could see it had twisted in the process. Almost in slow motion, the great slab of concrete, with its black tarseal surface, responded to the forces of gravity. Gathering speed, it dropped towards the ground thirty metres below. The weight and the downward momentum neatly severed the bridge surface between the piers. As the dust settled we could see that our charges, placed as they were next to one of the big piers, had also knocked out a big lump of the pier itself leaving that as an unstable platform for what remained of the bridge on the opposite side.

It was a great result. It would be impossible for ZAPU to retreat back towards Lusaka.

They were trapped.

As the dust cloud from our explosion spiralled into the air, Red Leader and his Hawker Hunters were closing in to administer the last rites to ZAPU. In the first wave, rockets destroyed the big mobile SAMs. Then they turned and attacked the armoured personnel carriers with their deadly 30-millimetre front guns firing a mixture of armour-piercing and incendiary rounds.

When they ran out of ammunition the Hunters returned to base to rearm and refuel. But there was no respite for ZAPU. The Rhodesian Air Force had also put its number two training squadron in the air. Flying elderly, two-seater Vampire jets, these pilots were now deployed on a genuine mission instead of the routine live-firing exercises over their firing range. They too carried rockets and had 20-millimetre front guns. As the Hunters streaked home to refuel, the Vampires struck the softer targets at the back of the advancing column with deadly effect. The fuel tankers exploded and burned. The fires spread from one vehicle to another. Black acrid smoke filled the air. As the troops fled from the vehicles, the Vampires attacked with their 20-millimetre front guns. They strafed the vehicle column and fleeing men without mercy and few would escape.

The Vampires had less endurance than the Hunters and were much less of a weapons' platform, so it was not long before they too had to return to base to refuel and rearm for the second round.

The Hunters returned and this time used their rockets on the tanks stuck at the bridge in front of the advance, and then on those being carried on the low-loader transporter vehicles. The Vampires came in again, and finally the Hunters for the third and last time.

Smoke filled the sky on the Zambian escarpment above the Zambezi River, from the burning ZAPU vehicles and weaponry supplied by Mother Russia, and from the bushfires the air attacks had also started.

There would be no recovery from this.

As a military and terrorist threat, ZAPU had been eliminated.

With the ZAPU opportunity vaporised, his country broken and isolated, Zambian President Kaunda had no choice but to go to the negotiating table.

Meanwhile, we had to get home. The map showed the contours of the escarpment hills, closing up to the west of us on both sides of the Zambezi River and eventually joining at the eastern edge of Kariba Gorge.

We knew the banks of the Zambezi River near the Chirundu Bridge were well populated, and while that direct route would have been the shortest way home we wanted no contact or conflict with locals. Far better, we reasoned, to stick with our well-proven strategy of being invisible; while it would take three or four days longer to get out of the area, we decided to track along the edge of the northern escarpment hills towards the gorge.

Rex had a forty-two-kilometre start on us. He sent back useful information such as where they had found waterholes and tracks we should follow.

There were not a lot of game animals as the area was uncontrolled and local hunters had been active for many years. That made life more difficult for us. Without the buffalo and elephants, the ancient game trails we usually shared had become overgrown with thick, low thorn scrub that was generally difficult and sometimes impenetrable.

So we picked our way through it for five days as we headed slowly towards the Zambezi.

Rex was taken out by helicopter three days before us. He had found a hidden clearing in the foothills well away from the local population that inhabited the river line. It was a safe place for the Alouette to come into, and it was not long before he and his team were back in the security of the military base at Kariba.

After a long but uneventful hike, we eventually used the same place for the final act of our own exfiltration.

Our mission had been an overwhelming success and we were unscathed.

We had engineered the final destruction of ZAPU. There would be no comeback for them after this annihilation. They were no longer part of this second scramble for Africa. Their tanks would never roll into the tribal lands as they had threatened. The Mashona tribal chiefs could rest easy. ZAPU and the Ndebele tribe they represented were out of the game.

We celebrated at the time. But events would prove that in truth it was a hollow victory.

The success of our operations against ZAPU effectively handed the future of Zimbabwe on a plate to the Chinese-backed ZANU faction. And while the ink on the independence documents was still drying, their Korean-trained Fifth Brigade drove into Bulawayo.

Old mineshafts filled up with bodies as the Mashona tribe wreaked revenge on the hated Ndebele.

# The English Lord: Richard Cecil

O perating as we did in several different countries in central Africa, it was handy to have a foreign minister on our side at a time when Henry Kissinger was zooming around trying to save the world. A time also when the British media, particularly, was dominated by liberal hand-wringing journalists, many of whom were anti-establishment in the extreme.

Unsurprisingly, the SAS were not heroes to these people. They were definitely not on our side. In fact, one I met later in London was actively involved with the enemy.

While we generally worked well under the radar, stories did sometimes get out and go to press. We had been disparagingly described as 'merce-naries' in one article, and we knew the same journalists would have no hes-itation in distorting the facts to accuse us of atrocities. Terrorist training camps with defensive trenches and anti-aircraft guns could, for example, magically become pitiful refugee camps. But such stories sold newspapers and the truth was regarded as irrelevant.

In contrast, Rhodesian Foreign Minister Pieter 'PK' van der Byl was a straight shooter and, having served in the British Army, was always a wel-come guest at our headquarters or occasionally at a base in the field. His eloquence and razor-sharp wit made him great company. If we were out in the bush somewhere he'd find time to collect our mail before coming out and to get a bottle of single malt Scotch for the camp table.

PK particularly enjoyed his association with the SAS, because we were up to things only a privileged few knew about. From our point of view, he was often an invaluable source of advice or a conduit through which we could get political approval for operations in the Portuguese territories of Angola and Mozambique. He sometimes organised unofficial help from the South Africans: it was he who organised our submarine ride from Cape Town to Beira so we could blow up the *Vladivostok* incognito.

PK spent New Year's Eve 1976 with us in a base camp on the Mozambique border, where I had half the squadron trying to intercept some terror-ists intelligence had said were heading our way. It was a pleasant evening;

we swapped stories on the state of our part of Africa, and there was plenty of humour with the lads I'd kept back as a reaction force reserve.

Before leaving the next day, he asked when I expected to be back in town and explained he had some visitors arriving from overseas whom he would like me to meet.

A few weeks later, I was invited to dinner at his home in the tree-lined suburbs of Salisbury – now Harare. There were three other guests, all fit looking men in their early 30s – the same sort of age as me.

PK firstly introduced me to Jacques, a short, dark-haired Frenchman who was in Rhodesia 'on business'; then to Nick Downey, British 22 SAS and now a freelance cameraman. Finally, PK turned to the taller of the two Englishmen and introduced Richard ... 'Lord Cecil' he added almost as an afterthought.

The title didn't mean anything to me at the time and Richard clearly wasn't expecting any airs and graces as we shook hands. I felt relaxed with all of them, and over dinner PK skilfully managed the conversation so we all learned about each other while discussing the war and the state of our respective nations, much as we had done with him on New Year's Eve.

Richard, I learned, had been a Sandhurst graduate who had been commissioned into the Grenadier Guards, then joined the Guards Squadron of 22 SAS. He had been on active service in Northern Ireland and was unimpressed with the soft approach the British military were taking there, and the apparent lack of support for the tougher stance of the British Parachute Regiment. The hand-wringing brigade had been busy over there as well.

Richard had injured his knee in a parachute jump and subsequently decided to leave the army for a career as a freelance journalist.

Richard and Nick had teamed up and obtained a commission from the *Daily Telegraph*, in England, to cover the conflicts in central Africa. The *Telegraph* wanted real-time reports on acts of terrorism, and the responsive action of the security forces, to counter the bias of the left-wing press and elements of the Labour Party.

PK was very much in favour of this and it was easy to understand why. He'd talked Rhodesian leader Ian Smith into accepting majority rule for the country, but it wouldn't happen while hostilities continued, so a series of peace talks had been arranged with the British Foreign Office. Some positive reporting to counter the recurrent negative sentiment of the left-wing press would do nothing but good.

The Frenchman left fairly early after dinner and we retired to the lounge where PK took control and explained the real purpose of the evening.

'Mick,' he said, 'Richard and Nick can help the situation here significantly with their reports for the *Daily Telegraph*, but we need your help as a fellow SAS officer to achieve this. Firstly they need your help and advice on how best to get into Rhodesia, and once here they will need further help from you to access the operational areas where they can get amongst the action and make their reports.'

I listened with interest but puzzled over the bit about getting into Rhodesia.

Richard stood up and took over from PK.

'To explain things for you, our plan is to buy a light aircraft in England and fly it out to Rhodesia. We hope you can help us with that. PK has told us you have a very good handle on intelligence and know where the terrorist bases are located in central and east Africa better than anyone. Places a light aircraft should avoid.

'Mick, we desperately need your help with the dangerous late stages of our flight plan into Rhodesia.'

I nodded my head in agreement. 'No problem, Richard. Easy.'

'Once in the country,' he continued, 'our plan is to fly the plane into the operational bases around Rhodesia. From there our hope is to join the Fireforce reaction teams on the ground and follow them into action against the terrorist groups. We'll film proceedings for TV and newsreels and we'll take photographs of the action to go with our written reports.

'We are unfamiliar with the way you operate here in Africa and need to prepare ourselves before committing to this. Our own safety aside, the better prepared we are the more likely we are to get the OK from the Rhodesian Army top brass to do all this.

'PK has told us something of your remarkable exploits in this part of the world, and suggested that as we were SAS in England it would be appropriate for the SAS here to take us under their wing and prepare us for this venture. Can you help us, Mick?'

I was about to reply with 'Not so easy' when PK interjected.

'Mick,' he said, 'is it possible for Richard and Nick to be attached to your SAS squadron, perhaps as seconded intelligence staff working under you?'

I could see his logic. As badged SAS men they would be readily accepted by the military units in the operational areas and what they were doing would be regarded as another arm of 'psy-ops', where with tame hyenas and spirit mediums in bat caves we had already gained a certain notoriety. This was the same sort of game, but one played on the international stage and I was all for it.

On top of that I liked these two Englishmen.

I liked the idea of what they hoped to do and it wasn't hard to see the value of the contribution they could make. But most of all I really enjoyed the sheer adventure of it all.

It was a *Boy's Own* story and these two guys were *Boy's Own* characters. But there was a big difference; they were well-educated and well-trained SAS men, they were well resourced, they had a ton of enthusiasm and they were determined to do it.

I took a sip of my drink to buy a little thinking time.

'PK. Richard. Nick. Let me start by saying that I like what you are trying to do and I particularly like why you are doing this, so you can count me in and I'll do my best to help as I can. It's not going to be easy, though.

'These days operations within Rhodesia are largely reactionary. Units of the Rhodesian Light Infantry commandos and the Rhodesian African Rifles regular army troops are positioned at all the major operational bases. They are there as a 'Fireforce' and as soon as contact with a terrorist group is reported they roar into action.

'They are often deployed by helicopter. Their officers go in the front of a gunship and have become very skilled at controlling the ground action from the air. They are fantastic troops and the 'Fireforce' concept has been a great success. You'll really enjoy working with them and I don't see too many problems with that.

'However, with the escalation of the conflict came the problem of a shortage of helicopters. But there has never been any shortage of innovation with the Rhodesians and they decided that deployment by parachute was a viable option.

'Both the RLI and the RAR were told they could volunteer to be para-trained and, to their credit, they volunteered to the last man in both units. It was remarkable.

'As a result, DC3 Dakotas are now stationed at the forward airfields to deploy the Fireforce by parachute. These are operational jumps at 400 feet above the ground and sometimes under fire. I did a few of these jumps with them as we were asked to lend a hand with the para training, and it was all done for real while the units were deployed in the operational areas.

'It is highly effective, but not for the faint-hearted. With the possibility of being under fire, it's in everyone's best interest to get on the ground as quickly as possible and the aircraft don't want to hang around in the danger zone. We consequently changed the rules on DZ (drop zone) quality: rocks were unacceptable. In the context of the Rhodesian environment, it isn't usually a problem because much of the country is covered in low woodland that won't do much damage to paratroopers.'

I paused to let this sink in, knowing Richard and Nick would never have experienced anything like it, and I told them that.

'You are both experienced parachutists. But Richard, are you physically up to this?' I asked. 'You left 22 SAS because of a knee injury and there are no soft English pastures here. The ground where you'll be going is usually hard.'

Richard responded by assuring me his injury was healed and he was as fit as he had ever been.

He'd need to be, but I wasn't going to leave that to chance.

I believed I could deliver what they wanted, but it was conditional on them successfully completing a parachute refresher-training course.

And it was over to PK to sell the idea to the senior military command who would give the final approval for letting them loose in the operational area.

The die was cast.

Meanwhile, Richard had first to put in place a few essentials: he needed to buy a plane, and perhaps more importantly, *he also had to learn how to fly one!*

Later that year I learned my grandfather was dying of cancer, so I took some leave and went back to England to see him for the last time. A veteran of the First World War, Grandpa was finally defeated by the Woodbine cigarettes he'd smoked for most of his life. I knew he was just hanging on to see me and it broke my heart to see a strong, tough man so withered and frail.

He lasted less than two days.

After the ambulance had taken his body away, I let the wind of Morecombe Bay blow away my tears as I walked amongst the oystercatchers and redshanks we had once watched together.

I had told Richard of my visit and was invited to his home in Hertfordshire: Hatfield House. By then I knew a lot more about the Salisbury family. Their name was given to the capital city of Rhodesia and to the city centre, Cecil Square.

I had read about the Marquis of Salisbury, the Lord High Treasurer of England who took Queen Elizabeth I to the throne. But it didn't really prepare me for the experience of spending a few days at what was a combination of a great hotel, a remarkable art gallery, a museum and a beautiful English country estate.

Lady Salisbury I met briefly, just before she left for a hunt in Leicestershire. She was a beautiful, young-looking woman with a warm personality, and even though we had only just met she treated me as if I was an old school friend of Richard's who had been visiting them for years.

Lord Salisbury seemed to be much older. He was genuinely interested in Rhodesia and listened attentively as I gave him and his three sons one of my intelligence briefings. I had taken large-scale map coverage with me to give to Richard and pinned it up on a panelled wall, so they could see where the action was in Rhodesia and the neighbouring states of Mozambique and Tanzania.

I had done many such briefings, but none in so grand an environment. As I turned to the map to point out where we had recently cleaned out the Frelimo guerrillas on the Malawi border, for the Portuguese, I glanced through the window and there, beyond the long, manicured lawns, was the old oak tree where a young Queen Elizabeth sat waiting for the news of her succession.

Richard, by then, had purchased a plane and was having daily flying lessons. I went along to inspect the machine and witness progress in the air. He had bought an Auster, a small, high-winged single engine aircraft that had been built as an artillery spotting plane in the Second World War and powered by not much more than a large elastic band.

Richard explained that the plan was to replace the back seat of the aircraft with an extra fuel tank, which would give it the range needed to complete some of the long flight legs on the trip across Africa.

'Richard,' I replied while discussing all this, 'I think the plane will be ideal for the job in Rhodesia. In fact, it's great and not unlike the Cessnas we use for air recce work, but why do you have to fly it there? Why not just put it on a ship to South Africa? Bringing it up from there is easy and a hell of a lot safer.'

'Out of the question, Mick,' he replied. 'We are SAS and we're flying it out from England.'

Vic Diamond was a friend and Air Malawi pilot. Every day he flew his BAC 1-11 airliner between Salisbury and Blantyre, so knew the country and knew the ropes with the local civil aviation authorities. He was a top guy and I needed help, so one evening I told him about Richard and the plan to fly his plane with the elastic band across Africa and into Rhodesia.

Vic surprised me with his immediate enthusiasm for the project, so together we looked at the maps and Vic made the flight plan for Richard. I wrote it all down, posted it off to England and it reached Richard not long after he had graduated from flying school.

On 29 December 1977, just before his departure from England, he posted a short note acknowledging receipt of the plan and congratulating us on our latest operation: a big camp attack where we killed over 1,000 guerrillas; it had been a massive blow to the opposition and was reported internationally. His letter advised that any updated information should be sent to a club in Kenya and that he hoped to see us around the end of January.

Richard and Nick only got as far as the Mediterranean island of Malta in the Auster. They were on the runway, waiting to take off after a commercial jetliner. As the small plane took to the air, they suddenly encountered residual ground turbulence created by the much larger plane that had just gone before them. The Auster flipped over and crashed.

Richard and Nick did well to survive, especially with all the fuel on board, but the aircraft was a write-off.

They arrived in Salisbury a month later off an SAA flight from Johannesburg. Without a plane they could still get into the operational areas, but it was now even more important for them to be allowed to parachute into the action with the Fireforce reaction teams.

I went up to the parachute training school that was commanded by air force Squadron Leader Derek de Kok and Frank Hales who had come over from 22 SAS. They were both totally professional and ran a great show. Having worked with these two men for nearly ten years I knew them well enough to do no more than put the facts on the table about Richard and Nick. By coincidence, we had an SAS parachute course starting just over two weeks later, and I asked if they could be included.

Derek and Frank enjoyed a conspiracy as much as the rest of us and immediately agreed, but there was one proviso. The two would be treated just the same as everyone, so if there was the slightest doubt regarding their physical ability to handle the course, they would be thrown out.

I had no doubt about Richard and Nick's general capability and experience, but they had just survived a plane crash and Richard hadn't really tested his knee with anything like what he was about to go through on the parachute course.

I needn't have worried.

We gave them both some hard physical training ahead of the course and they breezed through it.

On 21 April 1978 – so soon after their training – Richard was killed while moving into action with members of a Fireforce team.

A lone terrorist had the nerve to hide in the cover of long grass as Richard walked past, following the commandos in action in front of him. The terrorist gang member suddenly rose from behind and at point-blank range emptied his AK-47 magazine into Richard's back. He had no chance and died almost immediately from multiple bullet wounds.

The SAS motto is 'Who Dares Wins' – and that's true. But sadly not every time.

# Rex Nyongo's Luck

'OK, take her up, Mick,' said PB from the left-hand seat of the Cessna 180.

I pushed the throttle in towards the dashboard, released the brakes and we surged forward on the grass runway. The tailwheel came up quickly and in no time we were airborne.

I pulled in the flaps while PB adjusted the trim as we climbed slowly above the rural police base. 'Keep a steady climb up to 2,500 feet,' he said, 'and head for that big brick on the horizon while I get our maps sorted out.'

The 'big brick' was *Chiramba Kadoma* – the Ayer's Rock of the Zambezi Valley.

PB was Rhodesian Air Force Squadron Leader Peter Brown, and nobody did aerial reconnaissance better. His camouflaged Cessna 180 was the perfect plane for the job: it was quiet, fuel-efficient, and the high wing gave an unimpeded view of the ground below.

We had been given radio intercept intelligence suggesting the Musengezi River, on the west side of *Chiramba Kadoma*, in the Zambezi Valley was about to be used as an incursion route by a ZANU terrorist group from a base on the Zambian side of the Zambezi River known as *Mapapai* – the pawpaw tree.

The brigadier had given us the job of intercepting the terrorists. Our plan was to deploy onto the upper reaches of the Musengezi River then advance downstream towards their base. If we didn't meet the terrorists en route, we had clearance to cross into Zambia and destroy the *Mapapai* base, and we had every intention of doing just that regardless of what happened along the way.

It was three days before the start of the operation, and I had jumped at the chance of an air recce over the area with PB when I learned that both he and the Cessna were available.

The two of us had flown together many times, and on a couple of missions had come under fire from the ground. Nothing serious: we had an RPG7 whistle past, but well wide of us, on one occasion in Mozambique.

On another, we watched as two figures wearing blue overalls fired hopefully at us with their AK-47s.

When we first started this form of air recce work, PB said he needed me to control the aircraft while he was plotting tracks and camp locations on the maps.

I was more than happy to do that. But pointed out that as we had already been under fire on some of these missions, I thought he should teach me how to land and take-off as well as working the plane in cruise mode.

PB agreed, and I took off that morning in perfect conditions.

We reached the rugged escarpment of the Zambezi Valley, the most southerly extent of the Great Rift Valley system. As we crossed the broken foothills, we could see the Musengezi River with plenty of water in it flowing north across the flat valley floor towards the Zambezi.

A small herd of elephants raised their trunks towards us as we flew over a clearing and a warthog family dashed for the cover of their burrow. White egrets flew towards a nesting colony on the river. For a few moments, a very large vulture came alongside the Cessna and stared intently at us.

The rains had brought lush growth to the woodland, making it difficult to locate tracks and camps hidden beneath the green canopy.

PB and I had done this before. We knew you couldn't see anything looking directly down on the leaves and branches, so we would fly off to one side and angle our view so we could see under the canopy. We had learned what a terrorist camp looked like and where they preferred to build them.

We had dropped down to 800 feet and were flying parallel with the river. There were game tracks but nothing unusual. Ahead of us the river bent sharply back on itself; in the loop it made was a thick covering of trees. It was the perfect place for a camp.

PB steered the aircraft away from the river to get a better look under the canopy. Then his excited voice came over my headset: 'There's a camp. Three, four, five, six – probably more – the usual A-frame thatch bivvies.'

I took over the controls of the Cessna as PB plotted the location on the topo maps and we kept heading north towards the Zambezi.

A few minutes later PB again turned on the headset.

'Mick,' he said. 'I reckon you may have missed the boat. That camp is new – some of the grass roofing is still green. In this location, it will be a transit camp they'll use when moving between the Zambezi and their operational area. The camp looks deserted, which means the gang could be well on their way into the tribal lands, and your operation is still two days away.'

We turned round and headed back to base. I felt a bit depressed about the reality check PB had given me, but we needed to alert the operational commanders of what we had found and, if possible, get our SAS team into the area sooner than planned.

The big question now, however, was where should we start?

In the event the terrorists obligingly answered that one for us.

It was late afternoon. We were at a joint operations control centre, putting the final touches to our gear ahead of a first-light helicopter deployment, when I was called urgently to the operations room.

The brigadier was there with an air force wing commander.

'Mick,' he said. 'PB was right. The terrorist group we were expecting is now in the tribal lands. We have just received a report that a gang of nine, led by one calling himself Rex Nyongo, walked into St Albert's Mission School less than an hour ago. They assembled all the pupils and staff in the playground then shot the headmaster and the three teachers. They are now taking the 126 pupils away for training.'

He showed me on the map where this had taken place. The headwaters of the Musengezi River started less than a kilometre from the school.

'The two helicopters that were to take you in tomorrow are fully fuelled and we have already briefed the pilots. Get those kids back!' he ordered.

I ran from the Ops room and shouted to the boys.

They immediately realised there was a drama and gathered round.

Rex was away on leave with family, so I had brought in Sergeant Andy Chait – ex–South African Para Battalion – to fill the void. Andy was a cool head and a deadly shot. He and I were great rivals on the shooting range and always enjoyed the competition. Which he usually won.

'Mack, you, Fish, Simmo and Horse go with Andy. Fish, you take the radio. Karate, Pig Dog, Jonny and Nelson, you're with me. Move, guys. We're out of here in the next ten minutes. I'll sort out the maps for us and see you at the choppers.'

Within ten minutes the Alouette helicopters had lifted off. Settled in the front seat of the lead chopper, I put on the headset and called the Ops room. I asked for the brigadier and the wing commander.

They came on air and I told them I wanted to look at timings.

'Time now, 16.25,' I said looking at my Omega.

'What's the flying time to the mission school?' I asked.

'About twenty minutes, Mick, so your ETA will be around 16.45 hours,' came the wing commander's relaxed reply.

It was early March, meaning there were roughly equal day and night hours, so last light was probably 18.30. And if the weather was fine – which it was – the choppers would have a twilight flying horizon until after 19.00 hours.

'So we've got just over two hours to bring the kids home tonight. If we get lucky that might just be enough time.'

Could we do it? Would we get lucky?

I leaned back in my seat and watched the treetops whistle by as we skimmed above them at over 100 knots. Two hours wasn't much time, I realised, and we'd definitely need some luck to achieve anything that night.

But we did get lucky because moments later a police report came in. Three kids had run away from the gang and returned to the school.

They reported the gang was moving east along the escarpment, and they had heard them talking about Musengezi.

This was critical information. As he relayed it on to us, the brigadier finished by stating the obvious: 'You can't easily hide 120 kids and now we know where to look.'

In the air, meanwhile, over the closed-circuit radio, Andy and I had been discussing with the pilots what exactly we should do if and when we found the gang and the kids. The main issue was the safety of the kids, but we also had our own safety to think about.

Each Alouette had a 7.62-millimetre Fabrique Nationale GPMG mounted at the back left door, and the technicians were always keen to use it, but in this situation it would be way too traumatic. The kids had already witnessed their headmaster and teachers being executed. Gunfire from an aircraft would be too much. So it was decided that even if Rex Nyongo and his gang opened fire at the helicopters there would be no response until we were on the ground. We all prayed there would be a good landing zone when we wanted one.

Somebody was obviously listening to our prayers, because within fifteen minutes of swooping over the school and heading east along the top of the escarpment, we found the kids. We didn't get shot at and there were two great landing zones within 100 metres.

Andy and Horse were first out. They threw down their packs just before touchdown then jumped out and hit the ground running. A camouflaged figure carrying an AK-47 popped up and started firing. Kids screamed. Horse dropped to his knees and pulling the heavy weapon into his shoulder opened up with his MAG. Andy fired at the same time, and the terrorist was hurled backwards as the high velocity FN rounds smashed into his body. One less to worry about.

We saw the other terrorists running away, and Andy took off after them. 'Go! Go! Go!' I shouted to the others in his group, while Karate, Pig Dog and Nelson ran towards the screaming children huddled together on the ground.

Nelson was incredible with the kids. He spoke to them in their own Chishona language – commanding yet soothing. And while speaking he took several of them at a time in his big arms, holding them, stroking their woollen heads, bringing security and relief from a trauma no kid should ever have to experience.

Pig Dog, in his own unique Maori way, did the same. It didn't take long for us to have their confidence and a belief that maybe now all would be well.

While Nelson and Pig Dog settled the kids, Karate and I got on the radio back to base.

I told them we had 123 kids and were about to walk them quietly back to the school where they could be reunited with their parents.

Plus we had one dead terrorist and a pack full of explosives and ammunition.

Meanwhile Andy, with Mack and Fish in tow, were hotfooting it after the fleeing terrorists. No time for tracking. Andy just followed his own intuition, going where he would go if suddenly a helicopter with the SAS turned up to spoil the party.

He reached the edge of the escarpment. The ground sloped down at a steep angle, there were boulders everywhere. He could hear the noise of the gang fleeing ahead of him down the slope, but instead of running blindly after them he paused for a moment looking for a vantage point: a place where he might get a glimpse of the gang and hopefully get off a shot.

There was a slight rise thirty metres away and the ground looked more open. Andy sprinted forward to a large boulder that gave him cover and a firing platform for his rifle. Looking down he immediately saw two members of the gang. He picked the nearest one, who was bobbing up and down as he jumped over and around rocks and other obstacles on the descent.

Andy worked out where to fire and took aim. The terrorist emerged from behind a tree and was suddenly completely exposed.

He squeezed the trigger.

Sergeant Andy Chait didn't miss shots like that.

His bullet was already on its way and travelling over 800 metres per second towards the target. It would have been a millisecond or two away from contact when the terrorist tripped over a rock and went tumbling forward off his feet.

Andy saw what happened and knew he'd missed. He couldn't see the terrorist now down on the ground, so put several rounds into the general area where he thought he had fallen. He then ran forward towards the target, desperate for a second chance.

It wasn't to be. Andy picked up an abandoned pack and dragged it back up to the top of the escarpment. In the pack we found a copy of Mao's famous *Little Red Book* and on the inside cover was written the name, Rex Nyongo.

We'd missed the leader of the gang.

All this happened very quickly after our arrival. There were eight terrorists still at large. They may have successfully escaped from our initial attack, but what they wouldn't realise was that I knew where they would be going.

They'd be heading for the camp PB and I had found a few days earlier, in the loop on the Musengezi River. There could still be enough time to do something about it that night.

I grabbed the radio and explained this very quickly to the brigadier and the wing commander.

'Has the helicopter got enough fuel? Is there enough daylight flying time to get Andy Chait into the *Musengezi* camp then fly back home tonight?' I asked. 'And if so, are you happy for one of the aircraft to take us in?'

The wing commander called Ian Harvey, the senior of the two pilots now on the ground at the mission school, and asked the questions.

'Wait one,' Ian replied. 'We'll see what fuel we've got and what we can do. Don't worry about daylight. If we can find the fuel we will be coming home into the twilight, and there will be enough visible horizon for me.'

Meanwhile, I called over Andy and his team and told them what I had in mind. We gave them the rations and spare radio batteries my group were carrying as they could be in ambush for some time.

Andy would wait for Rex Nyongo inside his *Musengezi* camp.

When he arrived it would be payback time. Payback for what he'd done to the headmaster, the teachers and the kids.

And Andy wouldn't miss this time.

Ian Harvey came through with a positive response.

They had worked out a way to do it.

They took fuel from the second helicopter and put that into Ian's aircraft. It took a bit of time with the hand pumps they carried but he had enough for the mission. The second chopper was left with enough fuel to safely reach the local police base.

The brigadier gave us the green light. In the fading light of an eventful afternoon, Andy's team took up residence in the *Musengezi* terrorist camp.

All we had to do now was to wait for Rex Nyongo and the remnants of his gang to turn up.

Around 20.00 hours on that first night, there was a wild, electrical storm and the heavens opened. Andy and the boys were grateful for the shelter of the A-frame thatch bivvies where they lay in ambush. Andy thought about Rex Nyongo. For him, the rain would be good because his tracks would be washed out, but on the other hand he'd lost his pack. He had nothing except what he was wearing and the AK–47 he was carrying. He'd be wet and cold by now and would have no food. All logic said he would try to reach the shelter of this camp as quickly as possible.

Andy mentally pictured the map, and the ground between the mission school and the camp in the valley. As the crow flew it was between 25 and 30 kilometres away. It would be slow going, picking one's way down the steep slope of the escarpment in the dark, but once on the relatively flat valley floor there were game trails and much better progress would be made. Rex Nyongo and the other survivors of his gang could make it by late morning.

The rain stopped about an hour later and the night went quiet. There was a low rumbling behind the camp as the Musengezi River gathered some momentum from the storm water. A lone hyena howled in the distance.

Fourteen hours to wait.

At midnight the storm returned in earnest. Brilliant flashes of lightning illuminated the sky and great crashes of thunder shook the flimsy bivvies.

Then came the rain. It arrived as a vertical torrent. After a few minutes of this initial pounding it somehow intensified with a swirling ferocity none of the men had ever experienced. The lightning flashed and the thunder roared.

The madness lasted for about an hour while Andy and the boys curled up under their ponchos inside the flimsy, grass shelters. The rain eased but didn't stop. It continued steadily all night and was still going strong as the first light of a new day arrived.

The earlier rumbling behind the camp was now a roar as the Musengezi River flooded with fearsome power.

It continued to rain throughout the day and well into the second night. Conditions could not have been more miserable, and Rex Nyongo didn't turn up.

Andy's team stayed in the ambush for two days after the storm. By then they were just about out of food so we called it quits and brought them back to base.

I thanked the wing commander and the brigadier for letting us follow my hunch, and said I was sorry it didn't come off.

Both were philosophical about it: 'Rex Nyongo got lucky,' said the brigadier. 'There'll be another time for him. Meanwhile, we got all the children back safely; we killed one of the terrorists and chased the rest of his gang out of the area. It was a good outcome in that respect and I think we are on the positive side of the ledger.'

He was right, but I couldn't help feeling pretty hollow about the outcome. On top of that, the weather and flooding rivers also put paid to our plans for the *Mapapai* camp.

The story ended for Andy a few years later, in an attack on a large camp surrounded by deep defensive trenches. We had experience in clearing such trenches but it was high-risk and we sometimes took casualties.

Andy was shot in the thigh by a determined terrorist, who died milliseconds later as Andy's bullets tore through his chest.

The terrorist's shot had severed Andy's femoral artery. There was nothing we could do.

We sat with him as he slowly bled to death.

He was remarkably serene in dying. There was no panic, just a stoic acceptance that this was the end. We'd strapped up his thigh in a vain attempt to stem the bleeding. He gripped my hand and nodded when I told him the choppers were on the way.

He looked me in the eye and said, 'I still can't believe I missed that bastard, Rex Nyongo.'

Trying to lighten things up, I jokingly replied that even though I was a far better shot than him I too would probably have missed in the circumstances.

Andy's eyes lit up in a smile and his grip on my hand tightened. 'Mick,' he said. 'I missed Rex Nyongo by inches. You would have missed him by a fucking mile!'

The grip weakened. We'd had our last joke together and Andy had gone out the clear winner.

I wrote a condolence letter to his fiancée in the Orange Free State. Got a wonderfully warm South African reply, with an invitation to call and see them anytime I was anywhere near. I never did get to the Orange Free State and I still regret not trying harder to make that visit.

I didn't know at the time but the story was far from over for me.

Six years later, I had left the SAS and was trying my hand at a proper job with Dunlop Engineering Group in Coventry, England.

One of the English Sunday newspapers had published an emotive report about Rhodesian forces committing atrocities in their war zone. I thought of the mutilated bodies I had seen. Men and women beaten, sexually abused then executed by terrorist gangs, who forced their children to stand next to their parents and watch as they did their dirty work.

The article was garbage, and incensed me enough to put pen to paper and give them a few real facts about what was happening in central Africa.

A few days later I got a call from the newspaper.

They told me my letter would be published in the following Sunday's edition and thanked me for writing it. They said the article had been put together by a journalist called David Taggat, who was doing some work on the region and was keen to meet me.

Business took me down to London quite frequently, so they gave me David's phone number and suggested I call ahead of my next visit.

David Taggat was a Canadian about my age, obviously very bright, and I liked him immediately. He wasn't particularly proud of the article that brought us together, but said he wrote it to please other 'friends' who were sources of original information for a book he was writing about Robert Mugabe and Zimbabwe.

To maintain a perspective on events, David was interested in my take on what had happened during the conflicts in central Africa. The wars in Zimbabwe, Angola and Mozambique had finished by then, and without letting on too much about what we had been up to, I was happy enough to be of some help with his project.

Several weeks after our first meeting David again invited me to join him in London, saying he had some friends he especially wanted me to meet.

The party in his flat was in full swing by the time I arrived.

David firstly introduced me to a well-built African man, and I noticed the sparkle in his eye and the interested smile as David told him who I was.

My surprise showed with a short intake of breath as I learned he was Josiah Tongogara, the ZANU terrorist commander of operations.

He was totally relaxed and laughingly guessed I knew all about him.

'Except for where you were, Josiah!' I responded with a smile as I shook his hand.

'And thank goodness for that,' he replied. We both laughed, enjoying the unique moment of two adversaries meeting for the first time as people and without threats or weapons.

Josiah Tongogara was one of those charismatic personalities you meet now and then and our short meeting left me with a very positive impression. This was a man who could unite and lead Zimbabwe into a good future.

But he'd made a fatal mistake.

During the pre-independence Lancaster House talks in England, he stood up and told the squabbling political participants to go home and let him sort out a peace process for Zimbabwe.

He could have done it.

Tongogara would have made a great president, and supporters of the Mugabe faction knew that only too well. His Lancaster House statement was interpreted by them as a threat to the aspirations of their chosen leader, Robert Gabriel Mugabe.

Josiah Tongogara met his death in a brand new Mercedes on the main road south of Harare, conveniently close to the war veterans burial ground.

The official release stated that somehow the brakes or the steering failed and he had hit a power pole at high speed.

Josiah Tongogara ended up as just another casualty in the politics of Africa.

Meanwhile, back at the party in London, I was led to the second person David was keen for me to meet.

In contrast to the impressive Tongogara, this was a noisy, little black man who was already well through a bottle of Johnny Walker.

It was Rex Nyongo.

I could not contain my astonishment, and blurted out that he was the luckiest guy alive.

I told him about Andy Chait missing with that late afternoon shot on the escarpment near St Albert's Mission School, and then how I had sent the SAS team ahead to ambush the camp on the Musengezi I was sure he would go to.

'Rex, by all rights you should be dead.' Then, realising my opportunity: 'Where the hell did you go that night? Why didn't you go to the camp?'

My outburst brought on howls of inebriated laughter. Eventually he settled down, pointed a finger at me, and in the African style said, 'Ah! I was too clever for you.' This was followed by another fit of raucous laughter.

Then suddenly serious, he asked me if I remembered how hard it had rained at that time?

I nodded. 'It was a hell of a storm – flooded most of the Zambezi Valley.'

His eyes glazed for a few moments, I could see him mentally reliving the night.

'After the helicopters and the shooting and losing my pack I was very afraid, but I caught up with two of my comrades and we all headed down through the hills towards the camp on the Musengezi. At the camp we had built an underground cache where we had hidden some tinned food and ammunition for the AKs.

'At first we made good progress but then it started to rain. Initially, this did not trouble us because my comrades had their packs and gave me some clothing, but not long after that the rain became harder and harder. We were soaking wet, cold and hungry, but we kept on going to keep warm and to get closer to shelter and food at the *Musengezi* camp.

'We walked through the night, but then a great storm hit us. We thought we would die, but lucky for us we found a hollow baobab tree. The three of us squeezed inside the hollow and we sheltered until first light.

'It was still raining when we got out of the tree, but we were very hungry so pushed on in the rain towards the camp.

'Some hours later we reached the camp, but we were on the opposite side of the Musengezi River, which by now was in full flood. It was a wild raging torrent. There was even a drowned elephant in the river. There was no hope of getting across.'

Swirling the golden whisky in his glass, and suddenly sober, Rex recalled they'd been bitterly disappointed they could not reach the camp.

'We had no choice,' he said. 'We carried on walking for another two days until eventually we reached the Zambezi River. We shot an impala antelope and survived on the raw meat, but it took three days for the great river to subside before we could cross back into Zambia and return to the *Mapapai* base.'

In the driving rain of a miserable night, Rex Nyongo had again cheated death. He and the remnants of his terrorist gang had been less than 100 metres away from where Andy Chait lay waiting.

The story for Rex Nyongo ended in an appropriate way several years later.

Unlike Tongogara, Rex Nyongo was no physical or intellectual threat to the president.

He was the perfect 'Yes Man'.

Duly appointed Commander of the Zimbabwe Army, he was not slow to realise the opportunities his position presented in a landscape of farmer evictions and nationalisation of commercial enterprises without compensation.

He commanded the army. So long as he showed total support for his president, he too would be part of the redistribution of wealth the new leader was intent on achieving.

Rex Nyongo duly acquired many farms and several commercial enterprises, which he cleverly on-sold to buyers interested in – and capable of – running them for their true commercial worth. A clause in the sales agreements guaranteed security. In return, Rex took a percentage of the annual profit of each enterprise.

He became a very wealthy man.

However, as Rex got older his dependence on alcohol steadily increased and with that his respect and power started to decline.

The president knew he could not survive in power without the backing of the army. It was time to make some changes.

Not long after midnight, on a clear and cold winter evening, a black, late-model Mercedes and an old army Land Rover pulled up outside Rex Nyongo's mansion in the Greystone Park suburb of Harare where the Zimbabwe elite chose to live.

A sergeant got out of the Land Rover and ordered the guards at the house to get into the back of the vehicle. They would return to base where they would be given further orders. They climbed in and he drove away.

Only at that point did the door of the Mercedes open. A short, stocky man, powerfully built – intimidating – got out of the car. He was wearing the red cap band and collar dogs of a full colonel.

He went to the rear of the Mercedes and from the boot took out an AK–47. He put a full magazine on the firearm but, surprisingly, didn't cock the weapon. Instead, he pulled forward the stiletto bayonet and clicked it into place at the end of the gun barrel.

The colonel walked slowly into the house. All servants had been sent away, so he was on his own with Rex Nyongo somewhere in the building.

He walked slowly through the rooms of the ground floor then up to a mezzanine level with the bedrooms.

He found Rex still dressed, sprawled out on a huge bed, face up and snoring.

A half-empty bottle of expensive single malt whisky was on the bedside table with a half-full glass.

The colonel looked at Rex Nyongo's face briefly then he put the blade of the bayonet just beneath his sternum, lightly touching it, pausing as he adjusted his position to deliver the vital strike.

A deep breath, then he plunged the bayonet into Rex Nyongo's prostrate body, directly into the heart.

He held the bayonet there while the body convulsed, and with his strength was able to maintain the pressure until there was a little cough and blood flowed from the mouth. Still he held the bayonet pressure. The body was suddenly limp. Rex Nyongo was dead.

The colonel pulled out the bayonet of the AK–47. He went to the en suite bathroom and washed away the blood from the blade and the end of the rifle barrel in the handbasin. He wiped down the firearm with a bathroom towel and folded the bayonet back under the stock.

The colonel put the weapon down on the bed. He picked up the half glass of Scotch and drank it down in one gulp.

He searched the cupboards and drawers and in one found a bundle of US dollars. He didn't count, but flicking through the notes guessed there was at least 50,000.

Satisfied there would be nothing more of interest to find he picked up the bottle of Scotch and took that and the money to the Mercedes. He put them in the boot with his AK-47.

From the back seat of the car he then took out four twenty-litre jerrycans of petrol.

He put them in different places around the house.

First, he doused Rex Nyongo's body with fuel, then he used the empty whisky glass to throw petrol up into the base of the thatched roof above the bedroom. He worked his way through the house, spreading the fuel on the furniture and wooden floor tiles. The last jerrycan he used to make a trail to the front door.

Back at the Mercedes, in the driveway, he lit a Havana cigar he'd found in Rex's office. He had a couple of drags on it in appreciation, then hurled it through the open front door of the mansion.

The flames intensified as the heat eventually ignited the thatch roof. Fanned by the evening breeze the fire burned ferociously and at high temperature.

Rex Nyongo was cremated in his own house.

His luck had finally run out.